SISTER — MARSH
SAYS YOU'RE "STINKY",
BUT I DISAGREE.

HAPPY READING.

— B

THE SECRETS
OF THE KINGDOM

THE SECRETS OF THE KINGDOM

Religion and Concealment in the Bush Administration

Hugh B. Urban

ROWMAN & LITTLEFIELD PUBLISHERS, INC.

Lanham • Boulder • New York • Toronto • Plymouth, UK

ROWMAN & LITTLEFIELD PUBLISHERS, INC.

Published in the United States of America
by Rowman & Littlefield Publishers, Inc.
A wholly owned subsidary of The Rowman & Littlefield Publishing Group, Inc.
4501 Forbes Boulevard, Suite 200, Lanham, Maryland 20706
www.rowmanlittlefield.com

Estover Road, Plymouth PL6 7PY, United Kingdom

Copyright © 2007 by Rowman & Littlefield Publishers, Inc.

British Library Cataloguing in Publication Information Available

Library of Congress Cataloging-in-Publication Data
Urban, Hugh B.
  The secrets of the kingdom : religion and concealment in the Bush administration /
Hugh Urban.
      p. cm.
  Includes bibliographical references and index.
  ISBN-13: 978-0-7425-5246-3 (cloth : alk. paper)
  ISBN-10: 0-7425-5246-2 (cloth : alk. paper)
  ISBN-13: 978-0-7425-5247-0 (pbk. : alk. paper)
  ISBN-10: 0-7425-5247-0 (pbk. : alk. paper)
 1. Bush, George W. (George Walker), 1946—Religion. 2. Bush, George W. (George
Walker), 1946—Influence. 3. United States—Politics and government—2001- 4.
Religion and politics—United States—History—21st century. I. Title.
  E902.U73 2007
  973.931—dc22

                                                                    2006101200

Printed in the United States of America

⊗™ The paper used in this publication meets the minimum requirements of American
National Standard for Information Sciences—Permanence of Paper for Printed Library
Materials, ANSI/NISO Z39.48-1992.

For my mother and my late father,

who always taught me to think critically
about religion and politics,
even (especially) when I disagreed with them

Contents

Preface: An Obsession with Secrecy

Bush's Christ rules the world as well as the heart. . . . [T]he implication—one that unsettles those who desire to preserve a broad separation of church and state—is that institutions of faith "have an honored place in our plans and in our laws." If the presidency is a "bully pulpit," as Teddy Roosevelt proclaimed, no one in recent memory has pounded that pulpit for religion's role quite like the forty-third president.

—Stephen Mansfield, *The Faith of George W. Bush*

It has to be said: there has been nothing in our time like the Bush Administration's obsession with secrecy.

—Bill Moyers, "In the Kingdom of the Half-Blind"

THIS BOOK IS NOT, ultimately, about George W. Bush. I believe we now have more than enough Bush-bashing books and ample evidence of the weaknesses of this particular presidency. Although I discuss in great detail the activities of the current administration, this book is really about two very disturbing trends in the United States that have been with us since at least the beginning of the Cold War, but which have rapidly intensified during the past five years: a growing obsession with secrecy and a progressive erosion of the wall of separation between church and state. The presidency of George W. Bush simply represents the most extreme and most damaging example of these two trends. As such, this book is written not just for liberals or Democrats or Bush haters, but for any thoughtful citizen who is deeply concerned by what has happened in the United States over the past six years (which is roughly two-thirds of the population, according to most polls of 2006).

Until a few years ago, I would not have imagined myself writing a book about contemporary U.S. politics or the activities of the Bush administration. While I have long been interested in the topics of both religion and secrecy, most of the things I've written about to date have dealt with more traditional forms of religious secrecy, such as Freemasonry, Hindu and Buddhist Tantra, or Kabbalah—more to do, in other words, with the sort of secrecy found in *The Da Vinci Code* than with the NSA or the PATRIOT Act.[1] However, as I've closely watched the activities of this administration over the past six years, I have been increasingly disturbed by its mixture of obsessive secrecy and manipulation of religion for political gain.

At first, I found it simply astonishing that the same presidency dubbed by *Newsweek* "the most resolutely 'faith-based' in modern times"[2] could also be the most obsessively secretive of our times, that the same man who believes God called him to lead the nation could also shroud so many of his activities in unprecedented layers of concealment, that the same administration that promised moral values and honesty to its massive base of evangelical voters could have such a difficult time being straight with the American people. After six years of the Bush White House, we find that secrecy is at work at every level of this administration; it surrounds virtually all its activities, large or small, from the misuse of intelligence to justify a pre-emptive war to the vice president's shooting of his hunting companion. Much like Bush's trust in God, secrecy is one of this administration's basic articles of faith. Today, as I write this in 2006, we witness an almost daily series of revelations about the administration's obsessive secrecy, from the CIA's network of secret prisons to the NSA's wiretapping of U.S. citizens. Indeed, Bush, Cheney, Rove, and company seem to be leading us down a kind of Alice in Wonderland rabbit hole of endless dissimulation and false realities. As one senior White House aide bluntly told Ronald Suskind in 2004, "We're an empire now, and when we act, we create our own reality."[3] Or as comedian Al Franken put it, in somewhat more colorful terms, "If sunshine is the best disinfectant, then this administration has shoved us up the rectum of a rooster from Asia with a bad cough." However, not only liberal comics but also a great many conservative Republicans have been deeply unsettled by the intense secrecy and politicized religion of this administration. Many, such as John McCain, have expressed profound concern about its use of torture and secret prisons; others, such as Arlen Specter, warn that the secret NSA wiretapping could be a "program of big, Big Brother"; and key neoconservative theorists such as Francis Fukuyama have simply abandoned this administration's policy of pre-emptive war as a disaster and a "shambles."[4] Finally, even archconservatives such as Bruce Bartlett, the domestic policy adviser under Reagan and author of *Reaganomics,* have concluded that the Bush administration has less in common with traditional "conservatism" than with the obsessive secrecy of Nixon and the financial chicanery of Enron.[5]

Initially, this administration's powerful mixture of public religiosity and obsessive secrecy struck me as simple hypocrisy—the old story of an outward display of piety and a secret indulgence in vice, which is neither new nor unique to our current politicians. The more I thought about it, however, the more I realized that the connection between religion and secrecy is more than just hypocrisy; it is an integral part of the way this White House has operated from its inception.

This first hit home for me when I was teaching an undergraduate class on religion and globalization at Ohio State University. We had been discussing the Iraq war and the false information that was used to justify the U.S.-led invasion. I had asked the students to critically analyze Mr. Bush's repeated use of religious rhetoric to justify the war—the "Axis of Evil," freedom as a "gift of the Almighty," and so forth. And we then examined some of the evidence that strongly suggested that our president had misled us, such as the Downing Street Minutes, which seemed to indicate a deliberate abuse of intelligence. I asked my students how they would reconcile this apparent contradiction between our president's religious rhetoric and the mounting evidence of secrecy, deception, and outright lies. One young woman—a self-identified evangelical Christian—gave an answer that suddenly helped me understand this administration and how it has so successfully persuaded its supporters: "President Bush wouldn't lie to us," she said, "he's a man of prayer. I trust him. I find it comforting to know that a man who talks to God is leading us."

As Thomas Franks has pointed out, one of the reasons Bush—and much of the Republican Party—has been so successful is the creation of an image of *authenticity, truthfulness,* and *honesty.*[6] Bush's display of religiosity, along with his support from evangelical leaders such as Pat Robertson, Ralph Reed, and James Robison, has been a key part of this image of authenticity. This is a large part of what has persuaded so many Americans to give him the benefit of the doubt, to look the other way, *to trust him,* even as more and more aspects of his administration have been clothed in secrecy and carried out beyond the public eye. After all, if we are a nation of "In God we trust," then if our president trusts in God, we can safely trust in him. Until very recently, this image of trust has worked quite well, helping Bush through two elections[7] and only seriously beginning to falter almost six years into his presidency.

But as that trust has rapidly crumbled along with the president's plummeting poll numbers, it has become clear to me that Bush's image of "trust" also serves to mask a deeper and much darker aspect of this administration, one that combines religious fervor and obsessive secrecy in a far more disturbing way. Indeed, this administration appears to have a fundamental belief its own divinely guided and exceptional status, one that places it above public scrutiny, congressional oversight, and even international law. Thus it has justified the use of secret prisons, secret torture, and secret wiretapping, all in the name of its divinely appointed mission to defeat "evil-doers" and spread freedom as "God's gift to humanity." Ultimately, it seems to me, both secrecy and religion in this administration are part of a much broader and more disturbing phenomenon, namely, *an unprecedented grab for executive power, accompanied by an equally unprecedented erosion of citizens' rights and privacy.* This phenomenon, I believe, has little in common with democracy. On the contrary, this is its very undoing.

Obviously, neither government secrecy nor the political use of religious rhetoric are new things in the United States, nor are they likely to disappear anytime soon, even with the close of Bush's second term. On the contrary, these are trends that have been growing—and growing threats to democracy—for the past fifty years. In the context of our apparently endless "War on Terror," they are certain to continue and become even more central issues as we enter the post-Bush era, no matter which party wins the next election. It seems unlikely that many Republicans would like to see such obsessive secrecy, politicized religion, government surveillance, and unchecked executive power in the hands of Hillary Clinton, any more than most Democrats would like to see it in the hands of another Republican president. These are trends that any thinking citizen should find deeply unsettling. Based on the results of the 2006 midterm elections, which most observers see as a clear referendum on President Bush and the Iraq war, a growing number of citizens do appear to find these trends extremely disturbing.

As Jon Stewart pointed out in his infamous appearance on *Crossfire* in 2004, the mainstream media are apparently unable or unwilling to help us very much in the struggle for open discourse and informed, rational debate.[8] Controlled as they are by five major corporations, the U.S. media are concerned far more with profit and providing infotainment than with a serious critical analysis of the role of religion and secrecy in contemporary politics. Therefore, with the apparent failure of the fourth estate, it is now largely up to ordinary citizens to resist obsessive government secrecy and invasive surveillance, to critique the manipulation of religion for political gain, and to argue *for* the recovery of a kind of "moral values" that would benefit all citizens, rich and poor, gay and straight, black and white, Christian and non-Christian equally. Here, I will argue for a form of deliberative and communicative democracy that is, I believe, the very opposite of the sort of secretive, arrogant, and extremist politics that drive our current White House. In this sense, this book can be considered one of the "weapons of openness" that Niels Bohr believed could combat the "weapons of secrecy" wielded by oppressive political regimes.[9]

In writing this book, I have tried as far as possible to avoid extensive theoretical discussions, academic jargon, and excessive footnoting. My aim here is to open a debate among a broad public audience, not among a few academics. Readers who would like to see a more theoretical and extensively documented argument can read some of my articles, where I have developed some of these arguments in more technical detail.[10]

Acknowledgments

There are a number of friends and relatives who have helped me tremendously in the conception and writing of this book. Foremost among them are Michael Barkun, Wendy Doniger, Tanya Erzen, Cathy Gutierrez, Gene Holland, David Horn, Paul C. Johnson, Bruce Lincoln, Marge Lynd, Charles Mathewes, Rebecca Moore, Phil Newman, Brian Romer, Brian Rotman, Barry Shank, Arthur Versluis, my mother and siblings, and most of all, my best pals, Nancy, Shakti, and Dorje.

Notes

1. Hugh B. Urban, *Tantra: Sex, Secrecy, Politics, and Power in the Study of Religion* (Berkeley: University of California Press, 2003); *Magia Sexualis: Sex, Magic, and Liberation in Modern Western Esotericism* (Berkeley: University of California Press, 2006).

2. Howard Fineman, "Bush and God," *Newsweek*, March 10, 2003, 25.

3. Ronald Suskind, "Faith, Certainty and the Presidency of George W. Bush," *New York Times Magazine*, October 17, 2004, 44.

4. See John McCain, "Torture's Terrible Toll," *Newsweek*, November 21, 2005; "Spy Phone Database Fallout Hits Bush," *Sydney Morning Herald*, May 12, 2006; Francis Fukuyama, "After Neoconservatism," *New York Times Magazine*, February 19, 2006, 62.

5. Bruce Bartlett, *Imposter: How George W. Bush Bankrupted America and Betrayed the Reagan Legacy* (New York: Doubleday, 2006), 102ff, 141ff.

6. Thomas Franks, *What's the Matter with America: The Resistible Rise of the American Right* (London: Vintage, 2005), 27.

7. There is, of course, much debate as to how much religion and moral values influenced the last two elections—and also much debate as to whether Bush even *won* the last elections, as disturbing evidence of electoral fraud in key states such as Florida and Ohio has emerged. See Mark Crispin Miller, *Fooled Again: How the Right Stole the 2004 Election and Why They'll Steal the Next One Too (Unless We Stop Them)* (New

York: Basic, 2005); Robert F. Kennedy Jr., "Was the 2004 Election Stolen?" *Rolling Stone*, June 2006.

8. As Stewart incisively put it in his exchange with Tucker Carlson, "See, the thing is, we need your help. Right now, you're helping the politicians and the corporations. . . . You're part of their strategies. You are partisan, what do you call it, hacks." *CNN Crossfire*, October 15, 2004, at transcripts.cnn.com/TRANSCRIPTS/0410/15/cf .01.html.

9. See Arthur Kantrowitz, "The Weapon of Openness," *Foresight* 4 (1989), at www .foresight.org/Updates/Background4.html.

10. Hugh B. Urban, "Religion and Secrecy in the Bush Administration: The Gentleman, the Prince, and the Simulacrum," *Esoterica* 7 (2005), at www.esoteric .msu.edu/VolumeVII/Secrecy.htm, and "America Left Behind: Bush, the Neoconservatives, and Evangelical Christian Fiction," *Journal of Religion and Society* 8 (2006), at moses.creighton.edu/JRS/2006/2006-2.html.

Introduction

The Kingdom of Secrets: Religion, Secrecy, and the Politics of Empire

The secret of the kingdom of God has been given to you. But to those on the outside everything is said in parables.

—Mark 4:11 (NIV)

Secrecy lies at the very core of power.

—Elias Canetti, *Crowds and Power*

THE PRESIDENCY OF GEORGE W. BUSH CONTAINS, at its very heart, a fundamental paradox and apparent contradiction. On the one hand, this is arguably the most outspokenly religious president in U.S. history, a man who claims not only to have been saved, but also to have been called by God to lead our country. Religious conviction informs virtually every aspect of his presidency, from his domestic faith-based initiatives to his equally faith-based foreign policy with his "crusade" against the "Axis of Evil" and his promise to bring freedom as a "gift from God" to benighted regions of the world such as Iraq. Indeed, much of the success of Mr. Bush in the past two elections has been credited to his image as a man of sincere faith, straightforward honesty, and moral conviction.[1]

Yet on the other hand, this is also by many accounts the most secretive administration in U.S. history, displaying an intense preoccupation with information control. President Bush and Vice President Cheney have been described by various observers as having not just an obsession but a "secrecy fetish."[2] Larry Klayman, chairman of Judicial Watch, has called this administration "the most secretive of our lifetime,"[3] while former Nixon legal adviser

John W. Dean concludes that it is "worse than Watergate."[4] This preoccupation with secrecy began with Bush's first days in office, as he fought to conceal his own Texas gubernatorial records and the presidential records of Reagan and then–Vice President George H. W. Bush; it continues to pervade virtually every aspect of this administration, from its highly secretive National Energy Development Policy to the bewildering flurry of dissimulation surrounding the pre-emptive invasion of Iraq. As Walter Cronkite aptly put it, "This administration—the most secretive since Richard Nixon's—suffers from a deepening credibility problem. . . . Looking back at the past three years reveals a pattern of secrecy and of dishonesty in the service of secrecy."[5]

This book explores the apparent contradiction between this president's intense display of religiosity and his administration's equally intense obsession with concealment. Such a book is at once much needed and extremely relevant at this historical moment. While there has been much written on Mr. Bush's religiosity and a fair amount on his preoccupation with secrecy, this is the first book to examine critically the complex interplay between religion and secrecy in the present White House. Intense religiosity and obsessive secrecy, I will suggest, are not only coexistent in this administration; they are in fact inextricably intertwined.

The Secrets of the Kingdom will argue that this apparent contradiction between the current administration's intense display of religiosity and its equally intense concern with secrecy is in fact only that—an apparent one. When we place it in the broader context of the U.S. government's preoccupation with secrecy over the past fifty years and the power of faith in American politics, it makes a great deal of sense. Excessive government secrecy has been a growing threat since the beginning of the Cold War, the new "War on Terror" simply giving it new license for abuse. Similarly, the political manipulation of religion has been with us for quite a while, particularly since the Reagan era and the rise of movements such as the Moral Majority and the Christian Coalition.

What seems unique about the current administration is that, under the guidance of strategists such as Karl Rove and Dick Cheney, it has transformed the political use of both secrecy and religion into a whole new science. Indeed, in a postindustrial age of information, the control of information has become both a key political strategy and a new form of warfare. And in a media-dominated "society of the spectacle,"[6] the projection of a particular kind of image—above all, an image of piety, compassion, and faith—has become the key to political success. The Bush administration has used the arts of information control and image projection in ways that have been extremely effective, but also deeply disturbing to those who wish to preserve a free and open democracy.

The link between religion and secrecy becomes even clearer if we look at the role of the neoconservative movement in the current administration. Led by figures such as Irving Kristol, William Kristol, Paul Wolfowitz, and Donald Rumsfeld and powerful think tanks such as the Project for the New American Century, the neoconservatives are quite clear about the need for both strict secrecy in the political realm and strong religion in American society. One of the most influential but lesser-known neoconservative theorists is Michael Ledeen, who openly advocates a return to Machiavelli as the most appropriate model of governance—including Machiavelli's belief in the necessity of deception and the appearance of piety as essential political tools.

Meanwhile, the corporate media have largely played along with the construction of Bush's image as a man of strong faith and morality, while remaining stunningly uncritical of his administration's less admirable activities. Indeed, it seems difficult to believe that any administration could have gotten away with such a blatant disregard for truth without the complicity of a corporate-controlled media that seem either too timid or too complacent to seriously investigate this government's obsession with secrecy and dissimulation.

But most importantly, I will argue that much of the success—and also the failure—of this administration is due to the relatively vacuous figure of Mr. Bush himself. Combining a sort of divine certitude and religious zeal with an apparent disregard for government transparency or accountability, President Bush is a striking embodiment of this complex mixture of religious display and political secrecy. Above all, Mr. Bush serves as the key *structural link* that ties together the neoconservative ideologues and their strongest base of popular support, the Christian right. Using Max Weber's phrase, I will suggest that there is a kind of "elective affinity" between these two groups and that Mr. Bush serves as the primary link that helps join these two otherwise very different factions together. As a sort of religio-political ligament, Bush brings together the neoconservatives' intense concern with secrecy, information control, and surveillance with the evangelicals' push for a faith-based government. His display of piety thus provides a sense of *divine justification and messianic certitude* for his party's political agendas, while at the same time *concealing and obfuscating* their often catastrophic consequences for our nation and the world. Both religion and secrecy, in Bush's case, are ultimately about *power*: on the one hand, the power that comes from the appeal to a transcendent, suprahuman but also unseen divine authority and, on the other hand, the power that comes from the control of knowledge and the calculated concealment of valuable information.

In sum, the central role of religion and secrecy in the Bush administration does not represent so much a radical departure from U.S. politics as an intensification of certain trends that have been with us since at least the beginning of the Cold War. It should, however, serve as a wake-up call. In the context of the ongoing (perhaps perpetual) War on Terror, these issues are not likely to go away any time soon, even with the end of Bush's second term. On the contrary, the questions of government secrecy, individual rights to privacy, and the role of religion in politics are likely to become far more rather than less intense in the post-Bush era, no matter which party wins in 2008. It is therefore imperative that we begin seriously examining those questions, looking not just at the role of religion and secrecy in the present administration, but also at their larger implications for democracy as a whole.

In God We Trust? Religion, Secrecy, and the Paradoxes of American Democracy

> The cause we serve is right, because it is the cause of all mankind. The momentum of freedom in our world is unmistakable—and it is not carried forward by our power alone. We can trust in that greater Power who guides the unfolding of the years. And in all that is to come, we can know that His purposes are just and true.
>
> —George W. Bush, *State of the Union Address*, January 20, 2004

> All men having power ought to be distrusted to a certain degree.
>
> —James Madison, speech in the Constitutional Convention, July 11, 1787

The complex mixture of religion and secrecy is surely nothing new in the history of the United States. If anything, the Bush White House represents the most acute and extreme example of several much larger tensions that have been with us for a long time and that strike to the heart of our democracy. The most important among these are the tension between a vibrantly religious society and a government that respects the separation of church and state, and the tension between the need for political secrecy and the need for openness in a democratic society.

What is unique about the Bush administration, I believe, is that the delicate balances both between church and state and between secrecy and openness have been overturned significantly—and without any sense of misgiving or apology. In the post-9/11 world, secrecy is now the rule, like it or not. Likewise, in the era of small government and faith-based initiatives, the separation of church and state has become increasingly undermined, if not dismantled altogether. But don't worry, we are told, *Trust us. Have faith in us,* just as Mr. Bush has placed his trust in God as the Author of history and the unseen, hidden, yet providential Guide of America's destiny. As then-governor Bush put it in his 1999 autobiography, "I could not be governor if I did not believe in a divine plan that supersedes all human plans. . . . My faith frees me. . . . Frees me to make decisions that others might not like."[7] *Trust*, we will see, is a crucial part of Bush's success—and also of his failure, as that trust is increasingly undermined by reality.

The Necessity and the Danger of Secrecy:
The Power of Concealment and the Aura of Power

> O divine art of subtlety and secrecy! Through you we learn to be invisible, through you inaudible; and hence we can hold the enemy's fate in our hands.
>
> —Sun Tzu, *The Art of War*

Secrecy is a very powerful but ambivalent and double-edged sort of political strategy, with both positive and negative implications. Derived from the Latin verb *secernere*, secrecy is by definition what "separates" and "divides"—what separates those who know from those who do not, those who are "in" on the secret and those who are outsiders. In virtually all esoteric organizations, from indigenous secret societies to the Freemasons or Yale's Skull and Bones, secrecy is a basic means of distinguishing those who are in possession of highly valued information from those who are not. As such, secrecy is inevitably tied to relations of power. If, as the twentieth-century philosopher Michel Foucault suggests, knowledge and power are always interrelated, then secrecy lies at their very nexus; indeed, one could say that "wherever there is power there is secrecy."[8] In this sense, secrecy is integral to the functioning of all modern political bureaucracies, which are typically organized by hierarchies of knowledge and power. As sociologist Max Weber observed over eighty years ago,

> Every bureaucracy seeks to increase the superiority of the professionally informed by keeping their knowledge and intentions secret. Bureaucratic administration always tends to be an administration of "secret sessions": in so far as it can, it hides its knowledge and action from criticism. . . . The concept of the "official secret" is the specific invention of the bureaucracy, and nothing is so fanatically defended. . . . In facing a parliament the bureaucracy, out of a sure power instinct, fights every attempt of the parliament to gain knowledge. . . . Bureaucracy naturally welcomes a poorly informed and hence powerless parliament.[9]

But this link between power, knowledge, and secrecy is more important than ever in our current information-based society. Today as never before, in a world of cell phones, the Internet, on-line banking, and massive data banks of digital information, control of the circulation of knowledge is intimately tied to the circulation of power. It is no accident, for example, that the highly controversial and now (ostensibly) defunct "Total Information Awareness" project of DARPA's Information Awareness Office used the phrase *scientia est potentia* ("knowledge is power") on its official seal.[10]

Most basically, we might say that secrecy can work in two closely related but seemingly opposite ways—what we might call secrecy as *the power of concealment* and secrecy as *the aura of power*. As concealment, secrecy often has a necessary power of protection, of safeguarding individuals and groups from external forces who might endanger them. As philosopher Sisella Bok notes, governments have always used secret deliberation in order to conduct important affairs of state without fear of outside interference. Concealment insulates bureaucracies from criticism and interference; "it allows them to correct mistakes and to reverse direction without costly, often embarrassing explanation and it permits them to cut corners with no questions being asked."[11]

But this power of concealment can be used not just as protection but also as a weapon. As Elias Canetti points out in his classic *Crowds and Power*, secrecy is also the very "core of power." As a strategy of disguise and dissimulation, secrecy is what allows the predator to conceal itself from its prey; and it is what allows one military or political party to mount a sneak attack on its enemy: "The act of lying in wait for prey is essentially secret. Hiding, or taking on the colour of its surroundings and betraying itself by no movement, the lurking creature disappears entirely, covering itself with secrecy as with a second skin."[12] Thus, the Chinese philosopher Sun Tzu observed 2,500 years ago in his classic *Art of War* that secrecy is one of the essential keys to military strategy, the "divine art" that allows one to outwit and destroy one's enemies.[13] As we will see, Sun Tzu's advice on the power of secrecy has been followed by many contemporary political strategists, from Christian Coalition president Ralph Reed to campaign strategist Karl Rove.

Yet while secrecy clearly serves as an effective strategy of concealment and obfuscation, it can also function in the opposite sense—that is, as a kind of *aura or adornment* of power. Paradoxically, *the display of secrecy* and the *advertisement* or *leaking* of secret knowledge can be used as its own kind of potent political tactic. As Max Frankel observes in his study of White House politics during the Nixon administration, the release of secret knowledge can be as effective a political weapon as the keeping of secrets: "Even harmless secrets were *coins of power* to be hoarded. . . . [T]he bigger a secret the greater its ultimate value."[14] In other words, the *leaking* and *circulation* of secrets is often a key source of political capital that can be strategically used or "spent" in order to enhance one's position in the larger field of power:

> Officials often provided classified information to journalists, sometimes to enhance their own prestige, sometimes to gain advantage in an internal dispute. . . .

[M]ost "leaking" was coming from the higher reaches of the system (We have Kennedy's testament that the Ship of State is the only ship that leaks from the top).[15]

In our own historical moment, surely the most infamous example of this use of secret information as a coin of power is the leak of CIA operative Valerie Plame, which has now been traced to several top White House officials. Leaking of secrets was in this case not simply a "coin of power," but also a weapon apparently used as cruel payback for her husband Joe Wilson's negative report on Iraq's alleged attempts to obtain uranium from Niger (which in turn called into question the evidence used to justify the entire Iraq war).[16]

Finally, secrecy also has its own sort of mysterious power—a power that often borders on the religious. As Georg Simmel noted one hundred years ago in his classic work on the sociology of secrecy, the possession of secret knowledge gives its owner a certain "aura" or "adornment" of power, a kind of mystery, prestige, and awe that sets one apart from ordinary human beings:

> The secret gives one a position of exception. . . . For the average man, all superior persons have something mysterious. . . . From secrecy, which shades all that is profound and significant, grows the typical error according to which everything mysterious is something important and essential. Before the unknown, man's natural impulse is to idealize and his natural fearfulness cooperate toward the same goal: to intensify the unknown through imagination.[17]

Secrecy in this sense is generally more often associated with traditional aristocracies than with modern democracies. While democracies depend on publicity and the transparency of their elected officials, "aristocracies exploit the psychological fact that the unknown itself appears to be fearsome, mighty, threatening"; indeed, they depend to a large degree on the fact that "secrecy and mystification amount to heightening the wall toward the outside and hence to strengthening the aristocratic character of the group."[18] The presence of widespread political secrecy within a democratic nation such as the United States could therefore be taken as a symptom that a new kind of aristocratic power is at work. Indeed, as Kevin Phillips suggests in *American Dynasty*, the Bush family can be seen as part of a kind of "neo-aristocratic" phenomenon in the United States, what he calls the "dynastization of wealth and politics," as more and more money and influence is placed in the hands of a few powerful families such as the Bushes. As in traditional aristocracies, this dynastization has gone hand in hand with increased government secrecy, which has been "rising like an antirepublican phoenix" in the twenty-first century.[19]

In American politics, of course, secrecy is by no means a new phenomenon. As Eric Alterman observes, secrecy has been a "key facet of American governance since literally before the nation's founding."[20] Even the Constitutional

Convention of 1789 was held behind closed doors, shut to reporters, with delegates forbidden to reveal the deliberations. Presidents have long invoked the authority of Article II, section 2 of the Constitution in order to restrict dissemination of information relating to defense and foreign policy, and most Americans would likely acknowledge that no modern state can reveal everything to everyone without compromising the security of its citizens.

Yet alongside this recognition of the need for secrecy, there have also been powerful voices reminding us of its inherent dangers. From James Madison on, presidents have warned repeatedly of the destructive and antidemocratic nature of excessive government secrecy. As President Kennedy famously put it in 1961, "The very word 'secrecy' is repugnant in a free and open society; and we are as a people inherently and historically opposed to secret societies, to secret oaths, and to secret proceedings."[21] President Truman put it even more succinctly: "Secrecy and a free, democratic government don't mix."[22]

One of the greatest dangers of secrecy is that it so often and so easily slips into simple lying. Indeed, lying could be considered its "close cousin and frequently its handmaiden and inspiration,"[23] and secrecy in turn the "guardian angel of calculated deception."[24] It is not difficult to make the transition from not speaking the truth at all to speaking an untruth, and U.S. presidential history provides no shortage of examples of this maneuver. Among the more infamous cases of presidential lying are Lyndon Johnson's concealing of his policy of escalation in Vietnam in 1964 and his far-reaching deceptions in orchestrating the Gulf of Tonkin resolution; Nixon's secret bombing of Cambodia in 1969; and Reagan's lies about sending arms to Iran and aid to the Nicaraguan Contras.[25] Indeed, despite their noble warnings about the dangers of secrecy, both Truman and Kennedy would become involved in some of the most complex games of dissimulation in U.S. history—Truman overseeing the creation of both the Central Intelligence Agency (CIA) and the ultrasecret National Security Agency (NSA), whose very existence was denied for over a generation, and Kennedy lying about the secret compromise made with the Soviets that settled the Cuban missile crisis. As Department of Defense official Arthur Sylvester said on behalf of President Kennedy during the Cuban missile crisis, "It's inherent in [the] government's right, if necessary, to lie to save itself."[26]

So we have long recognized both the necessity of secrecy in certain situations, particularly those concerning national security, and the inherent danger of secrecy and its tendency to slip into lying pure and simple. As Edward Shils argues in his classic study of secrecy during the Cold War, a healthy democracy requires a delicate balance between secrecy, privacy, and publicity—that is, a recognition that some sensitive information needs to be concealed, that citizens' rights to privacy must be protected, and that we should strive for transparency in government wherever possible. (Secrecy here refers to the *obligatory* concealment of acts or information—for example, the identity of a covert CIA operative—accompanied by sanctions in the events of disclosure. Privacy, conversely, refers to the *voluntary* concealment of acts or information—for example, sexual relations between consenting adults—typically without such sanctions.)[27] Yet what has occurred over the past fifty years, and above all in the wake of 9/11, is a significant *shift* in our attitude toward government secrecy, a shift from secrecy as a necessary evil that must be limited as far as possible to secrecy as standard operating procedure and status quo. This shift has gone hand in hand with a shift from lying as a rare, at times defensible act to lying as a normal and accepted part of U.S. politics. But perhaps most disturbing, it has also gone hand in hand with a rapid erosion of privacy on the part of ordinary citizens.

Eternal Hostility or Mutual Reinforcement?
Religion and Politics in the United States

> I have sworn upon the altar of God eternal hostility against every form of tyranny over the mind of men.
>
> —Thomas Jefferson, letter to Benjamin Rush

On the surface—and indeed, even etymologically—religion would appear to be the opposite of secrecy. If secrecy is what separates (*secernere*), then religion is what "reconnects" or "reunites" (*re-ligio*), what joins human beings into communities and links them to a perceived transcendent power. Yet, in fact, the two have much in common and have often gone hand in hand in American history.

While there are many, perhaps infinite, ways of defining religion, one of the more useful comes from historian of religion Bruce Lincoln. What makes specifically *religious* sorts of discourse unique, Lincoln suggests, is that they make a claim to a particular kind of authority, an authority that is believed to be transcendent, suprahuman, and therefore beyond human finitude and fallibility: "religious claims are the means by which certain objects, places, speakers, and speech-acts are invested with an authority, the source of which lies *outside the human.* That is, these claims create the appearance that their authorization comes from a realm beyond history, society, and politics, beyond the terrain in which interested and situated actors struggle over scarce resources."[28] Thus religious authority is uniquely powerful. Indeed, it can serve as the *ultimate motivator,* an authority that can persuade human beings to undertake both superhuman acts of compassion and horrific acts of violence. Religions can thus provide deep sources of personal meaning as well as an inspiration for movements of social justice, civil rights, or Gandhian nonviolent resistance; but they can also provide the inspiration for violence and a divine justification for young men to fly airplanes into skyscrapers or drive fertilizer bombs into buildings. Human beings rarely wage war in the name of Shakespeare or Picasso, but they frequently *do* in the name of Jesus, Allah, Shiva, and even Buddha. In this sense, religion, like secrecy, is to a certain degree also about *power*, indeed, an ultimate form of power.

But it is a kind of authority and power that is also unverifiable and beyond contestation. Like secrecy, such religious authority is inherently *unseen, hidden, and unknowable* to all but those who have it, or claim to have it. As Rudolph Otto defined it in his classic *The Idea of the Holy*, the sacred, or *mysterium*, "denotes merely that which is hidden or esoteric, that which is beyond conception or understanding."[29] Likewise, as William James put it in his *Varieties of Religious Experience*, religion in the broadest sense "consists of the belief that there is an unseen order and that our supreme good lies in harmoniously adjusting ourselves thereto."[30] In sum, like secrecy, religion is to a large degree precisely about the *power of what is hidden or unseen.*

A perfect example of this appeal to a divine but unseen authority occurred during the third debate in the 1999 Republican primary race, when Governor Bush was asked to name his favorite philosopher. While other candidates cited John Locke or the Founding Fathers, Bush replied simply "Christ, because he changed my heart." When the moderator suggested that perhaps the audience would like a bit more elaboration on his choice, he said simply, "Well, if they don't know, it's going to be hard to explain. When you turn your heart and life over to Christ, when you accept Christ as a savior, it changes your heart and changes your life. And that's what happened to me."[31] There were no further questions. In other words, Mr. Bush claimed to have a connection to God that is a matter of inner, private, personal experience—an experience that cannot be communicated to others, but only felt by those who have had it themselves. Christ for Bush is a higher authority who cannot be questioned or explained; He can only be understood by those who know Him directly. As we will see in chapter 1, Mr. Bush also claimed a divine calling in his decision to run for president; he appealed to the authority of "a higher Father" when he decided to invade Iraq—both claims that went largely unquestioned by the media. In theory, of course, such claims could be true. But they could also be used to mask and mystify other, perhaps less spiritual, sorts of motivations.

Like secrecy, religion has played a powerful but also deeply ambivalent role in American history from its inception. As David Chidester suggests, the tension between theocracy and democracy—like that between secrecy and openness—has been there since before the founding of the country, and it has by no means subsided in the contemporary era.[32] One of the most instructive examples of this tension is Thomas Jefferson, who was an outspoken critic of

theocracy or any other form of ideological tyranny. While running for president in 1800, Jefferson came under fierce attack from the powerful Protestant
clergy of New England, who knew that he was determined to disestablish state
churches and advocated religious equality. Called "anti-Christ," "atheist," and
"French infidel," Jefferson was the subject of sermons warning that he would
"discredit religion, overthrow the church and destroy the Bible."[33] It was in response to these extremist attacks that Jefferson swore his "eternal hostility" to
any form of tyranny over free thought, political or religious.[34]

Yet in all of this, there is another striking paradox; in declaring his eternal
hostility to the forces of intolerance, Jefferson still appealed to a divine authority and chose to "*swear upon the altar of God*." Thus he highlights the fundamental tension between religious faith and secularism, between the power
of religious authority and the needs of a pluralistic democracy, that runs
throughout the history of this country, much like the tension between secrecy
and openness. The "eternal hostility" between the vicious intolerance of extremism and the ideal of religious pluralism has obviously not disappeared
during the past two hundred years; if anything, it is now more intense than
ever before.

Today, whenever I discuss religion with European friends, they inevitably
express their amazement that the United States is still so fervently religious;
they are baffled that America seems to bear so little trace of the waves of Enlightenment rationalism, Marxist criticism, existentialist despair, and postmodern skepticism that have weakened religious faith in much of western Europe. Most polls show European countries declining rapidly in religious belief
and practice, with only about 5 percent of French and 15 percent of Italian citizens regularly attending religious services. According to a long-term European Values Study, "A mere 21 percent of Europeans hold religion to be 'very
important.' In France . . . the percentage is lower still, at slightly over 10 percent."[35] In the United States, conversely, religious fervor has not only remained
strong but has also apparently intensified over the past several decades. According to *U.S. News & World Report*, there are "more churches, synagogues,
temples, and mosques per capita in the United States than in any other nation
on Earth: one for about every 865 people," while "nearly two thirds of Americans say religion is very important in their lives, and close to half say they attend worship services at least once a week—the highest percentages since the
1960s."[36]

While there are many ways of explaining the surprising strength of religion
in the United States, part of it is surely tied to our deep-rooted belief in America's status as a unique, exceptional, even divinely appointed nation. John
Winthrop's image of America as the "city upon a hill," "in covenant with God,"
and ordained as the light to all nations is a powerful part of our national

imagination, and it has been used, revived, and reused by countless religious and political leaders to inspire Americans to support all manner of social, political, and military causes. As Ernest Tuveson has shown, this image of America as "Redeemer Nation" is as old as the republic, and it tends to resurface during dramatic and violent moments such as times of war: "Over the course of several centuries, this moral mandate has been expressed in conceptions of America as a 'city on a hill,' a 'righteous empire,' and the 'last best hope of humankind.'"[37] This narrative of America's divine mission in history recurs throughout the public discourse of American presidents, gaining a new momentum in the twentieth century. As we will see, it was dramatically intensified during the decades of the Cold War, tied to our struggle against the godless communists and their "Evil Empire," and it would be revived in an even more powerful way by Mr. Bush in the wake of 9/11.

The Cult of Secrecy: Religion and Secrecy during the Cold War

Secrecy . . . has become a god in this country, and those people who have secrets travel in a kind of fraternity, . . . and they will not speak to anyone else.

—Senator J. William Fulbright (1971)

We may be the generation that sees Armageddon.

—Ronald Reagan to Jim Bakker (1980)

While both religion and secrecy have been part of the American political system from its beginning, the two really first began to meld together during the decades of the Cold War. The intense concern with information control that we see in the Bush administration is arguably the most extreme version, or perhaps a logical trajectory, of a growing "cult of secrecy" that has been with us for a long time, particularly since the end of World War II. "During the Cold War," Alterman notes, presidential deception and secrecy became "routinized, defended in elite circles as a distasteful but necessary matter of realpolitik."[38] As Senator Fulbright put it in 1971, secrecy during the Cold War had achieved a dangerous kind of god-like, quasidivine status in our government, serving, much as in a traditional secret society, to divide those who know from those who do not.

Particularly after 1949, when the Soviet Union detonated its own atomic bomb, the threat of communism suddenly seemed not far off in some distant land, but an insidious presence that could strike on American soil itself. Indeed, the Red Menace was now seen as a terrifying, unseen presence that caught much of America—including clergymen and journalists, conservatives and liberals—in its fearful grip. As Stephen Whitfield suggests in *The Culture of the Cold War,* "The specter that, a century earlier, Marx and Engels had described as stalking Europe was extending itself to the United States."[39]

Of course, the Soviet Union was every bit as worried about the United States' own military power, and the result of their mutual paranoia was the growth of the most elaborate apparatus of secrecy, espionage, and counterespionage the world had ever seen. As Angus MacKenzie observes in his study of secrecy and the CIA, the use of the word "war" in our competition with the Soviets was an effective means to justify broad government secrecy and the restriction of constitutional rights:

> The U.S. government has always danced with the devil of secrecy during wartime. By attaching the word "war" to the economic and ideological race for world supremacy between the Soviet Union and the United States, a string of administrations continued this dance uninterrupted for fifty years. The cold war provided the foreign threat to justify the pervasive Washington belief that secrecy should have the greatest possible latitude and openness should be restricted as much as possible—constitutional liberties be damned.[40]

More than just a "war," however, this was portrayed as a conflict with an insidious, implacable enemy bent on nothing less than global domination. Such a war demanded the most extreme sorts of tactics and, above all, extreme use of secrecy, espionage, and deception. Thus General James Doolittle wrote in his 1954 report on the CIA that

> It is now clear that we are facing an implacable enemy whose avowed objective is world domination by whatever means and at whatever loss. There are no rules in such a game. Hitherto acceptable long-standing American concepts of "fair play" must be reconsidered. We must develop effective espionage and counter-espionage services and must learn to subvert, sabotage, and destroy our enemies by more clever, more sophisticated and more effective methods than those used against us.[41]

Within the United States itself, the fear of Communist infiltration was soon extended not just to undercover agents, but also to ordinary American citizens; thus the Federal Bureau of Investigation (FBI) began to compile dossiers on novelists who seemed unduly critical of their native land, and it even filmed patrons of left-wing bookstores. Under both the Truman and Eisenhower administrations, extensive security programs were put into place throughout the civil service. Political testing was also not uncommon, as both government agencies and private employers sought to distinguish between those who were truly patriotic and those who might harbor concealed un-American tendencies. And ordinary citizens were enlisted in the Cold War, called upon to identify those who displayed a lack of patriotic spirit or even suspicious degrees of "neutrality."[42]

Perhaps the epitome of the Cold War obsession with secrecy, security, and surveillance was the creation of the ultrasecret National Security Agency, an organization even larger and more powerful than the FBI or CIA. Ironically referred to as "No Such Agency," the NSA was created in utmost secrecy by President Truman, and its very existence was denied for decades. A 1976 report from the House Government Affairs Committee concluded that "much of the secrecy surrounding [the NSA's] operations is obsessive and unfounded,"[43] while historian Ronald Clark described this secrecy as "a near pathological passion for security."[44] Originally created to spy on foreign enemies, the NSA has long roused fears that its tremendous powers of surveillance could be turned inward, to monitor U.S. citizens, as well. Indeed, as NSA historian James Bamford warns, it is the "agency that could be Big Brother."[45] Over thirty years ago, members of Congress had expressed this concern. After investigating the agency in 1975, Senator Frank Church warned that its power of surveillance "could at any time be turned around on the American people, and no American would have any privacy left, such is the capability to monitor everything: telephone conversations, telegrams, it doesn't matter. There would be no place to hide." If a dictator ever took over, he warned, the NSA would enable him "to impose total tyranny, and there would be no way to fight back."[46]

As the Nixon administration clearly showed, these awesome powers of surveillance provided by the NSA, FBI, and CIA were indeed prone to abuse. In probably the most secretive administration prior to the current one, Nixon effectively "co-opted the NSA and the FBI to advance his own political and policy agendas,"[47] authorizing spying on antiwar groups, celebrities, and even congresspersons; indiscriminate circulation of dossiers on individuals; and the compilation of his own personal "enemies list." In the wake of Nixon's obsessive spying, Congress passed the Privacy Act of 1974, at a time of growing distrust of law enforcement and intelligence agencies that seemed more concerned with protecting executive power than with preserving citizens' liberties. In 1978, Congress then passed the Foreign Intelligence Surveillance Act (FISA), which was intended to deny the president the unchecked right to determine whether a proposed target met a legitimate "foreign intelligence" need and to ensure that all proposals to intercept such communications be approved by a special FISA court.[48]

Despite such efforts to constrain it, however, the U.S. security apparatus only expanded massively during the 1980s and '90s. By the end of the twentieth century, the American obsession with information control had grown into a vast and mind-boggling security complex containing billions of pieces of secret information and employing hundreds of thousands of secret makers. As one observer noted in 2001, even before the intense secrecy that would follow in the wake of 9/11,

> Our secrecy system is vast and complex. It affects virtually every facet of politics and public policy—and of our lives. The U.S. government creates an estimated six million secrets a year. . . . The super-secret National Security Agency stores its hard copies of satellite-intercepted messages in a half million cubic feet of building space. Military records starting at World War II consume twenty-seven acres of underground storage at a site in Maryland. The secret makers, those who can classify a document top secret with the hit of a stamp, are estimated at more than a half million. In vaults at the CIA, State Department, Justice Department, Pentagon, and other agencies, there are a staggering four to five *billion* secrets. . . .
> The secrecy system is out of control. Its growth seems unstoppable.[49]

Commenting on a report by the Commission on Protecting and Reducing Government Secrecy in 1997, Senator Daniel Patrick Moynihan concluded that the immense security apparatus of Cold War America had reached a point of absurdity: "The secrecy system has systematically denied American historians access to the records of American history. Often we find ourselves relying on archives of the former Soviet Union . . . to resolve questions of what was going on in Washington in mid-century. This is absurd."[50] Yet if the Cold War obsession with secrecy was "absurd," we can only wonder what adjective Senator Moynihan might have used to describe the far more intense obsession with concealment and surveillance that we now see in post-9/11 America.

The Evil Empire and God's Chosen Nation: Religion and Cold War America

> God is giving us a desperate choice, a choice of either revival or judgment. There is no alternative! . . . The world is divided into two camps! On the one side we see Communism, . . .[which] has declared war against God, against Christ, against the Bible and against all religion! . . . Unless the Western world has an old-fashioned revival, we cannot last.
>
> —Reverend Billy Graham (1949)

But the Cold War was not only an era of paranoia about communism, intensive secrecy, and surveillance; it was also an era of growing religiosity, indeed, a kind of religious nationalism that helped shape American culture over the past fifty years. More than any other Western country, the United States saw a remarkable increase in religious affiliation after World War II. Church membership rose from roughly 43 percent in 1920 to 82 percent by 1950, although it dropped to 69 percent by the end of the 1950s.[51]

One of the most threatening features of communism, for many clergymen and politicians of the 1950s and '60s, was its "godless and atheistic" nature. This made commitment to Christian faith even more critical for a sincere commitment to the American flag and the struggle against the Soviet menace. Thus, as part of the attempt to distinguish America as a religious nation from the godless communism of the Soviets, "Under God" was added to the Pledge of Allegiance in 1954 and "In God We Trust" to the dollar bill in 1957. As Michael Lienesch notes, the political rise of conservative Christianity in the United States went hand in hand with strong anticommunism as an article of faith. The Christian right arose almost simultaneously with the creation of the Soviet Union and flourished "more or less in tandem with the expansion of Soviet-style communism. . . . Communism has been a focal point for fundamentalist politics, serving to funnel more diffuse fears of atheism, evolutionism, and modernism into a single embodied enemy."[52]

Few preachers of the 1950s were more outspoken in their patriotism, anticommunism, and Christian fervor than Rev. Billy Graham. Throughout his sermons, Graham wedded a kind of old-fashioned Americanism with the Way of the Cross as the most effective shield against "Satan's version of religion," which was communism. "If you would be a true patriot, then become a Christian," he exhorted his audience; indeed, "Only as millions of Americans turn to Jesus Christ at this hour and accept him as Savior, can this nation possibly be spared the onslaught of a demon-possessed Communism."[53] As theologian Reinhold Niebhur observed, this anti-Communist, pro-American rhetoric was a consistent and central theme in Graham's sermons of the 1950s, so much so that "scarcely one of his Sunday afternoon sermons over a nine-year period has failed to touch on communism. . . . Almost every time he mentions the need or value of a revival he does so in connection with the spread of communism. And several times he has devoted a whole sermon to the death-duel between Christian America and atheistic Russia."[54]

Like many contemporary evangelicals whom we will meet in this book, Graham also equated American-style capitalism with American democracy and saw it as a key part of our global struggle with the demon-possessed Communist system. Indeed, "Christianity and capitalism are as inextricably interconnected as the spiritual conversion of souls and their worldly success as selves."[55] In this respect, Graham foresaw the alliance between conservative Republicans and evangelicals that would later emerge in the 1980s and '90s and now shapes much of the current administration.

Graham's powerful mixture of anti-Communist and pro-American, pro-capitalist religious rhetoric was revived in the early 1980s by televangelists such as Jerry Falwell. For Falwell, the confrontation between the ultimate power of Good, America, and the ultimate power of Evil, was truly one of biblical proportions, signaling the imminent End of Days. In a 1984 pamphlet entitled "Armageddon and the Coming War with Russia," Falwell warned that the ultimate military and apocalyptic scenario was about to unfold: "the stage is rapidly being set, even today in the Middle East, for the final conflict. Russia will invade Israel, communism will be defeated, the antichrist will appear and the 'final holocaust' at Armageddon will consume the Earth." Yet true Christians need not worry, he assured his readers, for they have the ultimate Ally and Protector on their side: "we're going up in the Rapture before any of it occurs."[56]

But it was not only religious leaders who saw the Cold War as a mighty struggle between good and evil, God's chosen nation and godless communism. Many political leaders used almost exactly the same language. Following our triumph over the evil of fascism in Europe, President Truman proclaimed America "the greatest nation on earth, . . . the greatest in History," indeed, a kind of millennial nation that would "continue for another thousand years as the greatest country in the world."[57] Truman's Cold War rhetoric made explicit use of religious language to portray America as God's chosen nation, created in God's image, in contrast to the tyrannical menace of communism. As he stated in his 1949 inaugural address,

> The American people stand firm in the faith which has inspired this Nation from the beginning. . . . We believe that all men are created equal because they are created in the image of God. . . . In the pursuit of these aims, the United States and other like-minded nations find themselves directly opposed by a regime with contrary aims and a totally different concept of life. That regime adheres to a false philosophy which purports to offer freedom, security, and greater opportunity to mankind. Misled by this philosophy, many peoples have sacrificed their liberties only to learn to their sorrow that deceit and mockery, poverty and tyranny, are their reward. That false philosophy is communism. . . . Events have brought our American democracy to new influence and new responsibilities. They will test our courage, our devotion to duty, and our concept of liberty. . . . Steadfast in our faith in the Almighty, we will advance toward a world where man's freedom is secure.[58]

This sort of good versus evil, America as God's chosen nation versus the tyranny of godless communism rhetoric persisted throughout the 1950s and '60s. As President Eisenhower denounced the evil of communism in 1956, "According to that doctrine, there is no God; there is no soul in man. . . . Communism is cruel, intolerant, materialistic." To defeat this menace would require Americans to engage in a struggle of epic proportions and ultimate significance, for the "forces of good and evil are massed and armed and opposed as rarely before in history."[59]

Finally, this invocation of powerful religious rhetoric reappeared in a new form in the 1980s with the presidency of Ronald Reagan. Indeed, one could say that "the union between the sacred and secular . . . defined Reagan's public discourse."[60] Much as Bush would twenty years later, Reagan painted the world in clear black-and-white terms, with America as the divinely chosen defender of freedom against the implacable enemy of the Evil Empire. As Lienesch suggests, "From the early 1950s, when the Hollywood actor narrated anti-Communist films for the Church League of America, to the mid-1980s, when he spoke . . . to the National Association of Evangelicals, Reagan articulated the anticommunism of the Christian Right."[61] With his opposition to abortion, support for school prayer, and war against the Evil Empire, Reagan offered the mix of domestic and foreign policies that appealed directly to conservative Christian leaders. And he in turn enthusiastically embraced the conservative Christian community, declaring in 1980, "I endorse you."[62]

Ironically, however, the combination of religion, secrecy, and intensive militarism during the Cold War would give rise to a new kind of "imperialism" that finally outmatched that of the "Evil Empire"—namely, the often unrecognized but historically unprecedented empire of the United States, with its armies, weapons, bases, spies, and economic influence spread to every corner of the globe. By 2000, in fact, the United States was spending more on its military than Russia, China, all European NATO states, and Israel *combined*. Increasingly over the past five years, both critics and sympathizers have begun to recognize that America has indeed emerged as a new imperial power, one with unprecedented global reach. "People are coming out of the closet on the word 'empire,'" Charles Krauthammer noted in 2002, for today America is "no mere international citizen" but "the dominant power in the world, more dominant than any since Rome."[63] As Chalmers Johnson argues in *The Sorrows of Empire*, the rise of America's imperial stature has been accomplished in large part through pervasive secrecy and the quiet spread of our military power to every corner of the globe:

> most Americans do not recognize . . . that the United States dominates the world
> through its military power. Due to government secrecy, they are often ignorant
> of the fact that their government garrisons the globe. They do not realize that a
> vast network of American military bases on every continent . . . constitutes a new
> form of empire.[64]

A powerful religious ideology and a powerful apparatus of secrecy are key elements of any empire. Historically, religion and empire have gone hand in hand. As Kevin Phillips notes, religion and imperialism are frequently interdependent: "kings have been succored by the type of religion that required bishops, imperialism has thrived under the power of the scepter."[65] The most powerful political formations, from Rome to imperial Spain or Britain, require the most powerful forms of religious authority to legitimate and justify them. At the same time, if *scientia est potentia*, then empires also require secrecy, that is, control over the powerful resources of knowledge and information. Indeed, religion, secrecy, and empire form a closely interrelated triangle of power, fusing appeal to divine authority with the aura of mystery that radiates from the hidden.

With the dawn of the twenty-first century, the forces of religion and secrecy had reemerged and intertwined in a new form, what the neoconservatives have euphemistically dubbed the "emerging imperium" or "benevolent empire" of the New American Century.[66]

The New Cold War? Generalized Secrecy and Extreme Religion Post-9/11

> Our keeping of secrets has often misled and confused our own people but has been ineffective in denying information to our enemies or competitors. . . .
>
> A short time ago, the Soviet Union was the most secretive organization in the world; it no longer exists. . . . This puts the United States in the uncomfortable position of holding the record in secrecy. It is urgent that we do something about this situation.
>
> —Edward Teller (1992)

With the collapse of the Soviet Union and the end of the Cold War, many Americans were hopeful that the intensive secrecy that had come to pervade all levels of government might become obsolete and gradually recede. As Senator Moynihan put it in 1996, "It is time to dismantle government secrecy, this most pervasive of Cold War–era regulations. It is time to begin building the supports for the era of openness that is already upon us."[67] While this seemed to many a possibility during the Clinton era, when many previously classified documents were declassified, the attacks of September 11, 2001, would soon dispel such optimism and usher in a new, even more intense period of secrecy. While 9/11 did not create a new kind of government secrecy, it did give a powerful new justification, intensification, and, as we will see, a kind of divine legitimation to a secrecy-industrial complex that had been growing for the previous fifty years. Today, we seem to have entered fully into the state of "generalized secrecy" and "unanswerable lies" that philosopher Guy Debord had described as the defining features of media-driven consumer society of the late twentieth century.[68]

While some, such as Moynihan, looked forward to a new era of openness, many others were far less eager to relinquish the tremendous power that the enormous Cold War security apparatus had built. Most of the key players in the current Bush administration—such as Cheney, Rumsfeld, and Wolfowitz—were veterans of several Cold War administrations going back to Nixon and had no particular interest in seeing the massive system of secrecy dismantled. Many of the neoconservatives, as we will see in the following chapters, seem to have an almost romantic nostalgia for the good old days of the Cold War, when we all thought we knew who was good and who was evil, when there were clear heroes and enemies, and when America's military might always seemed to be on the side of right.

Thus it is no surprise that the new Bush administration would soon resurrect a powerful sort of Reaganesque Cold War rhetoric. Above all in the wake of 9/11, President Bush made a clear analogy between the new global war against terror and the Cold War, suggesting that now, in our struggle against radical Islam, we are once again facing an implacable enemy that represents that exact opposite of everything America believes in:

> Because the war on terror will require resolve and patience, it will also require firm moral purpose. In this way our struggle is similar to the Cold War. Now, as then, our enemies are totalitarians, holding a creed of power with no place for human dignity. Now, as then, they seek to impose a joyless conformity, to control every life and all of life. America confronted imperial communism in many different ways. . . . Yet moral clarity was essential to our victory in the Cold War. . . . Some worry that it is somehow undiplomatic or impolite to speak the language of right and wrong. I disagree. . . . Moral truth is the same in every culture, in every time, and in every place.[69]

Here we see Mr. Bush setting up a series of absolute dichotomies alleged to be common to both the Cold War and the War on Terror: totalitarianism versus dignity, conformity versus freedom, wrong versus right, evil versus good. Yet even more clearly than the Cold War, this new War on Terror has been portrayed as a religious war—a war against what is variously described as "Islamic radicalism," "Muslim extremists," or "Islamism," with America as global crusader guided by the "Author of Freedom." As Lauren Rozen described Bush's rhetoric in 2005, "Trying to cast himself as a successor to Reagan battling the evil empire, Bush invoked a 'global struggle' against 'Islamic radicalism' that 'like the ideology of communism, contains inherent contradictions that doom it to failure.'"[70] And this new Cold War narrative, with its distinctly religious and anti-Islamic twist, has been happily embraced by many conservative Christians. In the words of Reverend Richard Cizik, vice president of the National Association of Evangelicals, "Evangelicals have substituted Islam for the Soviet Union. The Muslims have become the modern-day equivalent of the Evil Empire"[71]

At the same time, the secrecy that surrounds our new War on Terror is even more intense and pervasive than that of the Cold War. Indeed, secrecy is as vital a component of Mr. Bush's War as is religious faith, and the two are often inseparable. As we saw above, secrecy is a basic component of modern political bureaucracies: as Weber pointed out, secrecy creates hierarchies of knowledge and so reinforces the superiority of those in power by their possession of valued information. We also saw that religion can be defined in William James's sense as a "belief in an unseen order," a hidden or secret order, to which we should strive to conform. The post-9/11 Bush administration has tried to persuade the American public that *these two forms of secrecy or hiddenness are in fact one and the same.* In other words, it has tried to convince us that conformity to the hidden mystery of God's will and conformity to the hidden agenda of the administration are both part of the same divine plan, that we should not worry or think critically but simply *trust* in the latter, just as we trust in the former. Absolute faith in God and absolute faith in the president's power to lead us, we are told, are both demanded in this new epic struggle against evil, the War on Terror.

However, while the Cold War had a clear victor and a historical end, there is no apparent resolution to a war on "terror." Indeed, such a war is almost by definition endless (and we might even question whether it is possible to wage war on a tactic). Hence, unless we change the terms of the struggle, there is no foreseeable end to the state of generalized secrecy and politicized religion that now characterizes the United States. Such a state of perpetual war and pervasive secrecy is disastrous for any system of democracy. Indeed, many critics have described the present administration as moving rapidly away from a healthy, open democracy and rapidly in the direction of either theocracy or totalitarianism (indeed, even fascism).[72] While I do believe that it contains some dangerous elements of both theocracy and fascism, the current administration strikes me as something rather different—what we might simply call a *Bushist* regime. Such a regime combines extreme secrecy and invasive government with messianic religious fervor and imperial military might; it is a regime that seems primarily concerned not with "freedom" or "liberty," as it purports, but rather with the accumulation of power for itself and the stripping of power from ordinary citizens. Yet it is also one possessing a stunning hubris and that seems increasingly bent on its own self-destruction.

The Structure and Outline of the Book: An Attempt at Dehypnosis

You have to hand it to America. It has exercised a quite clinical manipulation of power worldwide while masquerading as a force for universal good. It's a brilliant, even witty, highly successful act of hypnosis.

—Harold Pinter, 2005 Nobel lecture

The chapters that follow critically analyze, deconstruct, and I would hope un-mask much of the religious rhetoric used by the Bush administration, exam-ining the deeper and often far less spiritual interests that lie beneath it. As Harold Pinter suggested in his 2005 Nobel lecture, we have all been to a de-gree hypnotized by our government's rhetoric of America as a force of uni-versal good, and it is perhaps time we begin waking ourselves up from this media-induced slumber.[73] The results of the 2006 midterm elections suggest that Americans are indeed beginning to shake off this slumber and are not at all happy with the reality to which they are awakening.

Thus, chapter 1, "Prodigal Son, American Moses," explores the role of reli-gion—both publicly displayed and subtly double-coded—in the current White House. The narrative that Mr. Bush and his biographers relate about his life and political career is based largely on the model of Moses—a man who, despite his lack of experience, has heard a divine call to lead his people and fight for freedom at a time of grave danger. Mr. Bush's use of religious rheto-ric became especially pronounced, however, in the wake of the 9/11 attacks, as he began increasingly to describe the world as a cosmic war between the forces of good and evil, freedom and terror. So impressive has been the president's display of faith that he has been recognized by some as the new head of the Christian Coalition in America. Conversely, the Christian Coalition and other conservative religious groups have emerged as the Republican Party's most powerful base of popular support, serving as unrivaled organizers of get-out-the-vote campaigns and local political drives.

Bush's use of religious rhetoric in his public discourse is, however, complex and ambivalent. It is quite explicit in some circumstances, as in his frequent references to "evil" and "evil-doers," and to freedom as "God's gift to human-ity." But it is at other times very subtly woven into his speeches through a strat-egy of "double-coding," which makes specific references to biblical passages and Christian hymns that are likely to be missed by the majority of Americans but are clearly heard by those who are steeped in Scripture.

In chapter 2, "No Need for Explanation," I then delve into the intensive se-crecy, or "secrecy fetish," that has characterized this administration from its inception. From Bush and Cheney's very first days in office, with the attempt to conceal Bush's own Texas gubernatorial records, to the highly secretive Bush-Cheney Energy Task Force, to its stealth war on the environment, to the manipulation of intelligence in the preemptive invasion of Iraq, to its con-cealment of prisoner abuse at Abu Ghraib and elsewhere, to the CIA's global network of secret prisons, secrecy characterizes every aspect of this adminis-tration. Indeed, the Bush administration appears to dissemble simply as a matter of policy.

At the same time, ironically, the past five years have also seen an intense new preoccupation with surveillance and a rapid erosion of individual rights to privacy. The most obvious example is the USA PATRIOT Act, which gives the government unprecedented new powers to access our personal records and conduct secret searches of our homes and offices. But still more troubling is the revelation that Mr. Bush secretly authorized the NSA to spy on thousands (perhaps millions) of U.S. citizens without court approval. In short, what we have witnessed in the past five years is a very disturbing reversal of the ideal of government transparency and individual privacy: even as our government has become increasingly secretive, our citizens' rights to privacy have been significantly diminished.

Chapter 3, "New American Century, New American Empire," examines the influence of the neoconservative movement in the shaping of the Bush's administration's aggressive foreign policy and its use of both religion and secrecy as political tools. The title of this chapter is borrowed from the powerful neoconservative think tank the Project for the New American Century and from Irving Kristol, the "godfather" of neoconservatism, who has described the contemporary United States as an "emerging Imperium." Kristol and others in the neoconservative circles are quite clear about the need for strong religion as a means to enforce social order and national pride, but they are no less clear about the need for secrecy as the basic mode in which contemporary politics must operate.

This chapter also attempts to clarify the influence of political theorists such as Leo Strauss and Albert Wohlstetter on neoconservative ideology. The influence of Strauss on the neoconservatives, and particularly the influence of his writings on secrecy and religion, have been fairly well documented (though often misrepresented). Wohlstetter's influence, however, is less well known. As a key architect of U.S. defense policy during the Cold War, Wohlstetter was a model for the character of Dr. Strangelove and the primary intellectual influence on Paul Wolfowitz, the architect of the current Iraq war. The neoconservative agenda promoted by Wolfowitz, Rumsfeld, and others represents a fusion of Strauss's esoteric ideology with Wohlstetter's aggressive military policy.

In chapter 4, "Machiavelli Meets the Religious Right," I look more specifically at the political manipulation of religious rhetoric and symbolism by key strategists in the Bush administration. The figures most commonly compared to Machiavelli are, of course, Karl Rove and Dick Cheney. However, the most explicit appeal to Machiavelli as a model for modern governance has come from the influential neoconservative theorist and member of the American Enterprise Institute, Michael Ledeen. Considered by many the "driving philosophical force behind the Iraq war," Ledeen was a key figure in the Iran-Contra scandal of the 1980s and has more recently been cited as a possible source for the forged documents suggesting that Iraq had attempted to obtain uranium from Niger. Ledeen also happens to be an outspoken admirer of the political works of Machiavelli. Above all, he admires Machiavelli's frank recognition that (a) secrecy and deception are essential skills needed by any effective leader and (b) the manipulation of religion is the most effective way to mobilize public opinion and generate support for war. Ledeen has in fact appeared repeatedly on Pat Robertson's *700 Club*, arguing most recently for the need to invade Iran as the next stage in the war on terror.

Chapter 5, "Never Say Lie," then examines the role of the corporate media in the ongoing projection of Bush's image as a man of strong faith, virtue, integrity, and compassion, while largely overlooking the pervasive secrecy and dissimulation in his administration. This needs to be understood in the context of the larger consolidation of the U.S. media, most of which are now owned by just five major corporations. This intense consolidation becomes especially problematic when some of those corporations happen to be strongly right leaning and politically motivated, such as the Fox media empire. Fox works quite hard to project a consistent image of Mr. Bush as a man of deep religious conviction and integrity, while vigorously deflecting any investigation into the pervasive dissimulation of his administration. In our postmodern society of the spectacle, in which news is increasingly more entertainment than critical analysis, Mr. Bush has become a kind of hyperreal figure whose pious words and staged public appearances have less and less connection to the actual activities of his administration.

In chapter 6, "America Left Behind," I look more specifically at the striking intersections between the agendas of the Christian right and the neoconservatives in contemporary U.S. foreign policy. Here I focus in particular on the wildly popular series of evangelical end-times fiction, *Left Behind*, by Tim LaHaye and Jerry Jenkins. One of the most influential evangelical figures in America and cofounder of the Moral Majority, LaHaye was also the first president of the powerful Council for National Policy (CNP). A highly secretive group, the CNP brings together leading conservative Christians and key Republican politicians, including Jerry Falwell, Pat Robertson, R. J. Rushdoony, Oliver North, Tom DeLay, Jesse Helms, and (formerly) John Ashcroft. In the twelve-volume *Left Behind* series, LaHaye combines an evangelical reading of the Book of Revelation with a powerful political message centered on the evils of the United Nations and the return of Christ in the Holy Land.

There is a striking parallel or "elective affinity" between the aggressive foreign policies of the neoconservatives and the millenarian vision of LaHaye's *Left Behind* series. The former seeks a "New American Century" and "benevolent hegemony" of the globe by U.S. power, ushered in by the preemptive invasion of Iraq; the latter seeks a "New Millennium" of divine rule ushered in by Christ's imminent return and apocalyptic war in the Middle East, first in Babylon and then in Jerusalem. The two find common ground in the faith-based, often messianic idealism of the Bush administration. Unfortunately, however, the aggressive foreign policies of the neoconservatives bear with them a profound double irony that strikes to the heart of this White House—the irony of an increasingly secretive and invasive government that bears less and less resemblance to its own Constitution, and one that risks bankrupting itself through its intense militarism, unrestrained deficit spending, and massively expensive war overseas.

Finally, in the conclusion, I argue that the disturbing mixture of religion and secrecy in the Bush White House should not be simply a cause for pessimistic despair, but rather a powerful motivation for change. Indeed, if Mr. Bush has ushered in a kind of "post-truth presidency," then we need to think long and hard about what we want democracy to look like in a post-Bush (ideally, "post-Bushist") era. The tremendous new powers of executive privilege and government surveillance claimed by this administration will not disappear after the 2008 election, even with the election of a democratic president—that is, unless ordinary citizens demand that these powers be taken away.

This is not, I believe, a question of Democrats versus Republicans or liberals versus conservatives; it is a question of concerned Americans safeguarding the model of democracy outlined in our Constitution by combating excessive secrecy on the part of government and protecting the rights to privacy and freedom of speech on the part of citizens. The past five years have witnessed an extreme intensification of the former and a disturbing restriction of the latter. In a very short time, this administration has moved us rapidly away from the model of an open democracy with a transparent government and rapidly in the direction of an authoritarian, secretive, militaristic regime driven more by extremist religious ideology than by rational debate. If we are to survive as a republic bearing any resemblance to the one outlined in our Constitution, this dangerous trend needs to be reversed. In this struggle, values, morality, and religious conviction can and must play a significant role, but not as political tools to be wielded by partisan strategists to manipulate voters. Rather, the language of "values" needs to be rescued and reclaimed from partisan politics in order to inform much more immediate sorts of moral issues, such as poverty, war, health care, and protecting the environment at a time of ecological crisis. These are issues that are by no means exclusively "religious," but they are ones to which both religious believers and morally committed nonreligious citizens must respond.

Notes

1. See Stephen Mansfield, *The Faith of George W. Bush* (New York: Tarcher, 2003). Both *Newsweek* and *Time* have done cover stories on Bush's religiosity: "Bush and God," *Newsweek*, March 10, 2003; "Faith, God and the Oval Office," *Time*, June 21, 2004.

2. Jim Hightower, "Bush's Fetish for Secrecy," *Seattle Press*, April 22, 2003, at www.seattlepress.com/article-10186.html. See Pat M. Holt, "Someone, Blow the Whistle on Bush's Excessive Secrecy," *Christian Science Monitor*, February 6, 2003, at www.csmonitor.com/2003/0206/p09s02-coop.html.

3. Larry Klayman, chairman of Judicial Watch, in Alan Elsner, "Bush Expands Government Secrecy, Arouses Critics," *Reuters*, September 3, 2002, at www.fas.org/sgp/news/2002/09/re090302.html.

4. John W. Dean, *Worse Than Watergate: The Secret Presidency of George W. Bush* (New York: Little, Brown, 2004).

5. Walter Cronkite, " Secrecy, Lies and Credibility," King Features Syndicate, April 1, 2004, at www.yankton.net/stories/040104/opE_20040401035.shtml. See Christopher H. Schmitt and Edward T. Pound, "Keeping Secrets: The Bush Administration Is Doing the Public's Business Out of the Public Eye," *U.S. News & World Report*, December 22, 2003, at www.usnews.com/usnews/news/articles/031222/22secrecy.htm.

6. See Guy Debord, *The Society of the Spectacle* (Detroit: Black & Red, 1983).

7. George W. Bush, *Charge to Keep* (New York: Morrow, 1999), 6.

8. Michael Taussig, *Defacement: Public Secrecy and the Labor of the Negative* (Stanford: Stanford University Press, 1999), 7. See Michel Foucault, *The History of Sexuality: An Introduction* (New York: Vintage, 1990), 86: "power is tolerable only on condition that it mask a substantial part of itself. Its success is proportional to its ability to hide its own mechanisms. Would power be accepted if it were entirely cynical? For it, secrecy is not in the nature of an abuse; it is indispensable to its operation."

9. Max Weber, *Economy and Society* (1922), in Hans H. Gerth and C. Wright Mills, *From Max Weber: Essays in Sociology* (New York: Oxford University Press, 1958), 233–234.

10. "TIA: Total Information Awareness," ACLU.org, January 16, 2004, at www.aclu.org/privacy/spying/14956res20040116.html. DARPA is the Defense Advanced Research Projects Agency, an independent branch of the Defense Department.

11. Sisella Bok, *Secrets: On the Ethics of Concealment and Revelation* (New York: Pantheon, 1983), 177.

12. Elias Canetti, *Crowds and Power* (New York: Viking, 1962), 290.

13. Sun Tzu, *The Art of War*, translated by Lionel Giles (El Paso: Norte, 2005), VI.9.

14. Max Frankel, "Top Secret," *New York Times Magazine*, June 16, 1996, my italics. Paul C. Johnson has aptly called this sort of advertisement of concealed knowledge "secretism," or the "divulgence of a reputation of secret knowledge," in *Secrets, Gossip, and Gods: The Transformation of Brazilian Candomblé* (New York: Oxford University Press, 2005), 9.

15. Daniel Patrick Moynihan, *Secrecy: The American Experience* (New Haven: Yale University Press, 1998), 168.

16. See Joseph C. Wilson, "What I Didn't Find in Africa," *New York Times*, July 6, 2003, section 4, 1; Daniel Schorr, "Rove Leak Is Just Part of a Larger Scandal," *Christian Science Monitor*, July 15, 2005, at www.csmonitor.com/2005/0715/p09s02-cods.html.

17. Georg Simmel, "The Secret and the Secret Society," in *The Sociology of Georg Simmel*, edited by Kurt H. Wolff (New York: Free Press, 1950), 332–33. As Michael Taussig observes, secrecy thus often overlaps with religion, for secrecy creates an aura of suprahuman transcendence and "a powerful yet invisible presence"; the secret works by a "magnification of reality, by means of the sensation that behind the appearance of things there is a deeper, mysterious reality that we may here call the sacred, if not religion." Taussig, "Transgression," in *Critical Terms for Religious Studies*, Mark C. Taylor, ed. (Chicago: University of Chicago Press, 1998), 355–356.

18. Simmel, "Secret," 365.

19. Kevin Phillips, *American Dynasty: Aristocracy, Fortune, and the Politics of Deceit in the House of Bush* (New York: Viking, 2004), 328.

20. Eric Alterman, *When Presidents Lie: A History of Official Deception and Its Consequences* (New York: Viking, 2004), 15.

21. John F. Kennedy, Address before the American Newspaper Publishers Association, New York, April 27, 1961, at www.jfklibrary.org/j042761.htm.

22. Harry S. Truman, quoted in "The American Experience: Truman," *PBS.org*, at www.pbs.org/wgbh/amex/truman/tguide/tg_quotes.html.

23. Alterman, *When Presidents Lie*, 15.

24. Phillips, *American Dynasty*, 328.

25. James Pfiffner, "The Contemporary Presidency: Presidential Lies," *Presidential Studies Quarterly* 29, no.4 (1999): 903–917. On Reagan's lies about Iran-Contra, see Lawrence Walsh, "Final Report of the Independent Counsel for Iran/Contra Matters," August 4, 1993, at www.fas.org/irp/offdocs/walsh/.

26. John M. Orman, *Presidential Secrecy and Deception: Beyond the Power to Persuade* (Westport, CT: Greenwood, 1980), 46.

27. Edward Shils, *The Torment of Secrecy: The Background and Consequences of America's Security Policies* (Glencoe, IL: Free Press, 1956), 27.

28 Bruce Lincoln, *Authority: Construction and Corrosion* (Chicago: University of Chicago Press, 1994), 112.

29. Rudolph Otto, *The Idea of the Holy* (New York: Oxford University Press, 1958), 13. Likewise, Kees Bolle notes that secrecy is "the mystery at the heart of all religions." Bolle, *Secrecy in Religions* (Leiden, Netherlands: Brill, 1987), 2.

30. William James, *The Varieties of Religious Experience: A Study in Human Nature* (New York: Modern Library, 1902), 53.

31. "The Jesus Factor," written, produced, and directed by Raney Aronson, *PBS Frontline*, at www.pbs.org/wgbh/pages/frontline/shows/jesus/etc/script.html.

32. David Chidester, *Patterns of Power: Religion and Politics in American Culture* (Englewood Cliffs, NJ: Prentice Hall, 1988), 13–15.

33. Charles B. Stanford, *The Religious Life of Thomas Jefferson* (Charlottesville: University Press of Virginia, 1984), 1. See also Dumas Malone, *Jefferson the President: The First Term, 1801–1805* (Little, Brown, 1970), 190.

34. Thomas Jefferson, letter to Dr. Benjamin Rush, in Stanford, *Religious Life of Thomas Jefferson*, 2.

35. Brian C. Anderson, "Secular Europe, Religious America," *Public Interest* (Spring 2004), at www.findarticles.com/p/articles/mi_m0377/is_155/ai_n6143340.

36. Jeffrey L. Sheler, "Faith in America," *U.S. News & World Report*, May 6, 2002, at www.usnewsclassroom.com/issue/020506/misc/6religion.htm.

37. Michael Lienesch, *Redeeming America: Piety and Politics in the New Christian Right* (Chapel Hill: University of North Carolina Press, 1993), 196; see Ernest Tuveson, *Redeemer Nation: The Idea of America's Millennial Role* (Chicago: Midway Reprints, 1980). As Andrew Bacevich comments, "From the age of Winthrop to the age of George W. Bush, an abiding religious sensibility has informed America's image of itself and of its providential mission." Bacevich, *The New American Militarism: How Americans Are Seduced by War* (New York: Oxford University Press, 2005), 122.

38. Alterman, *When Presidents Lie*, 17. See John M. Orman, *Presidential Secrecy and Deception: Beyond the Power to Persuade* (Westport, CT: Greenwood, 1980), 4.

39. Stephen J. Whitfield, *The Culture of the Cold War* (Baltimore: Johns Hopkins University Press, 1996), 1.

40. Angus MaKenzie, *Secrets: The CIA's War at Home* (University of California Press, 1997), 201. See Richard O. Curry, ed., *Freedom at Risk: Secrecy, Censorship, and Repression in the 1980s* (Philadelphia: Temple University Press, 1988), 8; Athan G. Theoharis, ed., *A Culture of Secrecy: The Government versus the People's Right to Know* (University Press of Kansas, 1998).

41. "Report on the Covert Activities of the Central Intelligence Agency," September 30, 1954, Appendix A; published as *The Doolittle Report* (Washington: Infantry Journal Press, 1954).

42. Whitfield, *Culture of the Cold War*, 11–12.

43. U.S. House of Representatives Committee on Government Operations, Draft Report, *Interception of International Telecommunications by the National Security Agency*, 1976, 23.

44. Ronald Clark, *The Man Who Broke Purple* (Boston: Little, Brown, 1977), 249.

45. James Bamford, "The Agency That Could Be Big Brother," *New York Times*, December 25, 2005, at www.nytimes.com.

46. Frank Church, in Bamford, "Agency That Could Be Big Brother."

47. Athan G. Theoharis, "The FISA Files," *Nation*, March 6, 2006, at www.thenation.com/doc/20060306/theoharris.

48. Theoharis, "FISA Files."

49. Philip H. Melanson, *Secrecy Wars: National Security, Privacy, and the Public's Right to Know* (Washington: Brassey's, 2001), 2–3.

50. Quoted in Theoharis, ed., *Culture of Secrecy*, 13.

51. Whitfield, *Culture of the Cold War*, 83.

52. Lienesch, *Redeeming America*, 211. See Whitfield, *Culture of the Cold War*, 10.

53. Billy Graham, in Whitfield, *Culture of the Cold War*, 81.

54. Reinhold Niebhur, in Whitfield, *Culture of the Cold War*, 79–80.

55. Whitfield, *Culture of the Cold War*, 80–81.

56. Jerry Falwell, "Armageddon and the Coming War with Russia," quoted in *Oakland Tribune*, October 23, 1984. See Jerry Falwell, *Listen America!* (Garden City, NY: Doubleday, 1980), 84–85.

57. Harry S. Truman, in Donald W. White, *The American Century: The Rise and Decline of the United States as a World Power* (New Haven: Yale University Press, 1999), 21.

58. Harry S. Truman, "Inaugural Address," January 20, 1949, at www.bartleby.com/124/pres53.html.

59. Dwight D. Eisenhower, *Peace and Justice* (New York: Columbia University Press, 1961), 159, 25.

60. David Domke, *God Willing? Political Fundamentalism in the White House, the War on the Terror, and the Echoing Press* (New Haven: Yale University Press, 2004), 8.

61. Lienesch, *Redeeming America*, 211.

62. Domke, *God Willing?*, 8.

63. Charles Krauthammer, in Emily Eakin, "All Roads Lead to D.C.," *New York Times*, "Week in Review," March 31, 2002; Krauthammer, "The Bush Doctrine," *Time*, March 5, 2001. See also Iain Boal, T. J. Clark, Joseph Matthews, and Michael Watts, *Afflicted Powers: Capital and Spectacle in a New Age of War* (London: Verso, 2006), 84–85.

64. Chalmers Johnson, *Sorrows of Empire: Militarism, Secrecy, and the End of the Republic* (New York: Metropolitan, 2004), 1. See Andrew J. Bacevich, *American Empire: The Realities and Consequences of U.S. Diplomacy* (Cambridge, MA: Harvard University Press, 2002).

65. Phillips, *American Dynasty*, 60. See Kevin Phillips, *American Theocracy: The Peril and Politics of Radical Religion, Oil, and Borrowed Money in the 21st Century* (New York: Viking, 2006), 220–221. See Joan M. Martin and Linda L. Barnes, "Introduction: Religion and Empire," *Journal of the American Academy of Religion* 71, no.1 (2003): 3–12.

66. Robert Kagan, "The Benevolent Empire," *Foreign Policy* (Summer 1998), 24–35.

67. Moynihan, *Secrecy*, 227.

68. Guy Debord, *Comments on the Society of the Spectacle* (London: Verso, 1990), 12. See also Boal et al., *Afflicted Powers*, 21–23.

69. "Bush Delivers Graduation Speech at West Point," June 1, 2002, at www.whitehouse.gov/news/releases/2002/06/20020601-3.html.

70. Laura Rozen, "Bush Talks about Evil Doers on C-Span 3," October 6, 2005, at www.villagevoice.com/news/0541,rozen,68685,2.html.

71. Quoted in Laura Goodstein, "Seeing Islam as 'Evil' Faith, Evangelicals Seek Converts," *New York Times*, May 27, 2003.

72. See Phillips, *American Theocracy*; Michelle Goldberg, *Kingdom Coming: The Rise of Christian Nationalism* (New York: Norton, 2006), 54–55, 179.

73. Harold Pinter, "Art, Truth and Politics," 2005 Nobel lecture, at nobelprize.org/literature/laureates/2005/pinter-lecture-e.html.

1

Prodigal Son, American Moses: The Faith-Based Presidency of George W. Bush

I feel like God wants me to run for president. I can't explain it, but I sense my country is going to need me. Something is going to happen, and, at that time, my country is going to need me. I know it won't be easy, on me or my family, but God wants me to do it.

—George W. Bush to preacher James Robison in 1999

God must really hate Al Gore.

—former Bill Clinton speechwriter,
quoted by Jeffrey Goldberg, "The Believer"

WHEN I FIRST BEGAN LISTENING to George W. Bush's public statements and reading the various accounts of his life and political career, I was not particularly struck by their religious nature. Nor, probably, were most Americans. We have had many religious presidents—almost all of them have been religious, in fact—and the use of religious discourse does not appear to be a particularly partisan thing, but common to Democrats and Republicans fairly equally: Jimmy Carter was a born-again Christian, Ronald Reagan believed in Armageddon and endorsed the religious right, while Bill Clinton was not beyond invoking Jesus. As his former chief speechwriter Michael Gerson argues, Bush's use of religious language is simply due to the fact that he is "marinated in the American ideal" and the American belief that "human beings are created in the image of God and will not forever suffer the oppressor's sword."[1]

Yet there is something qualitatively different about President Bush, both in the way he uses religious rhetoric and in the way in which his administration has forged close ties with conservative evangelical Christians. For Bush, religion is not simply an accidental or secondary aspect of his political persona and his administration: it is central and definitive, providing a kind of guiding narrative for his entire decision to run for office and for most of his domestic and foreign policies. "We have had other 'religious presidents,'" Jeffrey Siker comments, "but no other President has so clearly perceived his calling in such epic Biblical terms."[2] As David Domke has shown, through a careful statistical comparison of Bush's public addresses with those of previous presidents from FDR to Clinton, American leaders have long invoked God in their political rhetoric; but no modern president has done so as consistently, frequently, or explicitly as President Bush—indeed, he has done it three to four times as often, by Domke's count.[3] Particularly in the wake of 9/11, Mr. Bush has described the entire world as a grand conflict between the forces of good and evil, freedom and terror, with the United States as God's appointed agent for the universal spread of liberty.

If we read Bush's autobiography and the various semihagiographic biographies written about him, we can see at least two guiding narratives in the description of his life and his decision to run for president. The first is the gospel narrative of the "prodigal son," the story of a young man who squandered his youth on booze and bad business, only to turn to Jesus and discover his true calling. The second narrative, which comes through in both his autobiography and in books such as *The Faith of George W. Bush*, is that of an American Moses—a man who, like Moses, was called by God to lead his people at a time when his country was going to need him.

Reading Bush's books and public speeches, however, is actually a surprisingly complicated task. For while he does sometimes make explicit use of religious rhetoric and appeals to "the Almighty," his speeches often employ a subtle technique of "double-coding"; that is, they often make subtle reference to specific biblical passages and hymns that are likely to be missed by most Americans but are clearly heard by those who are steeped in Scripture.[4]

Thus, in order to understand the role of faith in Mr. Bush's life and political career, we first have to place him within the broader context of the conservative Christian movement that Michael Lienesch calls the "New Christian Right," which has exerted a quiet but increasingly powerful influence in American politics since the 1980s. In many ways, President Bush is both the fulfillment and the ideal embodiment of the political aspirations long held by evangelical leaders such as Pat Robertson, Ralph Reed, and the Christian Coalition. Indeed, many critics warn that Bush's faith-based presidency is taking us dangerously in the direction of the theocratic or theonomic society envisioned by the most extreme end of the Christian spectrum, such as the Dominionists and Reconstructionists. While such fears are clearly exaggerated, I do think there are some striking affinities between Bush's faith-based policies and the Reconstructionists' call for a broader Christianization of American society.

Since at least 1999, many conservative Christians have embraced Bush's powerful use of religious rhetoric and lent him strong support, arguably helping him to win the past two elections. As a man of prayer, a simple man, a man who believes himself to have been called by God, Bush offers the image of a politician that seems to be beyond the messy, deceptive, lying world of mainstream politics—an image of "a flawed Everyman," as one biographer put it.[5] Indeed, his image has been built largely on an ideal of trust, sincerity, and genuineness. According to Pew Research Center polls of 2004 and 2005, the word Americans most often associated with Bush was "honest."[6] As Thomas Franks has recently argued, one of the primary reasons Bush has been so successful is that he fulfills some imagined ideal of *authenticity*—the ordinary guy you could go have a beer with, as opposed to the latte-drinking liberals who don't understand the problems of the working man: "While liberals commit endless acts of hubris . . . the humble people of the red states go about their unpretentious business, eating down-home foods . . . whistling while they work, and knowing they are under the secure watch of George W. Bush, a man they love as their own."[7] And the Bush administration has clearly used this image of faith, truth, and authenticity to persuade Americans to accept a wide array of dubious propositions—from the preemptive invasion of Iraq, to tax cuts that primarily benefit our wealthiest citizens, to the NSA's secret spying program. As a *New York Times* editorial put it, "We can't think of a president who has gone to the American people more often than George W. Bush has to ask them to forget about things like democracy, judicial process, and the balance of powers—and just trust him."[8]

But how much of this image of faith, authenticity, and trust is really George W. Bush, and how much is the construction of political strategists such as Karl Rove, the guidance of Cheney's "hand behind the throne," or the rhetorical flourishes of speechwriters such as Michael Gerson? How much of Bush's discourse of freedom as "God's gift to humanity" is the result of his own theological deliberations, and how much the result of neoconservative ideology? The answer, I think, is complex. While I do not doubt the sincerity of Mr. Bush's personal faith, I do think he is bound up with complex religious, political, and economic forces that he probably does not entirely understand. Bush's "faith" represents the fusion of a number of different influences and interests, including not only his own professed belief in the divine, but also the guidance of campaign strategists, speechwriters, evangelical supporters, and political tacticians, each of whom has an interest in the projection of Bush as a man of faith. This and the remaining chapters will explore these complex relations in detail.

Building the Secret Kingdom:
The Quiet Rise of the New Christian Right

> The first strategy and in many ways the most important strategy for evan-
> gelicals is secrecy. Sun Tzu says that's what you have to do in an effective
> war and that's essentially what we're involved in, we're involved in a war. It's
> not a war fought with bullets, it's a war fought with ballots.
>
> —Ralph Reed, to the Montana Christian Coalition (1996)

Neither George W. Bush's outspoken religious faith nor his administration's
blurring of the lines between church and state are entirely new phenomena.
Rather, they are expressions of a much broader movement in the United States
that has long roots in our history and has emerged as a surprisingly powerful
political force since the 1980s. As former speechwriter David Frum put it, "His
culture is that of modern evangelicalism. To understand Bush's White House
you need to understand the predominance of this belief."[9] This New Christian
Right is itself only the most recent manifestation of currents in American
Protestantism that can be traced to the earliest days of the Republic, ebbing
and waning in various periods of U.S. history, emerging powerfully in the
early twentieth century with the war against biblical criticism and Darwin, but
perhaps achieving its most powerful form in the 1970s and '80s. Following the
cultural revolutions of the 1960s, the Christian right reemerged "with a
vengeance" and also with a clear social and political agenda.[10] As President
Bush noted in a session with Christian editors and writers in 2004, "Something's happening in America. . . . The thing they say different now than four
years ago is, 'Mr. President, we pray for you.' . . . When I'm shaking those
hands, I bet you every other person . . . says, 'Mr. President, my family prays
for you.'"[11] What Bush was in fact describing here is a much broader phenomenon in America, an infusion of Christian faith into political discourse
and action that has been at work for the past twenty-five years.

Arising at the same time as the revival of political conservatism during the
late 1970s and '80s, this New Christian Right represents a powerful alliance
between conservative political activists and prominent religious figures. Led
by political professionals such as Paul Weyrich of the Committee for the Survival of a Free Congress and Howard Phillips of the Conservative Caucus,
these "New Right" conservatives practiced an activist brand of politics that
sought to build a mass movement based on moral concerns; thus, Lienesch
observes, they saw "potential for an alliance between secular and religious
conservatives."[12] They were thus able to recruit to their cause some of America's most popular preachers and televangelists, including Jerry Falwell of the
Old Time Gospel Hour, Pat Robertson of the *700 Club*, and James Robison, a

popular Texas television preacher. Working through organizations such as Falwell's Moral Majority (founded in 1979) and, later, Ralph Reed's Christian Coalition (1989), the religious agendas of the New Christian Right fit in very well with the domestic and foreign political agendas of the Reagan era: "coinciding with the resurgent conservatism represented by Ronald Reagan, religious conservatives carried on a campaign that combined anticommunism, support for conservative economic reforms, and a platform of social politics that included opposition to abortion, homosexuality, and pornography."[13] With Reagan, they shared the vision of America's divine role in world history, as a redeemer nation with a historic mission to combat evil and a calling, as Robison put it, "to save the world" by first saving America.[14]

Already by the late 1970s, evangelical leaders had begun to realize the power of this quiet, grassroots, locally based movement. As Robertson put it, realizing the immense reach of his *700 Club* and its millions of viewers: "We have enough votes to run the country." James Bakker of the *PTL Club* was equally ambitious: "Our goal is to influence all viable [presidential] candidates on issues important to the church. . . . We want appointments in government."[15] Explicitly wedding a strong conservative faith with strong conservative politics, the New Right was able to capture some of America's most powerful national symbols, such as patriotism, the family, motherhood, virtue, and moral rectitude, and so managed to build a massive popular movement aimed at nothing short of reclaiming America for Jesus Christ.

However, the rise of the New Christian Right and its role in U.S. politics has been accomplished in a remarkably quiet and unpublicized way. Far from a monolithic or homogenous movement, the New Christian Right is an extremely complex, diverse, and loose coalition of a wide range of conservative organizations, from the Christian Coalition to Focus on the Family, to the Chalcedon Foundation, to the Center for Reclaiming America. Rather than a centralized, top-down movement, this is more like what Rev. Tim LaHaye calls "a host of independent, locally sponsored and funded organizations that work in unison,"[16] operating at a grassroots level.

As Ralph Reed put it in 1996, speaking to the Montana Christian Coalition, the first and most important strategy for an effective Christian political movement is secrecy. Following Sun Tzu, he invoked secrecy as the most powerful weapon in this "war" to retake America.[17] This theme of secrecy, or what Frederick Clarkson calls "stealth tactics" and "covert operations," runs throughout the politics of the New Christian Right. In the words of Arne Christenson, legislative aide to Congressman Vin Weber (R-MN), "In America, effective political influence is often won through gradual infiltration rather than a swift ascension to power."[18] Thus Antonio Rivera, the New York Christian Coalition political adviser in 1992, urged members to place themselves in influential positions, advising that "you keep your personal views to yourself until the Christian community is ready to rise up, and then wow! They're gonna be devastated."[19] These sorts of stealth tactics include targeting low-profile elections that attract few voters, focusing get-out-the-vote efforts on specific churches (often providing voting cards to tell parishioners how to vote), and instructing the candidates to hide their views from the public by avoiding public appearances and refusing to fill out questionnaires. Many evangelicals are even willing to invoke Maoist-style political tactics, by building small, loosely knit, and quiet "cells" in order to wage a broader war against the dominant system. As Richard Cizik, research director for the National Association of Evangelicals, put it, "Many that I know here in Washington of the Religious Right are now quick to admit that Mao was right when he said that in a revolution, if you take the countryside, the capital will fall."[20]

Apparently, these stealth tactics have worked quite well. According to the journal *Campaigns and Elections* in 1994, eighteen state Republican Party organizations were classified as strongly under the control of Christian conservatives and thirteen as moderately so. By 2002, *Campaigns and Elections* had found that the first number had stayed the same, but the second one had doubled, for a total of forty-four state parties largely under the sway of the Christian right.[21]

The War for Dominion: The Secret Kingdom of Dominion Theology

> We are simply to speak forth our God-restored authority, preparing for an even more amazing era.
>
> —Pat Robertson, *The Secret Kingdom*

Among the many diverse organizations and theological movements associated with the New Christian Right, two of the most influential have been the groups roughly categorized as Dominion Theology and Christian Reconstructionism. The Dominionists take their cue from one passage of Scripture in particular, *Genesis* 1:26–27. As Robertson describes his own personal revelation in his 1982 book, *The Secret Kingdom*, "I was praying and fasting some years ago, seeking to understand God's purpose more fully. I heard His voice, level and conversational, 'What do I desire for man?'" The Lord then told him to read *Genesis* 1:26–27, in which God says, "Let us make man in our image, after our likeness, and let them have dominion over the fish of the sea and over the fowl of the air, and over the cattle, and over all the earth, and over every creeping thing that creepeth upon the earth."[22]

While most Christians take this to mean that humans are given dominion over the natural world, Robertson and others like him see this as a directive for Christians to exercise dominion over society and human beings, as well: "This was a kingdom law. God wants man to . . . rule the way he was created to rule."[23] God's plan, he tells us, is that His followers should be "exalted to positions of power"; and so he commands his reader, "As a follower of the Son of God, assume the authority, power and dominion that God intends for men to exercise."[24]

This also means, however, that the very idea of a "wall of separation between church and state" is a falsehood—indeed, a dangerous heresy that must be rejected outright. As Robertson argued in 1993, "There is no such thing in the Constitution. It's a lie of the left, and we're not going to take it anymore."[25] Rather than Jefferson and the Bill of Rights, Robertson looks to the Puritans and pre-Revolutionary America for his ideal Christian society. America has "the finest concept of ordered liberty the world has ever known," because "for two hundred years prior to our Constitution, all of the leadership of this nation had been steeped in the biblical principles of the Old and New Testaments"[26] (ironically, Robertson overlooks the fact that his home state of Virginia actively persecuted and jailed Baptists, especially preachers such as himself, in the 1760s).[27]

Robertson was confident that this grassroots movement of politically driven Christians would soon take the helm of U.S. government. In early 1991, he predicted a scenario in which "a coalition of Evangelicals and pro-family Roman Catholics" would take over the rebuilding of the Republican Party and have enough political strength by the year 2000 to win the presidency and a majority in Congress.[28] Even Robertson may have been surprised by the accuracy of his predictions.

Reconstructing America: R. J. Rushdoony and Christian Reconstructionism

God has a plan for the conquest of all things by his covenant people. This plan is His law. It leaves no area of life and activity untouched, and it predestines victory.

—R. J. Rushdoony, *God's Plan for Victory*

While figures such as Pat Robertson are well known to most American readers, other figures, such as R. J. Rushdoony and Christian Reconstructionism, are far less familiar. And they are also far more extreme in their view of the ideal Christian and biblically governed society. Whereas the Dominionists foresee an imminent Christian takeover of U.S. politics, Reconstructionists look forward to nothing short of a complete remaking of society, one based on Old Testament law in all its minute detail and modeled on ancient Israel as the blueprint for a God-centered nation.

Despite his relative obscurity today, Rushdoony's work has been remarkably influential in the shaping of the New Christian Right. Born in 1916 in New York, Rushdoony came from a family that traced its lineage back to fourth-century Armenia, the first nation to accept Christianity as its state religion. Rushdoony's "Chalcedon Foundation" has been dubbed by *Newsweek* "*the* think thank of the Religious Right," and his many enormous books have been endorsed by Falwell as "a tool Christians need" for the difficulties that confront society. As theologian Richard John Neuhaus observes, Reconstructionism has quietly moved from "eccentric marginality to a position of some influence" and could become "the dominant system of thought in the religious right."[29] Indeed, some observers even credit Rushdoony and his son-in-law Gary North for providing the theological justification for the Christianization of politics that has become the central theme of the New Christian Right; largely through their writings, "the concept that Christians are Biblically mandated to occupy all secular institutions has become the *central unifying ideology* for the Christian Right."[30]

Reconstructionism could be thought of as the far-right end of the Christian far right, the most fundamental of the fundamentalists, a movement that would put the Dominionist ideal of a total Christian society into practice in the most minute details of everyday life, governed by Old Testament law. As Rushdoony argues in his monumental *Institutes of Biblical Law*, true dominion demands that every aspect of human life submit to God's law and that every non-Christian institution be eradicated as evil:

> The first step in the mandate is to bring men the word of God and for God to re-generate them. The second step is to demolish every kind of theory, humanistic, evolutionary, idolatrous or otherwise, and every kind of rampart of opposition to the dominion of God in Christ. The world and men must be brought into captivity to Christ, under the dominion of the Kingdom of God and the law of that kingdom. Third, this requires that . . . we administer justice upon all disobedience in every area of life where we encounter it. To deny the cultural mandate is to deny Christ and surrender the world to Satan.[31]

In contrast to most contemporary evangelical movements, Reconstructionism also holds a postmillenarian view of history and the final judgment. Whereas the premillenarians believe Jesus will first return to defeat the Antichrist before the apocalypse and the thousand years of divine rule, postmillenarians such as Rushdoony believe that all of human society must first be conquered and submit to God's law for a millennium of divine rule before Jesus will return. "Postmillennialism," as Rushdoony defines it,

> is the belief that Christ, with His coming, His atonement . . . creates in His re-deemed people a force for the reconquest of all things. The dominion that Adam

first received and then lost by his fall will be restored to redeemed man. God's people will then have a long reign over the entire earth, after which, when all enemies have been put under Christ's feet, the end shall come, and the last enemy, death, will be destroyed.[32]

Although it is often characterized as a "theocratic" worldview, it is perhaps better described as "theonomic," that is, an ideal of society ruled by divine law. Indeed, the Reconstructionist view of the state is actually quite *minimalist*. While society is to be ruled by Biblical law and God's word, the state can do nothing to reform men; the state's function is to do little more than "punish and restrain evil."[33]

Whether we describe it as "theocratic" or "theonomic," however, Reconstructionism is explicitly and unapologetically *undemocratic*. Rushdoony is quite explicit in his condemnation of democracy, which he sees as nonbiblical and based on a flawed theology and anthropology. In short, democracy substitutes fallible human law and human judgment for God's infallible law and judgment, thereby overlooking man's inherent depravity: "democracy has no solution to the problem of human depravity and often fails even to admit the problem."[34] In effect, democracy puts man in God's place. Rather than modern American democracy, Rushdoony looks to colonial New England and the Puritans for the closest American approximation of a biblically ruled community. Democracy is in fact a modern and dangerous form of humanistic arrogance that can only lead to social chaos: "The heresy of democracy has since then worked havoc in church and state, and it has worked towards reducing society to anarchy."[35]

Yet despite their hostility toward democracy, the Reconstructionists are on the whole quite procapitalist. Like Graham, Falwell, and most other conservative Christians of the past fifty years, the Reconstructionists see free-market capitalism not just as good but as itself "rooted in Christianity" and the most appropriate economic system for a divinely ruled society. Indeed, Gary North founded his own "Institute for Christian Economics" in Tyler, Texas, and wrote massive volumes on capitalist interpretations of Scripture. In his words, capitalism and Christianity have arisen hand in hand as part of a divine covenant:

If capitalism is not Christian, then why did it arise only in the Christian West? . . . And how does it happen that Christianity, which is the only true religion, and the only religion that "works" eternally, is not the only possible source of the best system of economics in man's history. . . . Could it be that there is no covenantal relationship between Christianity and economic freedom, which is *only* produced by free market capitalism?[36]

Like others among the New Christian Right, the Reconstructionists believe that the most effective way to achieve their goal of the reconquest of society is through a kind of "stealth" movement or "infiltration" of the system. As North put it, Christians should not attempt a direct frontal assault on the top levels of government, but rather work quietly from the bottom up "to help smooth the transition to Christian political leadership. . . . Christians must begin to organize politically within the present party structure, and they must begin to infiltrate the existing institutional order."[37] On the whole, Reconstructionists seem to work slowly, with a more long-term goal of converting the whole of government and society: "they tend to operate strategically, and because their plans require careful step-by-step planning . . . they tend to attract individuals inclined toward covert activity who are mature enough to wait for long-term political pay-offs."[38]

We might note here that Rushdoony also suggests that it is in certain instances permissible for Christians to practice secrecy or even lie in order to achieve a higher good. In his *Institutes of Biblical Law*, Rushdoony uses the example of the story of Rahab (Joshua 2:1–24), the Canaanite harlot who hid two Israelite spies from the forces of the king of Jericho, and thereby helped bring about the Israelites' conquest of Canaan. In Rushdoony's interpretation, the story shows that the obligation to be truthful "does not apply to acts of war. Spying is legitimate, as are deceptive tactics in warfare."[39] As Clarkson observes, Christianity is, for Rushdoony, always in a sense "at war" with the forces of secularism and non-Christian faiths; therefore, secrecy and deception are always justifiable in defense of the good.[40]

Not surprisingly, the quiet but powerful rise of movements such as Dominionism and Reconstructionism—with their explicit rejection of a separation of church and state—has been worrying to many Americans. As President Carter argued in 2005, "There is obviously a widespread, carefully planned, and unapologetic crusade under way from both sides to merge fundamentalist Christians with the right wing of the Republican Party. . . . [T]his melding of church and state is of deep concern to those who have always relished their separation as one of our moral values."[41] Perhaps nowhere is this merging of far-right Christianity with the far right of the Republican Party more evident than in the presidency of George W. Bush.

From Prodigal Son to America's Moses:
Bush's Recommitment to Christ and Calling to the Presidency

My life is changed. I had a drinking problem. . . . It could have destroyed my life. But I've given my life to Christ.

—George W. Bush, to James Robison

> The minister said that America is starved for honest leaders. He told the story of Moses, asked by God to lead his people to the land of milk and honey.
>
> —George W. Bush, *A Charge to Keep*

Political candidates always tell stories about themselves and allow their campaign strategists to construct narratives around them. What is most interesting about George W. Bush, however, is that he is the first president in our history whose personal and political narratives have been constructed primarily around biblical themes. President Kennedy, for example, claimed to be a politician who happened to be Catholic and would not allow his religious faith to color his political decisions. Bush, conversely, has presented himself from the outset as a *Christian who just happens to have become a politician*—a man of faith who did not even *want* to run for office until he heard a call from above.

The primary narrative that has been created around Bush combines several major biblical tropes in a very effective way. The first and better known of these is the trope of the prodigal son—the man who squanders his youth on bad business and alcohol, only to turn to God and find his rightful place in his own father's former occupation. This narrative has been very carefully constructed by Mr. Bush and his biographers. While acknowledging his "drinking problem," for example, he states clearly that he was not an "alcoholic." But it was just enough of a problem to make him question his life's priorities and turn to God for a new direction. According to his 1999 autobiography, *A Charge to Keep* (ghostwritten by Karen Hughes, a Presbyterian church elder), Bush had become mired in the world of business and booze, and so turned in his darker hours to the study of Scripture. The beginning of this conversion occurred during a weekend in the summer of 1985, when evangelist Billy Graham visited George and Laura at their summer house in Maine. The reverend, with his magnetic presence and warmth, planted a "seed of salvation" in his soul that soon blossomed into a new birth:

> Reverend Graham planted a mustard seed in my soul, a seed that grew over the next year. He led me to the path, and I began walking. And it was the beginning of a change in my life. . . . [T]hat weekend my faith took on a new meaning. It was the beginning of a new walk where I would recommit my heart to Jesus Christ.[42]

It's worth noting here that at roughly the same time in the mid-1980s, Reverend Graham, like other evangelicals, had also made a powerful appeal for Christians to begin assuming political offices in the United States. As he told

Pat Robertson's audience on the *700 Club* on April 29, 1985, just months before he "planted the seed" in George W.,

> The time has come when evangelicals are going to have to think about getting organized corporately. . . . I'm for evangelicals running for public office and getting control of the Congress, getting control of the bureaucracy, getting control of the executive branch. . . . I would like to see every true believer involved in politics in some way.[43]

Ten years later, George W. would heed this call by running for governor, and then, in keeping with the narrative of the prodigal son, he would finally return to his "father's house" in Washington.

Interestingly enough, however, there is another less well-known account of the prodigal son's turning to Jesus—one that reads much more like a classic "born-again" experience. This took place a year earlier in 1984, when the famous evangelist Arthur Blessitt was visiting Midland, Texas. Known in the 1960s as "the Minister of Sunset Strip" for his preaching to Hollywood's hookers and hippies, Blessitt had become world renowned for carrying a huge cross on long walks around the word (in 2002, he carried a twelve-foot cross over 38,800 miles in 284 nations, winning a place in the *Guinness Book of World Records* for "The World's Longest Walk"). In April 1984, Blessitt came to preach at "Decision '84," a political summit for evangelicals. After hearing his message on the radio, Bush requested a private meeting with the preacher. Over lunch, Blessitt asked him, "If you died this moment, do you have the assurance you would go to heaven?" When Bush said no, Blessitt proceeded to explain how he could have that assurance and "know for sure that you are saved." "I like that," said Bush. Blessitt then asked Bush to join him in prayer, after which George W. accepted Christ as his savior and declared himself a "true believer in and follower of Jesus."[44] At the end, Bush was smiling and Blessitt began rejoicing. "It was an awesome and glorious moment," the evangelist recalled. Strangely, however, Blessitt decided it was best not to speak publicly about Bush's early conversion experience, and he kept it secret for seventeen years. It was only after *A Charge to Keep* was published, "with Bush writing so strongly about his faith," that Blessitt decided that "the time for secrecy had passed."[45]

It is not entirely clear why Mr. Bush and his ghostwriter chose to highlight the Billy Graham conversion story and keep the Blessitt story secret; but one can only suspect that a figure such as Graham provides a much more powerful spiritual legitimation than the "Minister of Sunset Strip"—and also one that appeals to a much broader audience of American voters than an idiosyncratic figure known best for carrying a giant cross around the world.

In addition to these prodigal son narratives, however, Bush's autobiography also contains a much more powerful narrative that is modeled on the story of Moses. This first appears in one very striking passage from *A Charge to Keep*, which recounts his decision to run for president. At a church service in January 1999, then-governor Bush heard a sermon by Pastor Mark Craig. The subject of the sermon was the famous story in *Exodus* 3–4, in which God appears to Moses in the burning bush, and despite Moses' lack of experience or skill, calls him to free Israel. "When God called Moses to deliver his people, he responded, 'Sorry God, I'm busy, I've got a family. . . .' Eventually, though, Moses relented and delivered a nation."[46] The pastor went on to link this passage to contemporary history, suggesting that, like Israel then, America today needs strong leaders with faith, integrity, and moral values: "People are starved for leadership," Pastor Craig said, "starved for leaders who have ethical and moral courage." While Bush himself downplayed the incident, suggesting that the pastor could have been talking to anyone, his mother Barbara knew better: "*He's talking to you*," she said.[47] As Bruce Lincoln suggests, this carefully constructed passage from Bush's well-timed autobiography contains a powerful but subtly double-coded message. Most readers might simply pass over it without much thought; yet an evangelical reader will recognize in this narrative a clear sign that Bush has heard the call and has been chosen for a higher purpose—that he has, like Moses, been called at a time when his people would need him.[48]

If we turn to Mansfield's presidential hagiography, *The Faith of George W. Bush*, it seems that this is in fact exactly the way many evangelicals interpreted the episode. Shortly after the Craig sermon, Mansfield recounts, Bush was visited in his governor's office by popular evangelist James Robison. But Bush was not alone that day; indeed, Mansfield tells us, they were joined by another important figure: "On the day that the evangelist entered Bush's office, he was surprised to find political strategist Karl Rove there as well." Bush then confided to Robison that he had a sense of divine calling to the White House: "I've heard the call. I believe God wants me to run for president." Indeed, going further, he linked it to a sense of an urgent mission: "I feel like God wants me to run for President. I can't explain it, but I sense my country is going to need me. Something is going to happen . . . but God wants me to do it."[49]

It is not insignificant that Bush made his announcement to these two men, Rove and Robison, the political tactician and the charismatic televangelist. Rove, of course, has served as Bush's political "brain" and brilliant campaign strategist. Part of Rove's strategy for the 2000 campaign was in fact an effort to "woo powerhouse evangelical pastors and Christian right leaders to Bush's side" and project the image of Bush the "compassionate conservative" as a new kind of Republican who could transform the GOP into a majority party.[50] Robison, conversely, was an extremely popular and well-connected televangelist who was known for bringing politicians and religious leaders together: "Robison had a gift for networking, for gathering people to pray and discuss the nation's problems. . . . He was particularly adept at connecting the Religious Right with conservative politicians and was even instrumental in encouraging Ronald Reagan to run for president in 1980."[51] Together, the political strategist Rove and the evangelist Robison then took Bush to meet a variety of religious leaders and receive their blessing for his newfound calling. Bush met with pastors of Pentecostal, Southern Baptist, and Charismatic backgrounds, and "before the meeting ended the pastors gathered around Bush and laid hands on him. . . . [T]he pastors prayed that God would bless him. . . . [T]ears were in Bush's eyes during the prayer."[52] According to Mansfield, there were many such gatherings. The Christian right had given the prodigal son and new Moses their blessing.

Bush in fact emerged as just the sort of true Christian leader that many evangelicals, such as Robertson, Reed, and Robison, had hoped would appear, serving as an ideal link between the New Christian Right and the Republican Party. As Craig Unger points out, George H. W. Bush had a good deal of trouble forming relations with the Christian right, who regarded his aristocratic Episcopalian airs with suspicion; yet the younger Bush had become perfectly attuned to the nuances of the evangelical world. Replacing his father's "visionless pragmatism with the Manichaean certitudes of Good and Evil, . . . Dubya's bond with the Christian right was a crucial part of what distinguished him from his father."[53] And it was surely one of the keys to his election in 2000.

Compassionate Conservatism: Crafting a Kinder, Gentler Republican Economic Policy

> Maybe disestablishment [of religion] wasn't such a good idea.
>
> —Marvin Olasky, "Patrick Henry's Idea"

From the start, then, Bush has led what Mansfield calls a fundamentally "faith-based presidency," one that demonstrates "the power of faith to change a life . . . and to help shape the destiny of a nation."[54] Apart from Rove and Cheney, most of Bush's inner circle is deeply religious or tied to the religious right. In addition to Karen Hughes, who is a church elder, former Chief of Staff Andrew Card is married to a Methodist minister; Secretary of State Condoleezza Rice is a preacher's daughter; former chief speechwriter Michael Gerson is a graduate of Wheaton College, known as the "evangelical Harvard"; and former Attorney General John Ashcroft is an active member of the Pentecostal Assemblies of God church. Faith has been an active part of this White House from the beginning. As BBC correspondent Justin Webb notes, "The Bush administration hums to the sound of prayer. Prayer meetings take place day and night."[55]

The cornerstone of Bush's political philosophy is the concept of "compassionate conservatism," a phrase first coined and then passed on to Bush by the influential evangelical writer Marvin Olasky. Often called "the most influential propagandist of the Christian right" and Bush's "unlikely guru," Olasky and his writings also helped inform the policies of the controversial Faith-Based and Community Initiatives, which offer unprecedented government financial support to religious organizations.[56] Olasky, we should note, was also significantly influenced by the work of R. J. Rushdoony and his ideal of a biblically governed society. While Olasky denies being a card-carrying Reconstructionist, he does cite Rushdoony in his writings and has clear affinities with Reconstructionist thought. Among other things, Olasky has suggested that the "disestablishment" of religion stated in the First Amendment was perhaps "not such a good idea" and has led to the erosion of religion in the public square; instead, he advocates a kind of "multiple establishment" of faith-based programs.[57]

While critics see these faith-based initiatives as a dangerous blurring of the boundaries between church and state, Olasky has argued that only religious organizations can offer genuine compassion and meet the spiritual needs of the least fortunate. Like many Republican politicians, Olasky argues that welfare tends to a create a sense of entitlement and thus dependency among the poor, "excusing the poor from the personal responsibility for their lives."[58] President Bush in turn whole-heartedly endorsed Olasky's ideas, wrote the forward to Olasky's book, *Compassionate Conservatism*, and repeated his rhetoric throughout his public addresses. As Bush put it, religious organizations can do things no state-run welfare program can, reaching peoples' inner hearts and avoiding the bureaucracy of government: "faith can move people in ways that government can't. I mean, government can write checks, but it can't put hope in people's hearts, or a sense of purpose in people's lives. That is done by people who have heard a call and who act on faith."[59]

The faith-based initiatives are, however, just part of a broader domestic policy that long predates the presidency of George W. Bush. Indeed, we might think of them as a kind of Christianized version of the push toward small government, privatization, tax cuts, and dismantling of the welfare state that has long been cherished by Republicans. In 1994, in fact, William J. Bennett, secretary of education under Reagan, gave Olasky's *Tragedy of American Compassion* to fellow Republican Newt Gingrich for Christmas; Gingrich in turn recommended it to incoming Republican members of Congress; and, as Jo Renee Formicola points out, "it is easy to see how Olasky's book had an impact on the Welfare Reform Act of 1996."[60] A similar logic and a similar Christianization of Republican economic policies underlies Bush's massive tax cuts. While critics argue that the tax cuts favor those with the highest incomes but leave less money for basic domestic programs, Bush's defenders, such as Michael Gerson, argue that such cuts accelerate the economy, reduce dependency on government hand-outs, and so are the best means of morally uplifting the poor.[61] In practice, then, "compassionate conservatism" does not look very much different from the earlier Republican policies of privatization and tax cuts for the wealthy; indeed, many critics see it as simply a "rebranding of conservatism with a human face," a conservatism no less determined to dismantle the programs of the New Deal and the Great Society, from Social Security to Medicare.[62] But it certainly does *sound* much nicer than slashing government "down to the size where we can drown it in a bathtub," as Grover Norquist famously put it. As Esther Kaplan comments,

> At the heart of Bush's faith-based project beats the gospel of privatization, the old-school right-wing ideal of pushing any responsibility for social welfare from the government to the private sector. . . . [F]irst push through tax cuts so drastic they empty the federal till, then force Congress to slash domestic spending. . . . [C]ompassionate conservatism in the form of faith-based grants and increased charitable deductions sounds far kinder and gentler than "starving the beast."[63]

But regardless of its name, the "beast" of government social programs has been "starved" much more drastically under Bush's presidency than under any previous Republican administration.[64]

Secrets and Parables: Double Coding and Religious Messages in Bush's Public Discourse

> He who has ears, let him hear.
>
> —Matthew 13:9 (NIV)

The public discourse of President Bush has from the very outset been infused with powerful religious language, themes, and imagery. Sometimes this religious language is quite explicit, but more often than not it is woven very subtly into his well-crafted speeches, usually in such a way that it is either not noticed by or not offensive to most Americans. Bush, of course, does not write his own speeches, nor is he a theologian. Most of his memorable speeches— and also the ones most loaded with religious imagery—are the work of

Michael Gerson, a devout Christian who graduated from Wheaton College. As Jeffrey Goldberg observes, "Gerson's life is built around prayer and faith and, so too, are his speeches."[65] It was Gerson, for example, who was responsible for Bush's famous phrase "the Axis of Evil," which he chose instead of "axis of hatred" because of its "more theological resonance."[66] But in most cases, Gerson's speeches for Bush are extremely careful to use religious language in very subtle ways; while they frequently refer to "the Almighty" and "the Creator," a close reading shows them to be very carefully nonsectarian and quite generic, never referring *explicitly* to Jesus Christ or to particular theological positions that might alienate a constituency. As Kaplan observes, "One of the administration's great political challenges is how to send its evangelical base these private or sub-rosa signals without seeming to openly express bigotry or religious intolerance or to openly declare a culture war."[67]

Much of Bush's public discourse, as Bruce Lincoln has shown, involves a form of "double coding" of religious themes in relatively innocuous-sounding rhetoric. That is, they often contain specific references to particular biblical passages, hymns, and Christian themes, which are clearly heard by those who are steeped in Scripture but largely missed by most American listeners. Thus Gerson "filled George W. Bush's delivery system with phrases that, while inoffensive to secular voters, directed more specific religious messages to the faithful. Examples . . . included 'whirlwind' (a medium for the voice of God in the Books of Job and Ezekiel), a 'work of mercy,' . . . and phrases like 'safely home' taken from hymns and gospel songs."[68] In an issue on "Bush and God," *Newsweek* listed a few of the many examples of this sort of double coding of biblical passages and Christian themes in Bush's speeches. Thus, in his January 2001 inaugural address, he told us that "an angel still rides in the whirlwind and directs this storm"—a direct reference to the whirlwind that serves as a medium for God's voice in the books of Job and Ezekiel. At the 9/11 remembrance ceremony in 2002, he declared "And the light shines in the darkness. And the darkness will not overcome it"—a direct reference to the first verses of the Book of John, referring to the coming of Christ. And in his 2003 state of the union address he described the "wonder-working power in the goodness and idealism and faith of the American people"—a direct quote from one of the oldest evangelical gospel songs.[69] Interestingly enough, the last two of these examples make a very striking theological move: whereas the "light shining in the darkness" and the "wonder-working power" originally referred to Jesus and God, Bush here uses them both to refer to *America*. It is now the *United States* that is the wondrous light of freedom fighting the powers of darkness and evil.

Gerson himself denies that Bush's speeches are "coded" in any particular way. As he put it, "There's an idea that we are constantly trying to sneak into

the President's speeches religious language, code words, that only our supporters understand. . . . But they are code words only if you don't know
them."[70] The implication, apparently, is that all Americans should be so
steeped in Scripture as to catch these subtle religious references. But in any
case, the people who know this language best are the evangelical Christians
who see in Bush an ideal kind of divinely guided leader.

War against the Evil-Doers: Divine Calling
and Religious Rhetoric in the War on Terror

I trust God speaks through me.

—George W. Bush at a speech before Old Order Amish in Lancaster, PA

You know, [my father, George H. W. Bush] is the wrong father to appeal to
in terms of strength. There is a higher father I appeal to.

—George W. Bush, explaining his decision to invade Iraq,
in Woodward, *Plan of Attack*

While religious themes run throughout Bush's public discourse from the beginning of his presidency, they emerged with a powerful new force in the wake
of the 9/11 attacks and in the build-up to the invasion of Iraq. In the post-9/11
world, America was no longer imagined as simply the beacon of freedom to
the world, but was now engaged in a cosmic battle between absolute forces of
good and evil, the shining light of America against the hateful forces of darkness and terror. According to Peter and Rochelle Schweitzer, a Bush family
member told them that the president sees this not just as a military confrontation but as "a religious war. He doesn't have a p.c. view of the war. His
view of this is that they are trying to kill the Christians. And we the Christians
will strike back with more force and more ferocity than they will ever know."[71]

At the same time, Mr. Bush appears to regard himself as divinely appointed
to play a kind of Moses-like role, leading his people at this moment of great
danger. Various people close to Bush have noted his sense of divine calling in
the war on terror. As a close acquaintance of Bush told the *New York Times*, "in
[Bush's] frame, this is what God has asked him to do . . . he has encountered
his reason for being, a conviction informed and shaped by the President's own
strain of Christianity."[72] Similarly, a former senior official who served in
Bush's first term spoke extensively with Seymour Hersh about the president's
deep religious faith and the Iraq war. After 9/11, he said, Bush felt that "God
put me here" to deal with the war on terror; after the Republican sweep in the
2002 elections, Bush saw the victory as a message from God that "he's the

man"; and after his reelection in 2004, "he spoke of it as another manifestation of divine purpose."[73] Finally, in one of the most stunning cases, the Israeli paper *Haaretz* quoted Palestinian prime minister Mahmoud Abbas after a meeting in which the president told him, "God told me to strike at al Qaida and I struck them, and then he instructed me to strike at Saddam, which I did, and now I am determined to solve the problem in the Middle East."[74] As we will see in chapter 6, Bush's sense of divine calling in the war on terror is not just deeply religious, but often sounds messianic as well.

If we examine Bush's post-9/11 speeches, we find that they contain a consistent but, again, often double-coded structure and narrative that reflects this divinely guided sense of mission. The most basic structure is a binary logic that divides the world today into two fundamental sides—good and evil, freedom and terror, American democracy and radical extremism. Indeed, few words appear more frequently in Bush's post-9/11 speeches than "evil" and "evil-doers." "My administration has a job to do and we're going to do it. We will rid the world of the evil-doers," he declared in September 2001.[75] "We are in a conflict between good and evil, and America will call evil by its name," he said in his 2002 West Point commencement address.[76] The term "evil," for Bush, suggests that the enemy is not simply bad; it means that the enemy is irrational, irredeemable, beyond reform. Such an enemy can only be destroyed. As he stated, in ruggedly down-home terms, in 2001, "The people who did this act on America . . . are evil people. They don't represent an ideology, they don't represent a legitimate political group of people. They're flat evil. That's all they can think about, is evil. And as a nation of good folks, we're going to hunt them down . . . and we will bring them to justice."[77] He is also clear that in this struggle between ultimate good and ultimate evil, there is no compromise. There is no middle ground. Everyone must take a side:

> There is no neutral ground . . . in the fight between civilization and terror, because there is no neutral ground between good and evil, freedom and slavery, and life and death.[78]

> Every nation, in every region, now has a decision to make. Either you are with us, or you are with the terrorists. . . . The course of this conflict is not known, yet its outcome is certain. Freedom and fear, justice and cruelty, have always been at war, and we know that God is not neutral between them.[79]

The binary logic of Bush's war on terror can thus be analyzed as in table 1.1.

Yet at the same time, in addition to this binary structure, Bush's public discourse contains a kind of linear narrative, one that is again subtly modeled on Christian ideals. Even more than a war of good against evil, the Iraq war is portrayed as part of a much larger narrative of human history, a key moment

TABLE 1.1

Good	Evil
Civilization	Terror
Freedom	Slavery, fear
Life	Death
America as agent of God's plan for history	Axis of Evil: Iraq, Iran, North Korea
Crusade (= religious war for Good)	Jihad (= religious war for Evil)

in the unfolding of freedom throughout the world, guided by the providential hand of God. In this sense, Bush has built upon the Cold War rhetoric of the triumph of America's God-given freedom over godless communism, but also pushed that rhetoric much further, to a kind of absolute and global level. During the Cold War, as George Will recently observed, "the survival of liberty meant the containment of tyranny. Now, Bush says, the survival of liberty must involve the expansion of liberty until 'our world' is scrubbed clean of tyranny."[80]

As Bush told the United Nations in 2002: "History has an Author who fills time and eternity with His purpose. We know that evil is real, but good will prevail against it."[81] Going further still, Bush also suggested that the United States is not a neutral bystander in this divine plan for history but has a very special, indeed, pivotal role to play in the unfolding of freedom throughout the world. As he stated in his third state of the union address, January 2003, in which he made the strongest case for the preemptive invasion of Iraq,

> We go forward with confidence, because this call of history has come to the right country. . . . Americans are a free people, who know that freedom is the right of every person and the future of every nation. The liberty we prize is not America's gift to the world, it is God's gift to humanity. . . . We do not claim to know all the ways of Providence, yet we can trust in them, placing our confidence in the loving God behind all of life, and all of history.[82]

An even stronger declaration appeared in his address to the National Endowment for Democracy in 2003, in which he suggested that "liberty is both the plan of heaven for humanity and the best hope for progress here on Earth." In this plan for humanity, America has been "called" to lead the world:

> The advance of freedom is the calling of our time. It is the calling of our country. . . . We believe that liberty is the design of nature. We believe that liberty is the direction of history. We believe that human fulfillment and excellence come in the responsible exercise of liberty. And we believe that freedom, the freedom we prize, is not for us alone. It is the right and the capacity of all mankind. And as we meet the terror and violence of the world, we can be certain the author of freedom is not indifferent to the fate of freedom.[83]

Implicit in these various statements are at least four very powerful religio-political ideas:

1. History is not random but has a specific goal and purpose;
2. History is guided by God;
3. God's plan for history is the spread of freedom to every nation; and
4. America has a special role to play in the unfolding of God's plan.

In sum, America has been called by God to lead the spread of freedom throughout the world, much as Bush had been called by God to lead the nation at this crucial historical moment—and, indeed, much as Moses had been called to lead the people of Israel to freedom. Finally, we might also add a fifth, unstated, but clearly implied, idea, namely, America must be willing to use military force in order to fulfill its role as the agent of God's plan for history.

This notion of America as having some special role in the world is not a new one. It is largely in keeping with the older ideal of America as a "chosen nation" and the "city on the hill ordained by God as the light of nations." In Bush's appropriation of it, this older idea of America's special role in God's plan seems to be combined with a form of millenarian theology. Much as that of postmillenarians such as R. J. Rushdoony, Bush's rhetoric suggests that we are moving progressively toward a divinely governed new world order, gradually realizing God's predestined plan right now in history. For postmillenarians such Rushdoony, as for Bush, God's plan for history is "the conquest of all things" and the infusion of His divine will into all institutions, including social and political institutions: it leaves "no area of life and activity untouched, and it predestines victory." Yet as we will see in chapter 6, this postmillenarian current in Bush's rhetoric is also mixed with a far more violent and destructive sort of premillenarian rhetoric of the sort that we find in Tim LaHaye's *Left Behind* novels.

God's Man at This Hour: Bush and the New Christian Right

I think President Bush is God's man at this hour.

—Tim Goeglin, quoted in Joel C. Rosenberg, *World*, October 6, 2001

Bush's powerful use of religious rhetoric, with its narrative of good versus evil and America as the bearer of God's gift of freedom, appears to have been quite effective indeed. Already when he first decided to run for the presidency, Bush and Rove had generated powerful support among the religious right for his domestic policies and his rhetoric of compassionate conservatism. According to Lou Sheldon, founder of the Traditional Values Coalition and a longtime activist for the religious right, Bush was not only generally in sync with Sheldon's overall agenda; indeed, Sheldon said, "George Bush *is* our agenda."[84]

Yet in the wake of 9/11, many began to see Mr. Bush as a divinely appointed leader, chosen to guide America in a historic battle against evil. On the day before Christmas 2001, the *Washington Post* reported that "Pat Robertson's resignation this month as President of the Christian Coalition confirmed the ascendance of a new leader of the religious right in America: George W. Bush."[85] Apparently, Robertson had stepped down because "the position has already been filled. . . . [T]he president] is that leader right now. There was already a great deal of identification with the president before 9-11 in the world of the Christian Right, and the nature of this war is such that it has heightened the sense that a man of God is in the White House."[86] In the words of Ralph Reed: "God knew something we didn't. . . . He had a knowledge nobody else had: He knew George Bush had the ability to lead in this compelling way."[87]

While Bush's support from the general evangelical community is fairly clear, his ties to the more extreme wing of the New Christian Right, such as Dominionism and Reconstructionism, is less so. While many inclined to conspiracy theory see Bush as the fulfillment of a kind of Reconstructionist dream of a theocratic takeover, I think the connections are far more complex and subtle. As we saw above, the genius behind Bush's "compassionate conservatism," Marvin Olasky, shows the influence of at least some Reconstructionist ideas and quotes Rushdoony in his work; yet he and most others close to Bush disavow being "Reconstructionists" themselves. Rather than a direct link, I think there is a more complex sort of "fit" or "elective affinity" between the faith-based policies of the Bush administration and the theonomic ideals of the Reconstructionists. As I note above, Bush's view of history and his narrative of a progressive unfolding of God's plan for humanity fits quite well with the postmillenarian view of history promoted by Reconstructionists. Beyond that, however, there are several other striking affinities between the two.

First, both emphasize the need for small, indeed, minimalist government that is not concerned with social welfare, but instead turns those matters over to the church. The state, for Rushdoony, is solely concerned with "the restraint of evil," serving as "a 'terror' to evil-doers," without which "hoodlums terrorize the country with riots and violence."[88] Such a view of the state seems to fit rather well with Mr. Bush's. Like Rushdoony, Bush was a known advocate of capital punishment as a means of administering justice and punishing "evildoers" in Texas; as President he has radically increased funding for defense and prisons, spending over $300 billion on a war to bring "evil doers to justice" in Iraq, while simultaneously slashing almost all social programs that benefit the poor.

Second, the Reconstructionists and the Bush administration also share a similar attitude toward the role of the church in society; both argue that the state can do little to reach people's hearts or regenerate the fallen, which is primarily the task of the church and faith-based organizations. Rushdoony also places enormous emphasis on the importance of Christian education (and is often cited as the father of the Christian home-schooling movement), while the Bush administration has given unprecedented support to Christian schools and to Christian-influenced education (such as abstinence-only education, which has spread rapidly in the past five years and is now taught in a staggering 30 percent of U.S. schools).[89]

Third, both Bush and the Reconstructionists share a fundamentally pro-capitalist, antitaxation, and antiregulation view of the economy. Like most of the New Christian Right, the Reconstructionists on the whole embrace a Republican ideal of low taxes, particularly for the wealthy, and deregulation of industry. As Lienesch observes, the economics of the New Christian Right "borrows from the supply-side economics of the Reagan era New Right"; indeed, "To these Christian capitalists, the neoconservative conception of capitalism as moral enterprise is an attractive argument, reinforcing their own view of capitalism as a religious endeavor."[90] Thus Pat Robertson was able to discover supply-side economics in Christian parables, arguing that investment is a sort of "social service, and that profit is a reward or payment for serving others. Encouraging people to invest and serve, God encourages profit and in fact expects people to seek as much of it as possible, using wealth to create more wealth."[91] Reconstructionists such as Gary North even go so far as to identify the origins of free-market capitalism with the Ten Commandments, which in his view "lay down the religious, legal, and economic foundations for the creation and long-term maintenance of a free market economy."[92]

In sum, while it seems unlikely that George W. Bush has been reading the *Institutes* of R. J. Rushdoony or even has much idea what Reconstructionism is about, there are clear affinities between the two. In the Bush administration, we might say, the far extreme of the Christian right and the far extreme of the Republican Party find they have much in common. As we will see in the next chapter, Bush would also appear to agree with Rushdoony that secrecy and lying are sometimes justifiable in the service of a higher good.

The Crumbling Wall: The Reestablishment of Religion in U.S. Politics?

A major change is under way. Laymen are active in the faith; the Christian family is coming into its own. . . . The battle is real, but the promises of victory are very great. The kingdom of this world shall indeed become the

Kingdom of our Lord, and of His Christ, for this is the victory that alone shall overcome the world.

—R. J. Rushdoony, *Christianity and the State*

The "faith of George W. Bush," as I think we've seen in this chapter, is by no means a simple or singular thing. While Bush and his biographers present him as a simple, uncomplicated man of piety, it seems clear that there are in fact many different forces at work in the image of Bush as a man of faith. These include campaign strategists such as Rove, ghostwriters and biographers such as Hughes and Mansfield, religious theorists such as Olasky, televangelists such as Robison and Robertson, grassroots Christian organizers such as Reed and the Christian Coalition, old-school "starve the beast" Republicans, and, as we will see in chapter 5, the corporate media. All of these together have helped construct the image of Bush as prodigal son and American Moses, as "God's man at this hour." But they have also worked to fundamentally erode the wall of separation between church and state. Indeed, many such as President Carter have warned that this represents a full-scale assault by both far right Christians and far right Republicans designed to tear down that wall brick by brick. Others, such as John Danforth, who had been an Episcopal priest before becoming a Missouri senator, warn that the Republican Party has itself become part of the Christian right:

Republicans have transformed our party into the political arm of Conservative Christians. . . . The problem is not with people or churches that are politically active. It is with a party that has gone so far in adopting a sectarian agenda that it has become the political extension of a religious movement.[93]

Still more disturbing, however, is the fact that our president—a civilian elected by the public (which is, of course, debatable)—appears to see himself in a kind of Mosaic and even messianic role, guided by God and waging a cosmic war against evil-doers. Indeed, as Jeffrey Siker points out, Mr. Bush seems to believe he has been granted "a clear vision of what is morally right and wrong, both personally and as the leader of the free world," as well as an ability to identify "evil-doers" wherever they dwell, whether the terrorists in foreign lands or the criminals to be executed in Texas: "some people simply deserve the wrathful judgment of God, and if God chooses to use him as the vehicle of punishment . . . so be it, whether for death row inmates in Texas or for governments such as Iraq. . . . White hats on one side, wanted posters on the other, with little doubt as to who's on which side of divine truth."[94] Yet such a conception of the presidency is extremely problematic, even disastrous, for a democratic political system, for it makes policy decisions a matter of divine and suprahuman authority rather than a matter of rational debate among mortal human beings: "it mandates an ideological shift away from open discussion, publicly responsible leadership, and humility, toward authoritarianism, publicly unmindful leadership, and arrogance."[95]

Finally, as we will see in chapter 2, this also raises disturbing questions as to how we are to reconcile this appeal to divine authority with an administration that is, in practice, obsessively secretive and seems to have an unprecedented tendency toward dissimulation.

Notes

1. Jeffrey Goldberg, "The Believer: George W. Bush's Loyal Speechwriter," *New Yorker*, February 13 and February 20, 2006, 64.

2. Jeffrey R. Siker, "President Bush, Biblical Faith, and the Politics of Religion," *Religious Studies News*, April 2003.

3. David Domke, "Religion and Race," paper presented at the conference "Fundamentalism: Race, Truth, and Democracy in a Global World," Ohio State University, March 2, 2006. See Domke, *God Willing? Political Fundamentalism in the White House, the War on the Terror, and the Echoing Press* (New Haven: Yale University Press 2004), 1–29.

4. See Bruce Lincoln, *Holy Terrors: Thinking about Religion after September 11* (Chicago: University of Chicago Press, 2003), 30–32.

5. Stephen Mansfield, *The Faith of George W. Bush* (New York: Tarcher, 2003), 166.

6. Public Opinion and Polls, *The Pew Charitable Trusts*, March 20, 2006, at www.pewtrusts.org. Former speechwriter David Frum sums Bush up with the words "decency, honesty, rectitude, courage, and tenacity." Frum, *The Right Man: The Surprise Presidency of George W. Bush* (New York: Random House, 2003), 272.

7. Thomas Franks, *What's the Matter with America? The Resistible Rise of the American Right* (London: Vintage, 2005), 27.

8. "The Trust Gap," *New York Times*, February 12, 2006, section 4, 13.

9. Frum, *The Right Man*, 17.

10. Martin Marty, "Fundamentalism Reborn: Faith and Fanaticism," *Saturday Review*, May 1980, 37–42.

11. Sheryl Henderson Blunt, "Bush Calls for Culture Change," *Christianity Today*, May 24, 2004, at www.christianitytoday.com/ct/2004/121/51.0.html.

12. Michael Lienesch, *Redeeming America: Piety and Politics in the New Christian Right* (Chapel Hill: University of North Carolina Press, 1993), 8.

13. Lienesch, *Redeeming America*, 5, 8.

14. Robison, *Save America to Save the World* (Wheaton, IL: Tyndale House, 1980), 112.

15. Frances Fitzgerald, " Reporter at Large: A Disciplined, Charging Army," *New Yorker*, May 18, 1981, 60.

16. LaHaye, cited in Kim A. Lawton, "Whatever Happened to the Religious Right," *Christianity Today*, December 15, 1989, 44. See Frederick's Clarkson's useful map of

the religious right's diverse orbits of influence, in "Expanding Universe," *Mother Jones*, December 2005, 44–45.

17. Joseph L. Conn, "Judgment Day," *Church and State* (September 1996), quoted in Frederick Clarkson, *Eternal Hostility: The Struggle between Democracy and Theocracy* (Monroe, ME: Common Courage, 1997), 24.

18. Arne Christenson, "Christians in Politics," *New Wine*, November 1986, 40.

19. Joe Conason, "Christian Coalition Enters New York City," *Freedom Writer*, May/June 1992, quoted in Clarkson, *Eternal Hostility*, 123.

20. Richard Cizik, quoted in Lawton, "Whatever Happened to the Religious Right," 44.

21. Jacob S. Hacker and Paul Pierson, *Off Center: The Republican Revolution and the Erosion of American Democracy* (New Haven: Yale University Press, 2005), 128.

22. Pat Robertson, *The Secret Kingdom* (Nashville: Nelson, 1982), 198.

23. Robertson, *Secret Kingdom*, 199.

24. Robertson, *Secret Kingdom*, 222.

25. Pat Robertson, quoted in Jimmy Carter, *Our Endangered Values: America's Moral Crisis* (New York: Simon & Schuster, 2005), 60.

26. Pat Robertson, *The New World Order* (Dallas: World Publications, 1991), 246.

27. Clarkson, *Eternal Hostility*, 27.

28. Pat Robertson, *Pat Robertson's Perspective*, March–April 1991, 6–7. See Bruce Barron and Anson Shupe, "Reasons for the Growing Popularity of Christian Reconstructionism: The Determination to Attain Dominion," in *Religion and Politics in Comparative Perspective: Revival of Religious Fundamentalism in East and West*, ed. Bronislaw Misztal and Anson Shupe (Westport, CT: Praeger, 1992), 86.

29. Rodney Clapp, *The Reconstructionist* (Downers Grove, IL: Intervarsity, 1987), 3, 4–5.

30. Sara Diamond, *Spiritual Warfare: The Politics of the Christian Right* (Boston: South End, 1989), 138.

31. R. J. Rushdoony, *The Institutes of Biblical Law*, vol. 1 (Nutley, NJ: Craig, 1973), 725.

32. R. J. Rushdoony, "Back to the Future," *New Wine*, November 1986, 24.

33. R. J. Rushdoony, *Law and Liberty* (Nutley, NJ: Craig, 1971), 3. Rushdoony himself does not speak of "theocracy," but his son-in-law, Gary North, explicitly embraces the term: "I certainly believe in biblical theocracy," North writes, and notes that Rushdoony himself "presents the case for biblical theocracy." North, *Political Polytheism: The Myth of Pluralism* (Tyler, TX: Institute for Christian Economics, 1989), x.

34. Rushdoony, *Institutes*, 1:765.

35. Rushdoony, *Institutes*, 1:100. Elsewhere, he writes, "Precisely because the Christian Church represents the contradictory view of man, the democratic state is implicitly hostile to Christianity. The rise of democracy has seen, on the one hand, the progressive abandonment of Christianity by many states in favor of humanism, and, on the other, a radical persecution of Christianity." Rushdoony, *Christianity and the State* (Velocity, CA: Ross House, 1986), 19.

36. Gary North, *Political Polytheism*, 177–178.

37. Gary North, "Comprehensive Redemption: A Theology of Social Acton," *Journal of Christian Reconstruction* (Summer 1981), quoted in Clarkson, *Eternal Hostility*, 122.

38. Diamond, *Spiritual Warfare*, 137.

39. Rushdoony, *Institutes*, 1:566.

40. Clarkson, *Eternal Hostility*, 122. Interestingly enough, some politicians, such as Michael Farris—"one of the most prominent Christian Right politicians in the U.S."—turned to the story of Rahab to defend the lies told during the Iran-Contra affair: "What Ollie North did was basically the moral equivalent of what the spies and Rahab did in Jericho." Farris, quoted in Clarkson, *Eternal Hostility*, 123.

41. Carter, *Our Endangered Values*, 64.

42. George W. Bush, *A Charge to Keep* (New York: Morrow, 1999), 136.

43. Billy Graham, *700 Club*, April 29, 1985, transcribed by Katherine Yurica, "The Despoiling of America," at www.yuricareport.com/Dominionism/TheDespoilingO-fAmerica.htm#_edn14.

44. Tim Dickinson, "A Prayer for W," *Mother Jones*, December 2005, 13–14; Mansfield, *Faith*, 64–65.

45. Mansfield, *Faith*, 65.

46. Mansfield, *Faith*, 107; Bush, *Charge to Keep*, 8–9.

47. Bush, *Charge to Keep*, 9; my italics.

48. Bruce Lincoln, "The Theology of George W. Bush," *Christian Century*, October 5, 2004.

49. Mansfield, *Faith*, 108, 109.

50. Esther Kaplan, *With God on Their Side: How Christian Fundamentalists Trampled Science, Policy, and Democracy in George Bush's White House* (New York: New Press, 2004), 70.

51. Mansfield, *Faith*, 108.

52. Mansfield, *Faith*, 110.

53. Craig Unger, *House of Bush, House of Saud: The Secret Relationship between the World's Two Most Powerful Dynasties* (New York: Scribner, 2004), 192–93.

54. Mansfield, *Faith*, front jacket.

55. Justin Webb, "America's Deep Christian Faith," *BBC News*, March 14, 2003, at news.bbc.co.uk/2/hi/programmes/from_our_own_correspondent/2850485.stm.

56. Max Blumenthal, "Avenging Angel of the Religious Right," *Salon.com*, June 6, 2004, at www.salon.com/news/feature/2004/01/06/ahmanson/.

57. Marvin Olasky, "Patrick Henry's Idea," *World Magazine*, July 8, 2000, at www.worldmag.com/articles/4008. On the influence of Rushdoony in Olasky's work, see Blumenthal, "Avenging Angel."

58. Jo Renee Formicola, "The Good in the Faith-Based Initiative," in *Faith-Based Initiatives and the Bush Administration: The Good, the Bad, and the Ugly*, ed. Jo Renee Formicola, Mary C. Seegers, and Paul Weber (Lanham: Rowman & Littlefield, 2003), 30.

59. "President Promotes Faith-Based Initiative," April 11, 2002, at www.whitehouse.gov/news/releases/2002/04/20020411-5.html.

60. Formicola, "Good in the Faith-Based Initiative," 30.

61. Goldberg, "Believer," 57.

62. Joe Conason, "Where's the Compassion," *Nation*, September 15, 2003, at www.thenation.com/doc/20030915/conason.

63. Kaplan, *With God on Their Side*, 45–46.

64. As Joe Conason comments, "Being a 'fiscal conservative' meant passing lop-sided tax cuts for the wealthy few and leaving the federal budget in deficit for the foreseeable future. Being a 'family conservative' meant looking after certain families, particularly if their annual incomes are higher than $200,000 and their estates are valued at more than $2 million. And so far, being a 'compassionate conservative' appears to mean nothing very different from being a hardhearted, stingy, old-fashioned conservative. Bush's budgets prove that he still emphatically prefers cutting the taxes of wealthy individuals and corporations to maintaining living standards for poor and working-class families." Conason, "Where's the Compassion?"

65. Goldberg, "Believer," 64.

66. Goldberg, "Believer," 60.

67. Kaplan, *With God on Their Side*, 79.

68. Phillips, *American Dynasty*, 225. See Lincoln, *Holy Terrors*, 30–32.

69. Karen Yourish, "Delivering the 'Good News,'" *Newsweek*, March 10, 2003, 28.

70. Goldberg, "Believer," 64.

71. Peter Schweitzer and Rochelle Schweitzer, *The Bushes: Portrait of a Dynasty* (New York: Doubleday, 2004), 517.

72. Frank Bruni, "For Bush, a Mission and a Defining Moment," *New York Times*, September 22, 2001, A1.

73. Seymour Hersh, "Up in the Air," *New Yorker*, December 5, 2005, at www.newyorker.com/fact/content/articles/051205fa_fact.

74. Arnon Regular, "Road Map Is a Life Saver for Us," *Haaretz.com*, at www.haaretz.com.

75. George Bush, quoted in "Bush Vows to Rid the World of Evil-Doers," *CNN.com*, September 16, 2001, at archives.cnn.com/2001/US/09/16/gen.bush.terrorism/.

76. George Bush, quoted in "Bush Delivers Graduation Speech at West Point," June 1, 2002, at www.whitehouse.gov/news/releases/2002/06/20020601-3.html.

77. George Bush, Speech at the Federal Bureau of Investigation, September 25, 2001, in *"We Will Prevail": President George W. Bush on War, Terrorism, and Freedom* (New York: Continuum, 2003), 22.

78. George W. Bush, "President Bush Reaffirms Resolve to War on Terror," March 19, 2004, at www.whitehouse.gov/news/releases/2004/03/20040319-3.html.

79. George W. Bush, "Address to a Joint Session of Congress," September 23, 2001, at www.whitehouse.gov/news/releases/2001/09/20010920-8.html.

80. George Will, "The New Math: 28 + 35 = 43," *Newsweek*, January 31, 2006, at www.msnbc.msn.com/id/6856836/site/newsweek/.

81. Bush, *We Will Prevail*, 71–72, xxx.

82. Bush, *We Will Prevail*, 220–221.

83. George Bush, "Address to the National Endowment for Democracy," November 6, 2003, at www.whitehouse.gov/news/releases/2003/11/20031106-2.html.

84. Mark Crispin Miller, *Cruel and Unusual: Bush/Cheney's New World Order* (New York: Norton, 2004), 265.

85. Dana Milbank, "Religious Right Finds Its Center in Oval Office," *Washington Post*, December 24, 2001, A2.

86. Milbank, "Religious Right Finds Its Center."

87. Milbank, "Religious Right Finds Its Center."

88. Rushdoony, *Law and Liberty*, 5; Rushdoony, *Institutes*, 1:62.

89. See Janice Irvine, *Talk about Sex: The Battles over Sex Education in the United States* (Berkeley: University of California, 2004), xv. See Rushdoony, *The Messianic Character of American Education* (Nutley, NJ: Craig, 1963).

90. Lienesch, *Redeeming America*, 109.

91. Lienesch, *Redeeming America*, 109–110.

92. Gary North, *Sinai Strategy: Economics and the Ten Commandments* (Tyler, TX: Institute for Christian Economics, 1988), 211.

93. John Danforth, *New York Times* editorial, April 2005, in Carter, *Our Endangered Values*, 63.

94. Siker, "President Bush."

95. Domke, *God Willing?*, 5.

2

No Need for Explanation: Generalized Secrecy and Unanswerable Lies

I'm the commander—see, I don't need to explain—I do not need to explain why I say things. That's the interesting thing about being the president. Maybe somebody needs to explain to me why they say something, but I don't feel like I owe anybody an explanation.

—George W. Bush, quoted by Bob Woodward, *Bush at War*

There is very grave danger that an announced need for increased security will be seized upon by those anxious to expand its meaning to the very limits of official censorship and concealment.

—John F. Kennedy, address before the
American Newspaper Publishers Association

THERE ARE MANY WORDS one could think of to try to sum up the Bush administration. Supporters of the administration might choose words such as "faith," "determination," "integrity," or "commitment." Critics might think of words such as "arrogance," "hubris," or simply "greed" (according to a March 2006 Pew Research Center poll, the words Americans most associated with Bush had shifted from "honest" to "incompetent," "idiot," and "liar").[1] But one central theme that runs through this administration that few people, supporters or critics, could deny is secrecy. As Larry Klayman, chairman of Judicial Watch, put it, "This administration is the most secretive of our lifetime, even more secretive than the Nixon administration. They don't believe the American people or Congress have any right to information."[2]

While presidential secrecy is nothing new—and largely taken for granted since the beginning of the Cold War—the Bush administration represents a qualitative shift in the dynamics of political concealment. Secrecy today is no longer a kind of necessary evil, justified by the need to protect our national interests; secrecy has now become the standard mode of operation and a simple matter of policy. Indeed, concealment *is* to a large degree the policy. Secrecy is this administration's method of handling any situation, great or small, whether foreign policy or minor domestic affairs, whether the false intelligence used in the invasion of Iraq or the decision to wait almost an entire day to report the fact that the vice president had shot a man in the face with a shotgun.[3] If philosophers such as Debord had warned twenty years ago that media-driven postmodern society was entering a state of "generalized secrecy" and "unanswerable lies," today we seem to have entered the "post-truth presidency,"[4] in which our leaders do not just dissimulate, but barely make an effort to tell us the truth.

Much of this administration's obsession with secrecy has been justified as a necessary reaction to 9/11 and the need to defend our national security in this new war on terror. Yet Bush and Cheney's preoccupation with secrecy long predates 9/11. Like his father before him, Bush was a member of one of the country's most infamous secret societies, Yale's Skull and Bones (a society "so secret I can't say anything more," as he put it),[5] and so knew much about the value of secret organizations and tightly knit old-boys networks long before assuming office. As a kind of "Fount of Elitism, Hubris, and Secrecy," in which members were "conditioned to level with each other and to keep secrets from (or deceive) outsiders," Skull and Bones has played an important role in the sort of dynastic and aristocratic power that still lingers in America.[6] And there are clearly aspects of Bush's prepresidential life that he would no doubt like to remain secret, such as his close ties to Enron and Ken Lay ("Kenny boy," as he was known to the Bushes), who were his largest source of financial support in the 2000 election.[7]

Vice President Cheney is also no novice in the tactics of concealment. Often cited as the "hand behind the throne" or even "the man who *is* president," Cheney is a veteran of the Nixon administration and an outspoken advocate of executive power. Complaining that the past three decades have seen an erosion of presidential power, Cheney has argued that America today is hampered by the fact that we do not have *enough* secrecy and that "one of the problems we have as a government is our inability to keep secrets."[8] He and Bush have apparently done everything possible to expand that power of secret keeping. Whereas Clinton had signed a major declassification order in 1995, making thousands of historical documents publicly available, this administration has rapidly accelerated a program of *reclassification* of tens of thousands of documents—most of which, according to historians, are "innocuous," "mundane," even "silly," and of no security threat to anyone.[9]

But what is the reason for such pervasive secrecy regarding even the most mundane kinds of information? The answer, I think, lies in this administration's aggressive pursuit of power, with secrecy serving as both the "core" and the "aura" of power.

It would take a very long book, or perhaps several long books, to catalogue all the examples of secrecy, concealment, and dissimulation in this administration. But even a glance at the most egregious examples—ranging from the Bush-Cheney Energy Task Force to the CIA's network of secret prisons—provides ample evidence that concealment is a particular obsession of this administration. What is perhaps even more disturbing, however, is that this powerful push for government secrecy has gone had in hand with an *equally powerful push for government surveillance and encroachment upon our civil liberties.* Particularly in the wake of 9/11, with new measures such as the USA PATRIOT Act and the NSA's secret wiretapping program, government secrecy has been *radically expanded* even as our personal privacy has been *dramatically reduced.*

This obsession with secrecy, I will argue, is both intimately related to and yet stunningly at odds with President Bush's avowed faith and commitment to truth. On the one hand, Bush's public display of piety has been extremely effective in persuading many Americans to support his various domestic and foreign policies—to *have faith* that he is doing the right thing even when much of it is beyond the public gaze and without congressional oversight, *to look the other way,* even as his administration has vastly expanded executive power. Yet, at the same time, any thinking citizen can see that there are profound tensions, if not blatant contradictions, here—contradictions between a rhetoric of compassion and the realities of preemptive war based on misleading intelligence, between the ideal of faith-based initiatives and the realities of tax cuts that benefit the wealthiest Americans accompanied by the slashing of social programs that benefit the poorest. As we stagger through Bush's second term, it seems that many Americans are beginning to seriously question that trust.[10] As doubts about the reasons for the invasion of Iraq, the legality of NSA spying, and the morality of torture undermine this trust, all but the most faithful supporters seem increasingly uncomfortable with such a secretive, unaccountable, and invasive model of presidential power.

Working the Dark Side: Generalized Secrecy and Unanswerable Lies

We also have to work . . . sort of the dark side, if you will. We've got to spend time in the shadows in the intelligence world. A lot of what needs to be done here will have to be done quietly, without any discussion, using sources and methods that are available to our intelligence agencies.... [I]t's going to be vital for us to use any means at our disposal, basically, to achieve our objective.

—Dick Cheney, interview on *Meet the Press*, September 16, 2001

Secrecy is the first essential in affairs of state.

—Cardinal Richelieu, "Maxims"

While neither Bush nor Cheney was a stranger to secrecy before taking office, the real obsession with concealment began from the first days they stepped into the White House in 2001. According to *U.S. News & World Report*, on day one of the Bush presidency, Chief of Staff Andrew Card issued a directive to "wall off records and information previously in the public domain," as the administration "quietly but efficiently dropped a shroud of secrecy across many critical operations of the federal government—cloaking its own affairs from scrutiny and removing from the public domain important information on health, safety, and environmental matters. The result has been a reversal of a decades-long trend of openness in government."[11]

Bush's own first act as president was not to initiate a new economic strategy or a plan to combat terrorism, but instead a concerted effort to conceal his own Texas gubernatorial records. As soon as he received word of the Supreme Court's ruling on his election, George W. arranged for his records to be "gathered, placed on sixty large pallets, shrink-wrapped in heavy plastic and, with no announcement, quietly shipped off to his father's presidential library at Texas A & M University."[12]

Among his next decisions as president was a similar attempt to restrict access to the presidential records of Ronald Reagan (and of his then vice president father). According to the Presidential Records Act of 1978, these were to be released in January 2001. However, after requesting a series of extensions to review the many "legal questions" relating to the documents, Bush issued an executive order in November 2001 that created an entirely new standard for obtaining information about former presidents. Although the American Historical Association filed a lawsuit to acquire access to these records, the case has been refiled repeatedly and remains unresolved. Unless overturned, this newly expanded secrecy could allow presidential papers to remain sealed indefinitely; it would require that access to a former president's papers be approved by both the former president and the incumbent president; and it would allow representatives of former presidents to invoke executive privilege after a president is dead. As Robert Parry explains, this potentially gives him and his children a remarkable kind of "dynastic power" over a large period of history and a massive body of presidential secrets:

> Bush's order eventually could give him control over both his and his father's records covering 12 years of the Reagan-Bush era and . . . Bush's own presidential term. . . . Under Bush's approach, control over those two decades worth of secrets could eventually be put into the hands of Bush's daughters, . . . a kind of dynastic control over U.S. history.[13]

It is worth noting here just a few of the sensitive documents that Bush decided should remain secret: a six-page memo dated December 8, 1986, entitled "Talking Points on Iran/Contra Affairs" and a series of memos dated November 22 and December 1, 1988, one of which was entitled "Pardon for Oliver North, John Poindexter, and Joseph Fernandez."[14]

Follow the Money (If You Can): The Highly Secretive Energy Task Force

> There is no company in the country that stood to gain as much from the White House plan as Enron. The recent revelations regarding the extent of Enron's contacts with the White House have only underscored the need for full public disclosure.
>
> —Rep. Henry Waxman

One of the most secretive and controversial of the Bush administration's initiatives was its National Energy Policy Development Group. First unveiled in May 2001, the plans of the Energy Task Force clearly embodied Cheney's unapologetically pro-industry, antienvironmentalist agenda, focusing primarily on promoting oil, gas, and nuclear power, while largely ignoring alternative energy technologies, significantly weakening environmental regulations, and calling for the opening of environmentally sensitive areas such as the Arctic National Wildlife Refuge to oil drilling. Not surprisingly, all of this alarmed many environmentalists and members of Congress. The Government Accountability Office (GAO), headed by David Walker, therefore requested that the White House reveal who was consulted by Cheney and what was discussed. Cheney's blunt reply, however, was that the GAO had no authority to seek the information—a move that many see as a bold assertion of the administration's autonomy and its exemption from any sort of congressional oversight.[15]

However, Larry Klayman and Judicial Watch filed a second suit, which did proceed far enough to reveal that Cheney's Task Force had relied for advice almost exclusively on energy companies, many of them big GOP donors. From January to May 2001, Energy Secretary Spencer Abraham met with over one hundred representatives of energy companies, eighteen of which had contributed more than $16 million to the party since 1999. These include ChevronTexaco, ExxonMobil, British Petroleum, the Nuclear Energy Institute, Edison Electric Institute, and Enron. Consumer and environmental groups were barely contacted at all. Operating under a cloak of "Nixonian secrecy," the commission produced what the *Washington Monthly* referred to as an "all-drilling no-conservation" national energy plan.[16] One email sent by the secretary's top assistant even asked a lobbyist what he would do if he were "King or Il Duce." It was done.[17]

Such a plan, which called for massive investment in coal-fired power plants and billions in subsidies and tax cuts to encourage oil, nuclear, and coal production, was particularly of interest to companies such as Enron. Indeed, "no initiative interested Enron more, and Cheney welcomed the company's active participation in its deliberation."[18] As *CNN* reported in 2001, Enron and Bush had close ties in Texas well before Bush entered the White House, and they only grew closer through Cheney's secret energy policies:

> Enron . . . was only able to grow so big, so fast, because of the deregulation of energy companies instituted by then-Gov. George W. Bush. And Ken Lay rewarded his friend. He and Enron together were Bush's biggest contributor, giving $2 million to his campaigns for governor and president. Lay also loaned Bush his corporate jet. . . . Once in the White House, Bush responded generously. Ken Lay was the only energy executive to meet privately with Vice President Dick Cheney to help shape the administration's new energy policy.[19]

Thus in April 2001, Lay met with Cheney, handing him what many have called a "wish list" of corporate recommendations. This prompted Representative Henry Waxman of the House Committee on Government Reform to order an analysis of the memo, which revealed that Cheney's Task Force adopted almost all of the recommendations in seven of eight policy areas.

The Judicial Watch lawsuit also forced Cheney to cough up a few extremely revealing documents. The most important of these included detailed maps of Iraq's oil fields and lists of nations with oil interests in Iraq and neighboring countries. One of the projects, dated March 2001, was entitled "Foreign Suitors for Iraqi Oilfield Contracts."[20] As we will see in chapter 3, this was very likely part of a larger interest in controlling the significant portion of the world's oil supply located in Iraq and restructuring the broader politics of the Middle East itself.

Overall, Cheney's obstinate refusal to cooperate with Congress or any other external investigator was more than simply an attempt to hide unpopular business dealings (though it was certainly that). More important, it was also a bold assertion of executive autonomy and an early indication of the fundamentally secretive, nontransparent, and uninhibited form of presidential power that the Bush administration would assert for the next five years.

Stealth War on the Environment: From "Clear Skies" to "Healthy Forests"

This is stealth war on the environment in the name of ideology.

—Bill Moyers, interview with Amanda Griscom

Among the most astonishing examples of secrecy in the Bush administration has been its environmental policy, which is closely tied to its dealings with the energy industries. As John Dean observes, "no aspect of the Bush-Cheney hidden agenda is more disturbing than the stealth mistreatment of the environment."[21] Bush's dismal environmental record was already evident from his years as governor of Texas, when he was known for exempting some of the very worst polluters in the biggest polluting state from environmental regulation. However, as commander-in-chief, he would make this assault on the environment a national agenda. According to environmental lawyer Robert F. Kennedy Jr., the White House "has actively hidden its anti-environmental program behind the deceptive rhetoric, telegenic spokespeople, secrecy and the intimidation of scientists."[22] Noting over four hundred environmental rollbacks in just the previous three years, Kennedy describes the Bush assault on the environment as a form of stealth attack, carefully kept beyond the media and public gaze:

> Five years ago, if you asked the leaders of the major environmental groups in America, What's the gravest threat to the global environment?, they would have given you a range of answers: overpopulation, habitat destruction, global warming. Today, they will all tell you one thing: it's George W. Bush. This is the worst environmental president that we have ever had. . . . It is a concerted, deliberate attempt to eviscerate thirty years of environmental law. It is a stealth attack, one that's been hidden from the public.[23]

In short, Bush's environmental strategy could be summarized as dissimulation in action, a constant stream of deception and double-think: "Say one thing, do another. Never admit what you're up to. Rather, assert the opposite, repeatedly and despite all available evidence."[24]

Bush was greatly assisted in his stealth war on the environment by Republican pollster and public relations strategist Frank Luntz. Raising the use of "Orwellian language" to a kind of art form, Luntz helped craft an environmental rhetoric for Bush that was soothing and comforting yet largely disconnected from the reality of his policies. According to a memo sent by Luntz to Bush entitled "The Environment: A Cleaner, Safer, Healthier America," the administration would have to mask its agenda with far more euphemistic phrases. As Luntz put it, "it can be helpful to think of environmental and other issues in terms of 'story.' A compelling story, even if factually inaccurate, can be more emotionally compelling than a dry recitation of the truth. . . . The facts are beside the point. It's all in how you frame your argument."[25] Among the more remarkable sorts of "stories" that Luntz helped Bush tell are the "Clear Skies Act," which has actually *increased* air pollution by eliminating the requirement that every industrial facility clean up and postponed standards for meeting public health goals within twenty-five years, and the "Healthy Forests Act," which allows the timber industry to clear-cut forests in the name of "fire prevention."[26] Still more Orwellian is the administration's choice of people to head key positions overseeing our environmental resources, most of them former lobbyists for energy corporations. As Kennedy observes, "they have installed the worst, most irresponsible polluters in America, and the lobbyists from those companies, as the heads of virtually all the agencies and subsecretariats and even Cabinet positions that regulate or oversee our environment.[27] Thus Mark Rey, who previously lobbied for timber industries, was appointed undersecretary of agriculture for Natural Resources and Environment, in charge of forests; Patricia Lynn Scarlett, who previously lobbied for a wide range of corporate polluters, was made assistant secretary of the Interior for Policy, Management, and Budget, in charge of government regulations; and so on.

It would take a very long time to recount all the ways in which this administration has concealed its assaults upon the environment. Among the more incredible examples: concealing the fact that the air around Ground Zero was not safe and allowing citizens to return to homes and offices when it was in fact still very dangerous;[28] stifling Environmental Protection Agency (EPA) warnings about the dangers of deadly substances such as vermiculite, which contains lethal levels of asbestos fiber, 16 billion tons of which had been shipped throughout the United States;[29] and declaring that carbon dioxide— one of the principal causes of global warming, of which the United States is the world's greatest producer—is not legally "a pollutant that the EPA can site to regulate emissions from cars and power plants."[30] Finally, not only did the White House largely ignore the EPA's 2002 "Climate Action Report," which concluded that global warming is a reality, directly linked to greenhouse gas emissions, but it also censored the EPA's 2003 report by deleting or modifying key sections that provided disturbing data on global warming. This sort of censorship is clearly part of a larger pattern. In January 2006, NASA's top climate scientist James Hansen reported that the administration had tried to stop him from speaking out and actively worked to prevent Americans from grasping the catastrophic dangers posed by climate change: "They feel their job is to be this censor of information going out to the public," Hansen concluded.[31]

As many observers have noted, this administration's resistance to scientific evidence and the entire global community regarding climate change seems to have a kind of religious conviction behind it. According to Robert May, one of Great Britain's chief scientists and president of the Royal Society, the United States is trying to impose its own "fundamentalist ideology on the rest of the G-8."[32] As we will see in chapter 6, there is something disturbingly apocalyptic about Bush's apparent indifference to the massive evidence of global warming and the imminent probability of catastrophic climate change.

Stonewalling the 9/11 Investigation and Giving Fodder to Conspiracy Theories

> People are always coming up with stuff about holograms and planes shooting pods. That's what happens when the truth is systematically suppressed.
>
> —Monica Gabriella, whose husband was killed in the 9/11 attacks

If the Bush administration was unusually secretive when it came into office, it became markedly more concerned with the control of information in the wake of 9/11. The War on Terror has been used to justify a whole new wave of official concealment, ranging from secret immigration hearings and secret court proceedings to secret detentions; meanwhile, as John F. Stacks notes, public access to knowledge through the Freedom of Information Act has been "tightened so as to virtually gut the intention of the law."[33] On the Friday of Columbus Day weekend after 9/11, Attorney General John Ashcroft quietly issued an order urging all government agencies to deny whenever possible all Freedom of Information Act requests. In what some have called a "full scale assault on the public's right to know," secrecy has simply become "the preferred response."[34]

One of the most incredible examples of the administration's pervasive secrecy, and one of the most difficult to fathom, was its repeated effort to obstruct any external investigation of 9/11 itself. Indeed, perhaps the main reason for the wild proliferation of conspiracy theories surrounding 9/11—ranging from a Bush/Cheney "inside job," to an Israeli plot, to planes piloted by space aliens[35]—is simply the White House's intense secrecy and its refusal to participate in a full investigation. If anything, the administration seems to have gone out of its way to withhold information and to obfuscate rather than clarify the reasons for this national disaster.

Americans after 9/11 were left asking a myriad of disturbing questions about the attacks: how the hijackers were able to slip into the country past both the FBI and CIA, how they were able to receive the training to fly commercial aircraft, why our air defenses failed to follow standard protocol and scramble jets to meet the hijacked planes, why our president sat and read *My Pet Goat* with a group of children—and was *allowed* by his Secret Service to sit there as a potential target—even after he knew the nation was under attack, and so forth. And yet, incredibly, the White House seems to have done whatever it could to resist the demand for a full public investigation of the events. Despite the entreaties of the victims' families and a bipartisan group of congressmen, Mr. Bush vocally resisted forming an investigatory commission. He only relented in November 2002, a full year after the attacks and only after enormous political pressure was applied by a grassroots movement led by the families of the victims. When he finally did so, he initially chose to appoint none other than Henry Kissinger to head the commission—a move the *New York Times* suggested was clearly an attempt "to contain an investigation it has long opposed."[36] The White House also initially refused to allow National Security Adviser Condoleezza Rice to testify and finally relented only with the provision that "the panel agree not to seek testimony from other White House aides," even if that testimony was deemed critical to the investigation.[37] Mr. Bush himself agreed to testify only with Cheney at his side, and only on the condition that they not be forced to testify under oath. Meanwhile, the White House also denied requests for the Presidential Daily Briefs (PDB), and after months of negotiation allowed only four of the commissioners to see a mere 24 of the 360 PDBs dating back to 1998. According to the *Washington Post*, it also held back over 75 percent of the eleven thousand records from the Clinton era—records that Clinton himself had authorized the National Archives to gather and release to the commission.[38]

In light of this repeated stonewalling and bizarre denial of information regarding the worst terrorist attack in U.S. history, it is hardly surprising that a wide array of conspiracy theories has flourished over the past five years. Indeed, when I typed "9/11 conspiracy" into Google.com, I came up with over *six million* hits, and there seem to be almost as many books on the subject now in print. According to a 2004 Zogby poll, a full half of New Yorkers believe the administration had advance knowledge of the attacks but consciously failed to act; and we now have even reputable theologians and other academics seriously pursuing "alternative explanations" for 9/11.[39]

I am not an advocate of any particular conspiracy theory regarding 9/11 (other than that of staggering incompetence and ruthless opportunism), but I do believe that such theories are inevitable when our government works so hard to obstruct a serious, critical, and public discussion of how such a thing could have happened, who was at fault, and what could be done to prevent such disasters in the future. In light of the administration's extreme secrecy, and in light of the ways in which the administration subsequently used 9/11 to justify its preemptive invasion of Iraq, it is difficult not to agree with John W. Dean's conclusion that it seems likely that the administration had little incentive to *prevent* such a disaster, because they were already eager to *exploit* one when it came along.[40] As we will see in the following chapters, that is precisely what they did. One need not resort to any particular conspiracy theory to note that they would, in effect, "hi-jack" 9/11 for their own ends.

On a Mission from God: Manipulation of Intelligence in the Invasion of Iraq

They didn't like the intelligence they were getting and so they brought in people to write the stuff. They were so crazed and so far out of and so difficult to reason with—to the point of being bizarre. Dogmatic, as if they were on a mission from God.

—Former intelligence official quoted
in Seymour Hersh, "Selective Intelligence"

All warfare is based on deception.

—Sun Tzu, *The Art of War*

Surely the most catastrophic example of this administration's tendency toward dissimulation was its use of intelligence to justify a preemptive invasion of Iraq. Between August 2002 and January 2003, Bush and Cheney made repeated claims that Saddam Hussein had weapons of mass destruction and that Iraq had ties to Al Qaeda. Almost all of these claims have since been shown to be distorted, misleading, or simply false. Among the many examples: on September 7, 2002, Bush spoke of an International Atomic Energy Agency report indicating that Saddam was just "six months away from developing [a nuclear] weapon." Such a report did not exist.[41] On October 7, 2002, Bush gave a televised speech in Cincinnati that was filled with misleading statements, such as a claim that Iraq "has trained Al Qaida members in bomb making and poisons and deadly gases"—a claim that his own intelligence officials had disputed.[42] Finally, in his state of the union address on January 28, 2003, Bush presented eight alarming "facts" about Iraq's weapons of mass destruction (WMD), every one of which later turned out to involve exaggerated and misleading information.[43] The most egregious of these was the claim that Saddam had sought "significant quantities of uranium from Africa"—a claim the CIA already knew to be dubious, which had in fact been removed from the October 7 speech because of its unreliability. Only days later, Colin Powell refused to use that claim in his United Nations speech because of its lack of credibility (Powell did, however, use a good deal of other faulty evidence in that speech, such as satellite photos of "decontamination trucks" that were actually water trucks and an image of an Iraqi jet spraying "simulated anthrax" that turned out to be a leftover from before the 1991 Gulf War).[44]

What is perhaps most striking about Bush and Cheney's claims is their repeated insistence on the *certainty* of the case for war. The administration did not say "we think Saddam might have WMD" or "it's possible he could have links to Al-Qaeda"; rather, it was "We are *absolutely sure and there can be no doubt.*" As Bush put it in his address to the nation on March 17, 2003, "Intelligence gathered by this and other governments leaves no doubt that the Iraq regime continues to possess and conceal some of the most lethal weapons ever devised."[45] Or as Cheney claimed on *Meet the Press* on September 6, 2002, "Simply stated, there is no doubt that Saddam Hussein now has weapons of mass destruction," and "We do know, with absolute certainty, that he is using his procurement system to acquire the equipment he needs in order to enrich uranium to build a nuclear weapon."[46] Rumsfeld echoed the same refrain:— "We know they have weapons of mass destruction. . . . There isn't any debate about it"—as did Powell—"I'm absolutely sure there are weapons of mass destruction there."[47]

Still more incredibly, despite its claims being disproved by its own appointed weapons inspectors and by all credible sources, the administration has attempted to maintain the now absurd fiction that its prewar arguments were accurate. Asked in the summer of 2003, "Where are the weapons of mass destruction?" Bush replied, "We found them." Cheney, too, claimed months later that "conclusive evidence now demonstrates that Saddam Hussein did in fact have weapons of mass destruction."[48]

In fact, however, there was a great deal of doubt within the U.S. intelligence community from the very outset. According to a secret report of the Pentagon's Defense Intelligence Agency sent to Rumsfeld in September 2002, "There is no reliable information on . . . whether Iraq has—or will—establish its chemical warfare agent production facilities."[49] Moreover, there is now much evidence that the administration was applying enormous pressure on the intelligence community to provide them with the kind of information they wanted to hear, often at the expense of any sort of contrary evidence. According to Patrick Lang, former head of human intelligence at CIA, the administration had an almost religious faith in its war plans and exerted intense pressure on the intelligence community to provide the facts to fit its ideology:

They are such ideologues that they knew what the outcome should be and when they didn't get it from intelligence people they thought they were stupid. They start with an almost pseudo-religious faith. They wanted the intelligence agencies to produce material to show a threat.... Then they worked back to prove the case. It was the opposite of what the process should have been.[50]

Perhaps smokiest of the many smoking guns suggesting that the administration had manipulated intelligence was the release of the "Downing Street Minutes" in May 2005. According to this memo dated July 23, 2002, and labeled "secret and strictly personal," the administration had already made up its mind to invade Iraq and was quite willing to twist the facts to make its argument: "Bush wanted to remove Saddam, through military action, justified by the conjunction of terrorism and WMD. But the intelligence and facts were being fixed around the policy."[51]

As former Treasury Secretary Paul O'Neill and former terrorism tzar Richard Clarke have revealed, the invasion of Iraq really had nothing to do with 9/11 or WMD, except as a flimsy pretext. The administration was intent on removing Saddam long before 9/11—indeed, almost from its first days in office. According to O'Neill, the very first National Security Council (NSC) meeting at the White House, just a few days into Bush's presidency, focused on Iraq and even included a map for a postwar occupation, marking how oil fields would be carved up: "From the start we were building the case against Hussein and looking at how we could take him out.... It was all about finding *a way to do it*.... The President was saying, 'Fine. Go and find me a way to do it.'"[52] Long before the weapons inspectors had finished their investigation, while the diplomatic process was still underway, the president had made up his mind: "F__ Saddam. We're taking him out," as he put it in March 2002.[53]

Not only did the administration clearly manipulate information in order to make the case for war, but it also attacked those who tried to present contrary evidence. The most obvious case is Joseph Wilson, who investigated the claim—now known to be based on forged documents—that Iraq had attempted to obtain yellow-cake uranium from Niger. Following his devastating article, "What I didn't find in Africa," Wilson's wife, Valerie Plame, was outed by White House sources as a covert CIA operative—a move that destroyed her career and also endangered her life. Indeed, Special Counsel Patrick Fitzgerald described this leak as a "concerted action" by multiple people in the White House to use classified information as a weapon to "discredit, punish or seek revenge against" a critic of Bush's war in Iraq.[54] The profound irony in this is that we now know that Plame had been working specifically on Iran and its weapons programs. Incredibly, this same administration that has claimed to make national security its primary objective outed one of its own agents who had been working on one of the most sensitive and volatile aspects of the war on terror.[55]

In the initial stages of the investigations into the leak, President Bush had vowed that anyone involved in the leak would be fired (which he later revised to "if somebody committed a crime they will no longer work in my administration").[56] Yet, unbelievably, in April 2006, Special Counsel Fitzgerald found that *the president himself* had authorized Cheney's aide I. Lewis Libby to disclose "highly sensitive intelligence information to the news media in an attempt to discredit a CIA adviser whose views undermined the rationale for the invasion of Iraq." As Rep. Jane Harman of the House Permanent Select Committee on Intelligence put it, "it's breathtaking. The president is revealed as the leaker-in-chief."[57] While the administration insists that the president had legally declassified portions of our prewar intelligence on Iraq simply because "he wanted people to see the truth" about Iraq's weapons programs, most critical observers find this hard to believe. As the *New York Times* put it, "this president has never shown the slightest interest in disclosure, except when it suits his political purposes. He has run one of the most secretive administrations in history," and the only time he has revealed or declassified anything has been when it worked to his political advantage.[58]

But from the very beginning, the war in Iraq had less to do with national security than with the pursuit of power, both economic and symbolic. As such, it has been masked and obfuscated by the same sort of Orwellian rhetoric as Bush's environmental policy. As he put it in a speech of June 18, 2002, in words that might just as well have come straight out of *1984*:

> When we talk about war, we're really talking about peace. We want there to be peace. We want people to live in peace all around the world. . . . We believe in peace in the Middle East. We're going to be steadfast toward a vision that rejects terror and killing, and honors peace and hope. . . . [W]e don't conquer people, we liberate people—because we hold true to our values of life and liberty and the pursuit of happiness.[59]

Amazingly, this sort of backward rhetoric, combined with Mr. Bush's religious conviction that he is guided by a Higher Father, did persuade a large percentage of the American public and Congress to back the preemptive invasion of a nation that in reality posed us no threat.

The Torture of Secrecy: From Guantanamo to Abu Ghraib

> This new paradigm renders obsolete Geneva's strict limitations on questioning of enemy prisoners and renders quaint some of its provisions.

> —Alberto Gonzales (2002)

What masquerades as the motive for torture is a fiction.

—Elaine Scarry, *The Body in Pain*

In his classic work on the sociology of secrecy, Edward Shils described "the torment of secrecy" that pervaded Cold War America and its obsession with security. Writing in the 1950s, he warned that the delicate balance between secrecy, privacy, and publicity that held democracy together had been upset by the Cold War culture of concealment. In the post-9/11 world, however, it might be more appropriate to speak of the "torture of secrecy," as we now know that our government has been concealing—and in many cases *defending*—the use of torture as a weapon in the War on Terror.

On April 30, 2004, President Bush proudly declared that there were no longer the scars of dictatorial oppression in Iraq: "there are no longer torture chambers or rape rooms or mass graves in Iraq."[60] Unfortunately, he was quite wrong. There were in fact torture chambers, rape rooms, and mass graves in Iraq. The only difference was that they were no longer run by Saddam Hussein, but by Americans. While Saddam's hideous mass graves are widely known, America's are less publicized. In a retaliation for the gruesome killing of four American security contractors in Fallujah, for example, U.S. forces bombarded the city with five-hundred-pound bombs and raked its streets with cannon and machine-gun fire. As a result, two soccer fields in Fallujah—the only place to put the hundreds of bodies, many of them civilians—were transformed into mass graves. As *USA Today* reported, "Bodies were being buried in two soccer fields. . . . It was filled with row after row of graves."[61]

Sadly, Mr. Bush was also quite wrong about the existence of torture chambers and rape rooms. One of the most horrible secrets of the U.S. occupation of Iraq has been the cancerous spread of torture throughout our prisons, with apparent support from the highest levels of the administration. The decision to "work the dark side," as Cheney put it, was apparently made immediately after 9/11. In the wake of the attacks, more than 1,200 men and women throughout America, none of whom was ever convicted of any crime related to terrorism, were rounded up; not only have their identities been kept secret, but also they were never given the right to hear charges against them or have legal counsel. Today, almost five years later, we still have over five hundred people from forty nations held incommunicado at Guantanamo, almost all without legal counsel and no charges filed against them. Indeed, it was not until March 2006 that the Pentagon released the names of even some of the prisoners.[62]

As early as the summer of 2002, a CIA analyst visited Guantanamo and returned "convinced that we were committing war crimes" and that "more than half the people there didn't belong there. He found people lying in their own feces."[63] We now know that, since at least December 2002, similar abuse was taking place at other facilities in Iraq and Afghanistan, including threatening with dogs, repeated beatings, immersion in cold water, and electric shocks.[64] In some cases, such as the "Black Room" at the highly secretive Camp Nama facility near Baghdad, U.S. soldiers converted the Iraqi government's own torture chambers into interrogation cells. Placards on the walls of Camp Nama read "no blood no foul," meaning: "if you don't make them bleed, they can't prosecute for it." According to a *New York Times* report, the full nature of the abuse will likely never be known because of the "shroud of secrecy" that continues to surround the unit.[65]

Yet, despite recurring rumors of torture throughout 2003, the secret did not begin to come out until April 2004, when the now-infamous images of prisoner abuse at Abu Ghraib were released. According to General Antonio Taguba's report of April 4, 2004, classified "secret," U.S. soldiers at Abu Ghraib had committed a wide array of "egregious acts and grave breaches of international law," including punching, slapping, and kicking detainees; arranging detainees in sexual positions; forcing male detainees to wear women's underwear; forcing groups of male detainees to masturbate; placing a naked, hooded detainee on a box with electric wires attached to his fingers, toes, and penis; breaking chemical lights and pouring phosphorus on detainees; raping a female detainee; and sodomozing a detainee with a broomstick, among other atrocities.[66] As we see from the hundreds of photos and videotapes, much of the torture was filmed, adding to its humiliating and sickly spectral quality.

While the administration has repeatedly tried to blame the abuse on a few "hillbilly" soldiers out of control, there is compelling evidence that the secret chain of command stretches to the very top. According to the navy's former general counsel, Alberto Mora, navy intelligence officers reported in 2002 that interrogators at Guantanamo were engaging in "escalating levels of physical and psychological abuse rumored to have been authorized at a high level in Washington." Although Mora tried to warn the Pentagon of the problem of torture two years before the Abu Ghraib scandal, he found that the Justice Department had already negated his arguments with what he calls a "virtually unlimited theory of the extent of the president's commander in chief authority."[67] In fact, in January 2002, White House lawyer Alberto Gonzales had issued a memo urging the president to declare all aspects of the war in Afghanistan exempt from the strictures of the Geneva Conventions. Describing the struggle against terrorism as a "new kind of war," he argued that "the nature of the new war places a high premium on other factors, such as the ability to quickly obtain information from captured terrorists."[68] According to the *New York Times*, President Bush authorized this policy in a secret directive of 2001; and he also publicly declared that detainees at Guantanamo and elsewhere "will not be treated as prisoners of war" and so would not be protected by the Geneva Conventions.[69]

By an incredible feat of rhetorical acrobatics, at the very same time that the administration has obstinately denied the use of torture at U.S. facilities, it has issued numerous statements asserting that the president does have the authority to *defy* international law and *approve* the use of torture. In effect, they are saying: "We're certainly *not* torturing anybody and would never dream of doing such a thing. But legally we *could* do so if we wanted to." According to the Department of Defense,

> The president, despite domestic and international laws constraining the use of torture, has the authority as Commander in Chief to approve almost any physical or psychological actions during the interrogation, up to and including torture.[70]

Alberto Gonzales put the matter even more simply. The post-9/11 paradigm, he argued, demands new and more extreme measures that render previous rules against torture "quaint" and "obsolete."[71] Meanwhile, Mr. Cheney— whom the *Washington Post* dubbed "Vice-President for Torture"—has aggressively pushed for the legal authorization of human rights abuses by Americans, waging "an intense and largely unpublicized campaign to stop Congress, the Pentagon and the State Department from imposing more restrictive rules on the handling of terrorist suspects."[72]

At the same time, President Bush has authorized the creation of secret interrogation centers around the world, where highly secret special forces can operate outside of either public scrutiny or international law. As Seymour Hersh explains in *Chain of Command*,

> The President had signed a top-secret finding . . . authorizing the Department of Defense to set up a specially recruited clandestine team of Special Forces operatives and others who would defy diplomatic niceties and international law and snatch . . . 'high value' Al Qaeda operatives anywhere in the world. Equally secret interrogation centers would be set up in allied countries where harsh treatments were meted out, unconstrained by legal limits or public disclosure. The program was hidden inside the defense department as an "unacknowledged" special-access program or SAP, whose operational details were known only to a few in the Pentagon, the C.I.A., and the White House.[73]

Based on leaks to Hersh and other reporters, we now know that the CIA has been operating a hidden global internment network of secret prisons, or "black sites," with "ghost detainees" in various places, such as Thailand, Afghanistan, and parts of Eastern Europe. This new form of unconventional warfare is based on the logic of strict concealment; that is, it keeps "even basic information about the system secret from the public, foreign officials and nearly all members of Congress."[74] Hersh makes a compelling argument that special forces units such as these had also been at Abu Ghraib; indeed, the primary reason the administration worked so hard to cover up the Abu Ghraib abuse was that they could reveal a much darker secret about the brutal and illegal nature of America's war on terror: "The White House and Pentagon also would have to work together to prevent Congress and the press from unraveling an incendiary secret—that undercover members of an intelligence unit that operated in secret . . . had been at Abu Ghraib."[75]

In a deep and disturbing way, it would seem, the logic of torture is inextricably tied to the broader narrative of "Good versus Evil," America as divine force of freedom versus the demonic forces of terror, that pervades Bush's public discourse. As William T. Cavanaugh suggests in an article for *Christian Century*, torture is a key part of the larger narrative of American exceptionalism and the "othering of the enemy." While America is imagined as the exceptional nation, so inherently good and divinely guided that it would never harm anyone who did not deserve it, the tortured prisoner is imagined as so evil as to be deserving of his pain. As we see in the hundreds of images from Abu Ghraib, torture becomes a kind of hideous theatrical performance that transforms the prisoner into something subhuman—a screaming, irrational "other" that cannot be reasoned with, only degraded or destroyed (as Bush put it, the terrorists are "flat evil": "you can't negotiate with these people. . . . Therapy won't work").[76] In sum,

> Torture helps create the state of exception by ritually enacting power on the bodies of others. As the Abu Ghraib photos make plain, torture is a kind of theater in which victims are made to play the role of deviant. Stacked naked, chained to the floor, dragged around on leashes, made to howl with electrical shocks, the prisoners become what terrorists are in our imagination: depraved subhumans. Torture as theater provides its own justification: why should we bother with human fights when the enemy is less than human?[77]

At the same time, torture is intimately related to the broader dynamic of secrecy, power, and knowledge so central to this administration. If, as the Information Awareness Office tells us, "*scientia est potentia*," then the most powerful nation on earth requires the most knowledge and information; it cannot tolerate any enemy who withholds information from its gaze; and it will go to any lengths, using any degree of pain, to extract that information. As Elaine Scarry wrote twenty years ago in her classic work, *The Body in Pain*, torture is a key part of every totalitarian regime's "production of a

fantastic illusion of power," serving as a kind of "grotesque piece of com-
pensatory drama:"

> Torture consists of a primary physical act, the infliction of pain, and a primary
> verbal act, the interrogation. . . . Although the information sought in an interro-
> gation is almost never credited with being a *just* motive for torture, it is repeat-
> edly credited with being the motive for torture. But for every instance in which
> someone with critical information is interrogated, there are hundreds interro-
> gated who could know nothing of remote importance to the stability or self-
> image of the regime.[78]

This would appear to be much the same logic behind the United States' secret
torture campaign. While the administration obsessively defends its legal right
to torture as part of its war on terror, it has not in fact given us a single example of any useful information obtained through these extreme measures.
As Scarry suggests, that is never really the point of torture, anyway, which is a
much more vicious game of power and knowledge. Ultimately, torture has far
more to do with maintaining the illusion of power, particularly for political
regimes that are most uncertain, whose legitimacy is most in question: "The
physical pain is so incontestably real that is seems to confer its quality of 'in-
escapable reality' on that power that has brought it into being. It is, of course,
precisely because the reality of that power is so highly contestable, the regime
so unstable, that torture is being used."[79] The atrocities at Abu Ghraib suggest
that the use of torture is indeed largely about America's claim to absolute
power—and also about the unstable and contestable nature of that power in
the case of a preemptive war based on false information.

Yet, incredibly, even in the face of worldwide outrage, even in light of Viet-
nam-veteran John McCain's passionate plea to end torture and the law he
pushed to ban it, the Bush administration has continued to defend its right to
torture. Thus, in March 2006, the administration made the astonishing argument that "the new law that bans cruel, inhuman or degrading treatment of
detainees in U.S. custody" does not, in fact, apply at the Guantanamo prisons.[80] At the same time, according to a report released in March 2005 by
Human Rights First, the number of detainees in U.S. custody in Iraq and
Afghanistan had not decreased but in fact had *increased* from 6,000 to over
11,000 in just a few months, while the concealment of our detention operations intensified, showing "a trend toward greater secrecy, not less."[81] But still
more astonishing is the fact that when the *Washington Post* revealed the chain
of secret CIA prisons around the world, the reaction of Republican leaders of
Congress was not to open a full-scale investigation into the agency's abusive
and illegal activities; instead, it was to demand an investigation of the media's
leak of its secret program of global torture.[82]

Government Secrecy, Public Transparency:
The PATRIOT Act and Beyond

I believe there is something out there watching over us. Unfortunately it's
the government.

—Woody Allen

Privacy is dead, get over it.

—Scott McNealy, CEO of Sun Microsystems (2001)

In some ways even more disturbing than this obsession with secrecy, however,
is the striking increase of government surveillance and the reduction of rights
to privacy for ordinary citizens. The clearest example is the "Uniting and
Strengthening America by Providing Appropriate Tools Required to Intercept
and Obstruct Terrorism Act," better known by its ironic acronym, the USA
PATRIOT Act, championed by former Attorney General John Ashcroft. Although reviewed by no congressional committee, and too massive and complex for any congressperson to read, the act was rushed through both chambers with almost no discussion.

Among other things, the PATRIOT Act gives the government unprecedented power to detain noncitizens indefinitely; it allows the FBI to search citizens' homes or offices and conduct surveillance of phone and internet use
without proving probable cause; it grants authorities the power to require
bookstores and libraries to list the names of all books bought or borrowed;
and it gives government agencies the authority to conduct "Sneak and Peek"
searches, that is, to search our homes or offices without even letting us know
they've been there. As critics such as Howard Zinn have argued, this act thus
appears to be "the very opposite of patriotism, if patriotism means love of
your country and not the government, love of principles of democracy and
not the edicts of authority."[83] And not only Democrats and liberals, but even
many conservative Republicans have found the PATRIOT Act deeply troubling. Thus Arkansas congressman Ron Young warned that "in our desire for
security . . . we might be on the verge of giving up the freedoms which we're
trying to protect"; or as archconservative Grover Norquist put it, "for the administration to still answer the public's questions about how those powers are
being used with 'Just trust us' is insulting."[84] What is perhaps most disturbing
is that most of the controversial sections of the PATRIOT Act are not even focused on terror suspects; on the contrary, they apply to the general public.
And there is ample evidence that it is far more than terrorists who are now
being monitored. According to an FBI memo from 2002, recently released by

the ACLU, the government has been spying not just on suspected terrorists but also on many other "suspicious" individuals, including environmentalists and peace groups such as the Thomas Merton Center of Pittsburgh, whose only apparent crime was distributing anti–Iraq war leaflets.[85] NBC News likewise found that the Pentagon had targeted peace activists, antiwar protesters, and even a Quaker Meeting House in Florida. "This is incredible," said Rich Hersh, a member of the Quaker group monitored by the Pentagon, "It's an example of paranoia by our government. We're not doing anything illegal."[86]

Yet, incredibly, despite the tremendous new powers of surveillance granted by the PATRIOT Act, Mr. Bush is apparently still not satisfied. Indeed, he quietly found a new way to bypass even the minor safeguards contained in the act. When the bill came up to be reauthorized in March 2006, it included several oversight provisions to make sure the FBI did not abuse its powers to conduct secret searches of homes and offices, requiring the Justice Department to keep closer tabs on the FBI's activities. On March 9, Bush signed the reauthorization with much fanfare. But as soon as the reporters left, the White House quietly issued a "signing statement," which explains the president's interpretation of the new law. According to this statement, Bush does not in fact consider himself obliged to tell Congress how the PATRIOT Act is being used; indeed, he can withhold that information if he believes it might compromise national security or the "performance of the executive's duties." In sum, "The executive branch shall construe the provisions . . . that call for furnishing information to entities outside the executive branch . . . in a manner consistent with the president's constitutional authority to supervise the unitary executive branch and to withhold information." In other words, the president may ignore those oversight provisions and authorize secret, unaccountable forms of surveillance more or less at his discretion.[87]

In effect, under measures such as the PATRIOT Act, the concept of transparency has been *fundamentally reversed*; government has become increasingly secretive, while the public has become increasingly subject to surveillance. As Elaine Scarry aptly puts it, the PATRIOT Act "inverts the constitutional requirement that people's lives be private and the work of government officials be public. It instead crafts a set of conditions in which our inner lives become transparent and the workings of the government become opaque."[88] It is indeed ironic that the same attorney general (himself a Pentecostal Christian) who declared U.S. freedoms to be "not the grant of any government or document but . . . our endowment from God"[89] should have gone to such lengths to invade and restrict those freedoms. And it is doubly ironic that the same president who claims a divine calling to bring freedom to the world has granted himself the power to violate our freedoms whenever he sees fit.

Mining for Secrets: From Total Information Awareness to NSA Wiretapping

> I know the capacity that is there to make tyranny total in America, and we must see to it that this agency and all agencies that possess this technology operate within the law and under proper supervision, so that we never cross over that abyss. That is the abyss from which there is no return.
>
> —Senator Frank Church on the NSA (1975)

Since the 1970s, Americans have been aware of the dangers inherent in the awesome powers of surveillance offered by new information technologies. Already in 1975, Senator Church had warned that organizations such as the NSA could lead us into the abyss of tyranny and a total loss of privacy if not carefully overseen. In the wake of 9/11, the Bush administration took new measures that seem not to have crossed the abyss, but to have plummeted headlong into it.

In 2002, it was revealed that the Pentagon had begun a massive new surveillance program called Total Information Awareness (TIA). This data-mining program was led by John Poindexter, the former national security adviser under Reagan who had played a key role in devising the Iran-Contra arms deal. According to the *New York Times*, the TIA program "would permit intelligence analysts and law enforcement officials to mount a vast dragnet through electronic transaction data ranging from credit card information to veterinary records, in the United States and internationally."[90] Even apart from its Big Brother–ly nature, TIA generated public outrage with its official seal— a truly remarkable image that featured the eye in the pyramid from the back of the dollar bill casting its God-like gaze over the entire earth, accompanied by the phrase "*scientia est potentia.*" This image and the nature of the program were so shocking that TIA was defunded by Congress in 2003 and officially scrapped. However, according to James Bamford, a scholar and historian of the NSA, the data-mining project of Total Information was not so much scrapped as quietly continued in other guises.[91]

In the fall of 2005, we learned that Bush had authorized a secret program that would allow the NSA to bypass the FISA court and conduct eavesdropping on U.S. citizens without warrant. As Bamford suggests, this reflects a completely new paradigm for information gathering, one that is far more pervasive and invasive than anything imagined by the FISA law: "Rather than monitoring a dozen or so people for months at a time . . . the decision was made to begin secretly eavesdropping on hundreds, perhaps thousands, of people. . . . In essence, NSA seemed to be on a classic fishing expedition, precisely the type of abuse the FISA court was put in place to stop."[92] Yet, still more incredibly, in May 2006 we learned that this program was far more massive than previously thought, indeed, that the NSA had been tracking not just hundreds or thousands, but *tens of millions* of phone calls made by U.S. citizens, all without court order or congressional oversight.[93]

Ironically, President Bush had been asked over a year before about precisely this sort of abuse of intelligence. During his reelection campaign in April 2004, Bush spoke to reporters about the PATRIOT Act and assured them that it did not encroach on Americans' civil liberties:

> Any time you hear the United States government talking about wiretap, it requires—a wiretap requires a court order. Nothing has changed, by the way. When we're talking about chasing down terrorists, we're talking about getting a court order before we do so. . . . [W]hen you think Patriot Act, constitutional guarantees are in place when it comes to doing what is necessary to protect our homeland, because we value the Constitution.[94]

We now know that at the time he made this statement, Bush had already authorized the NSA to conduct wiretaps without court order and that the program had been going on for years. This statement, like so many others, is remarkable evidence of this president's ability to say one thing while simultaneously doing the exact opposite.

The administration, of course, has defended its need to wiretap without warrant as part of a War on Terror in which the FISA rules are too slow and cumbersome. But President Carter, who was in office when FISA was put into effect, has called Bush's actions simply "disgraceful and illegal," and his arguments in their defense flatly "ridiculous."[95] FISA, Carter points out, already allows the government to wiretap citizens immediately and then obtain a warrant retroactively. The only possible motivation for the secret NSA program is a much broader and more disturbing project of mass data mining that has no legal defense. According to Bruce Schneier, a renowned technology consultant dubbed "security guru" by *The Economist*, "Arguing that this is legal is basically saying we're in a police state."[96]

What is perhaps even more remarkable is the fact that the administration will apparently face no significant consequences for what many believe is a clear violation of FISA and an outrageous invasion of privacy. The Senate Intelligence Committee decided there would be no real investigation into how the program was operated, who was wiretapped, and whether it violates the law; instead, the committee's Republicans voted to form a subcommittee that would simply receive reports from the White House on any future warrantless surveillance. As *The New York Times* notes, "It's breathtakingly cynical. Faced with a president who is almost certainly breaking the law, the Senate sets up a panel to watch him do it and calls that control."[97] In his typically Orwellian style, the president not only did not reprimand anyone at the NSA, but actually chose Michael Hayden—the same man who ran the NSA's secret operation—as the new the head of the CIA. Indeed, rather than an investigation into whether the administration had violated the law, the exact opposite has happened: the White House has instead launched an investigation into the employees of the CIA and NSA and the reporters who *leaked* the information to determine whether *they* had violated the law by trying to inform the public that the government was spying on them without warrant.[98] Here we see the complete *inversion* of government transparency and citizens' rights to privacy: now it is the government's right to spy on us that is obstinately defended and the public's right to know what they're up to that is under attack.

Hidden Agendas and the Crumbling Trust: Making Sense of Bush's Secrecy

> Don't forget, the real business of the War is buying and selling. The murdering and the violence are self-policing and can be entrusted to non-professionals. The mass nature of wartime death is useful in many ways. It serves as a spectacle, as diversion from the real movements of the War. . . . The true war is a celebration of markets.
>
> —Thomas Pynchon, *Gravity's Rainbow*

> It's not just the church that needs evangelists. So does big oil.
>
> —Cartoon in *The New Yorker*, March 6, 2006

The pervasive secrecy that runs throughout the Bush administration is deeply disturbing for a number of reasons. Most basically, it raises the question of just what the heck are they up to? As former Attorney General William Rogers put it, "The public should view excessive secrecy among government officials as parents view sudden quiet when youngsters are playing. It is a sign of trouble."[99]

But, most important, this also raises the question of how we are to resolve a series of apparent contradictions: the contradiction between Mr. Bush's outward display of religious piety and his administration's apparent obsession with secrecy; between a president who claims to be a man of prayer and an administration that defends torture; between a claim to honesty and clear evidence of deceptions that led us into a disastrous war; between a rhetoric of "compassionate conservatism" and a record of environmental destruction and slashing of social programs that benefit the poor. As the *New York Times* pointed out in 2006, such obsessive dissimulation is fundamentally at odds with a president who has run so much of his campaign on an ideal of *trust*. In fact, "we can't think of a president who has deserved that trust less. This has been a central flaw of Mr. Bush's presidency."[100]

There are several ways we could try to reconcile these contradictions. One would be the mainstream Republican (and, as I will argue in chapter 5, mainstream media) view that this is simply how politics works. In other words, the president really is a sincere man of faith, but the harsh world of politics requires that he sometimes step into the messy realm of compromise, ambiguity, and occasional half-truths.

A second, perhaps more plausible, answer would be that Bush and his entire party are simply hypocrites. That is, they have cynically manipulated religious rhetoric to conceal what is actually going on, which is largely about *money*—namely, endless tax cuts for the rich, massive breaks for the energy industries, and slashed social programs for the poor. This is the critique often leveled by many Democrats and a few of the braver members of the media. As Jimmy Carter recently argued, this same president, who claims to be a compassionate conservative, has consistently pushed economic policies that overwhelmingly favor the wealthiest Americans and harm the poorest. The primary result of his "compassion" has been a rapidly widening gap between the very richest and the very poorest citizens, between the ever-inflating salaries of corporate CEOs and the dwindling wages of ordinary workers:

> Under the tax cuts pushed through Congress since 2000, for every dollar in reductions for a middle class family, the top 1 percent of households will receive $54 dollars, and those with $1 million or more income will receive $191 dollars. During the first three years, the number of Americans living in poverty increased by 3.5 million, while the income for the 400 wealthiest Americans jumped by 10 percent just in the year 2002. . . . [T]he salaries of corporate chief executive officers have gone from 40 times to 400 times the average worker's pay.[101]

Even John DiIulio, the former director of the Office of Faith-Based and Community Initiatives, was shocked by the hypocrisy of Bush's alleged "compassion." In a devastating letter to the president in 2002, he noted that "there is a virtual absence as yet of any policy accomplishments that might, to a fair-minded nonpartisan, count as the flesh on the bones of so-called compassionate conservatism."[102]

A stunning example of Bush's "compassion" in action was his "Deficit Reduction Act" of 2005, ostensibly designed to lower the federal deficit by $40 billion. So controversial was the act that Vice President Cheney was forced to fly halfway around the world to break the 50–50 tie on the vote in the Senate. The act lowers the deficit, but only by radically slashing almost every social program that benefits the poorest and neediest Americans, such as college students ($12.7 billion cut to student loans), single moms ($5 billion cut to state agencies to track down dead-beat dads for child support), the sick (premiums and copayments raised significantly), and foster parents ($343 million cut from foster care). Still more astonishing is the fact that this budget reduction bill came at the same time as a new wave of tax cuts that primarily benefit the very wealthiest Americans. As Tim Dickinson comments, this is yet another example of the twisted Orwellian logic of this administration:

> behind closed doors, House Ways and means Chairman Bill Thomas confided to a group of lobbyists that the GOP slashed social programs for the poor by $40 billion to help pay for $90 billion in new tax cuts—almost half of which will go to wealthy Americans with incomes in excess of $1 million. The net result of the Deficit Reduction Act will be a $50 billion *increase* in the deficit. In the bizarre world of President Bush's double-speak bills, the new spending measure takes its place along the Clear Skies Act, which sought to increase air pollution, and the Healthy Forests Initiative, which opened America's woodlands to more clear-cutting.[103]

Senator Kent Conrad, the ranking Democrat on the Senate Budget Committee, aptly commented on the disturbing irony in this: "I don't know of any religion practicing in America today that preaches from the pulpit that what one should do is take from the least among us to give to those who have the most. But that's what this budget is about. It's so profoundly wrong."[104]

It is therefore not surprising that critics such as Thomas Franks see the whole rhetoric of "religion" and "moral values" as a distraction or smoke screen. In Franks's view, it is largely a political ploy that has worked very effectively to persuade many working-class Americans that they are voting for "American family values" when in fact they are voting against their own economic self-interest: "The trick never ages; the illusion never wears off. *Vote* to stop abortion; *receive* a rollback in capital gains taxes. *Vote* to make our country strong again; *receive* deindustrialization." Republican politicians invoke God and the battle against gay marriage on the campaign trail, but once they're in office, they push through economic policies that benefit their corporate lobbyists:

> Old-fashioned values may count when conservatives appear on the stump, but once conservatives are in office the only old-fashioned situation they care to revive is an economic regimen of low wages and lax regulations. Over the last three decades they have smashed the welfare state, reduced the tax burden on corporations and the wealthy, and facilitated the country's return to a nineteenth century pattern of wealth distribution. . . . The leaders . . . may talk Christ, but they walk corporate. Values may "matter most" to voters, but they take a backseat to the needs of money once the elections are won.[105]

Surely there is much truth to this critique. One need only look at the activities of this administration over the past five years to see that most of its initiatives—from the secret Energy Task Force, to the stealth war on the environment, to the invasion of Iraq—have had far more to do with funneling ever more money to powerful corporate interests than with moral values. Indeed, it would be fair to say that the only thing this administration has actually "conserved" is wealth for those who are already rich; the only evidence of its "compassion" has been its generosity toward the gas, oil, and coal industries and its massive no-bid contracts to Halliburton. Even as taxpayers have been asked to foot the $300 billion bill for a war they were led into on false pretences, defense contractors such as Halliburton have seen their profits rise by a staggering 292.9 percent since 2004.[106] Still more cynically, then, one might say that the pious rhetoric of the "War on Terror" and "faith-based initiatives" has actually served to conceal what is really a form of economic war: *a war for the rich and a war on the poor.*

However, while this critique goes a long way to help explain the contradiction between Bush's religious rhetoric and his intense secrecy, the situation is far more complex than a simple matter of hypocrisy. The use of religious discourse and political secrecy is not, I think, simply about money (though it is certainly partly about money). More fundamentally, it is about *power*—the power that comes from control of knowledge and the power that comes from appeal to divine authority. As Michel Foucault observes, "power is tolerable only on condition that it mask a substantial part of itself. Its success is proportional to its ability to hide its own mechanisms. Would power be accepted if it were entirely cynical? For it, secrecy is not in the nature of an abuse; it is indispensable to its operation."[107] But this is also about a *radical shift* in the political balance of power. This administration's extreme secrecy has transferred tremendous power to the executive branch, even as its invasive surveillance has stripped more and more power away from ordinary citizens. Like the logic of torture that underlies Abu Ghraib, however, this administration's obsession with secrecy is rooted in a kind of religious faith—*a faith in America's exceptional status as a divinely guided nation and in this president's exceptional position as a divinely appointed leader,* one who is above any public scrutiny or oversight (and apparently also facts or reality). As we will see in the following chapters, moreover, there are also strong ideological forces at work in this administration for whom religion and secrecy are intimate parts of a broader vision of American power and its imperial role in the twenty-first century.

Notes

1. Public Opinion and Polls, *The Pew Charitable Trusts*, March 20, 2006.

2. Larry Klayman, quoted in Alan Elsner, "Bush Expands Government Secrecy, Arouses Critics," *Reuters*, September 3, 2002, at www.fas.org/sgp/news/2002/09/re090302.html.

3. As President Clinton noted of the Cheney shooting, "the administration has an enormous penchant for secrecy, for not telling anybody anything about anything." "Clinton: Secrecy Sparked Shooting Reaction," *ABC News*, February 19, 2006, at abc-news.go.com/Politics/wireStory?id=1638050.

4. Eric Alterman, *When Presidents Lie: A History of Official Deception and Its Consequences* (New York: Viking, 2004), 294.

5. George W. Bush, *A Charge to Keep* (New York: Morrow, 1999), 47.

6. Kevin Phillips, *American Dynasty: Aristocracy, Fortune, and the Politics of Deceit in the House of Bush* (New York: Viking, 2004), 344. As Walter Isaacson and Evan Thomas describe Bonesmen in regard to W. Averell Harriman, "So complete was his trust in the Bones's code of secrecy that in conversations at annual dinners he spoke openly about national security affairs. He refused, however, to tell his family anything about Bones." Isaacson and Thomas, *The Wise Men: Six Men and the World They Made.* (New York: Simon and Schuster, 1986), 82.

7. See below, and see Robert Bryce, *Pipe Dreams: Greed, Ego, and the Death of Enron* (New York: Public Affairs, 2002), 273.

8. Interview with Brit Hume, *Fox News*, February 15, 2006, at msnbc.msn .com/id/11373634/.

9. Scott Shane, "U.S. Reclassifies Many Documents in Secret Review," *New York Times*, February 20, 2006, A1.

10. "The Trust Gap," *New York Times*, February12, 2006, 4, 13.

11. Christopher H. Schmitt and Edward T. Pound, "Keeping Secrets," *U.S. News & World Report*, December 22, 2003. www.usnews.com/usnews/news/articles/031222/22secrecy.htm.

12. John Dean, *Worse than Watergate: The Secret Presidency of George W. Bush* (New York: Little, Brown, 2004), 56.

13. Robert Parry, *Secrecy and Privilege: Rise of the Bush Dynasty from Watergate to Iraq* (Arlington: Media Consortium, 2004), 354.

14. "Archive, Historians Ask Judge to Rethink Dismissal: Presidential Records Act Still Not Resolved," *National Security Archive*, April 30, 2004, at www.gwu.edu/~nsarchiv/news/20040430/index.htm.

15. See Dean, *Worse than Watergate*, 75–83; Carl Pope and Paul Rauber, *Strategic Ignorance: Why the Bush Administration Is Recklessly Destroying a Century of Environmental Progress* (San Francisco: Sierra Club Books, 2004), 108–111.

16. Joshua Mica Marshall, "Confidence Men," *Washington Monthly*, September 2002, at www.washingtonmonthly.com/features/2001/0209.marshall.html.

17. Jason S. Hacker and Paul Pierson, *Off Center: The Republican Revolution and the Erosion of American Democracy* (New Haven: Yale University Press, 2005), 82–83.

18. John Nichols, *Dick, the Man Who Is President* (New York: New Press, 2004), 180.

19. Bill Press, "Enron Makes Whitewater Look Like Peanuts," *CNN.com*, December 12, 2001, at archives.cnn.com/2001/ALLPOLITICS/12/12/column.billpress/. Frank Pellegrini, "Bush's Enron Problem," *Time.com*, January 10, 2002, at www.time.com/time/nation/article/0,8599,192920,00.html.

20. "Maps and Charts of Iraqi Oil Fields," *Judicial Watch*, March 7, 2006, at www .judicialwatch.org/printer_iraqi-oil-maps.shtml.

21. Dean, *Worse than Watergate*, 160.

22. Robert F. Kennedy Jr., "Crimes against Nature," *Rolling Stone*, December 11, 2003.

23. Robert F. Kennedy Jr., "For the Sake of Our Children," *EarthLight*, Winter 2005, at informeddissent.org/2005/02/.

24. Pope and Rauber, *Strategic Ignorance*, 24.

25. "Framing," *Center for Media and Democracy*, December 16, 2005, at www.sourcewatch.org/index.php?title=Framing.

26. Pope and Rauber, *Strategic Ignorance*, 85–89.

27. Kennedy, "For the Sake of Our Children."

28. Elizabeth Shogren, "EPA's 9/11 Air Rating Distorted, Report Says," *Los Angeles Times*, August 23, 2003, A1.

29. Andrew Schneider, "White House Budget Office Thwarts EPA Warning on Asbestos-Laced Insulation," *St. Louis Dispatch*, December 29, 2002.

30. Seth Bornstein, "Bush Giving Business a Boost; Environmental Rule Changes Fulfill Corporate Wish List," *Pittsburgh Post-Gazette*, September 21, 2003, A11.

31. Andrew C. Revkin, "Climate Expert Says NASA Tried to Silence Him," *New York Times*, January 29, 2006, A1. See Pope and Rauber, *Strategic Ignorance*, 163–165.

32. Juliet Epstein, "Climate Plan Splits U.S. and Europe," *Washington Post*, July 2, 2005, A4.

33. John F. Stacks, "Watchdogs on a Leash: Closing Doors on the Media," in Richard C. Leone and Greg Anrig Jr., eds. *The War on Our Freedoms: Civil Liberties in an Age of Terrorism* (New York: Public Affairs, 2003), 237.

34. Pope and Rauber, *Strategic Ignorance*, 169.

35. There is a vast body of literature on 9/11 conspiracy, ranging from the disturbingly serious to the just plain silly. See David Ray Griffin, *The New Pearl Harbor: Disturbing Questions about the Bush Administration and 9/11* (Northampton, MA: Interlink, 2004); Mark Jacobson, "The Ground Zero Grassy Knoll," *New York*, March 27, 2006, 28–35.

36. "The Kissinger Connection," *New York Times*, November 29, 2002, A38.

37. "Bush Allows Rice to Testify on 9/11 Public Session," *New York Times*, March 31, 2004, A1.

38. Dan Eggen and Dana Milbank, "White House Holds Back Clinton Papers," *Washington Post*, April 2, 2004, A2.

39. "Half of New Yorkers Believe U.S. Had Advance Knowledge of Impending 9/11 Attacks," *Zogby.com*, August 30, 2004, at www.zogby.com/news/ReadNews.dbm?ID=855. For an influential theologian's view, see Griffin, *New Pearl Harbor*.

40. Dean, *Worse than Watergate*, 110.

41. Dana Milbank, "For Bush, Facts Are Malleable," *Washington Post*, October 22, 2002, A1. See Joseph Cirincione, Jessica T. Mathews, and George Perkovich, *WMD in Iraq: Evidence and Implications* (Washington: Carnegie Endowment for International Peace, 2004).

42. Louis Fisher, "Deciding on War against Iraq," *Perspectives on Political Science* 32 (2003): 135. Bush also met with congressional leaders several times in late 2002, warning of the imminent threat posed by Iraq's WMD; at one classified briefing he told

senators that Saddam had not only biological and chemical weapons, but also the ability to use them against the East Coast of the United States via unmanned drone aircraft. John McCarthy, "Senators Were Told Iraqi Weapons Could Hit U.S.," *Florida Today*, December 17, 2003.

43. Dean, *Worse than Watergate*, 141–143, and appendix I, which systematically analyzes each of these eight "facts." See also Cirincione et al., *WMD in Iraq*.

44. Charles J. Hadley, "Powell's Case for Iraq War Falls Apart 6 Months Later," Associated Press, August 10, 2003, at www.fortwayne.com/mld/fortwayne/news/local/6502258.htm?

45. George W. Bush, "Address to the Nation," March 17, 2003, at www.white house.gov/news/releases/2003/03/20030317-7.html.

46. Walter Pincus and Dana Priest, "Bush, Aides Ignored CIA Caveats on Iraq," *Washington Post*, February 17, 2004, A17.

47. "DoD News Briefing—Rumsfeld and Gen. Pace," United States Department of Defense, September 26, 2002, at www.defenselink.mil/transcripts/2002/t09262002_t0926sd.html; "In Their Own Words," *PBS Frontline*, at www.pbs.org/wgbh/pages/frontline/shows/truth/why/said.html.

48. Alterman, *When Presidents Lie*, 300.

49. Robert Scheer, "Bad Iraq Data from Start to Finish," *Nation*, June 11, 2003, at www.thenation.com/doc/20030623/scheer20030610.

50. Patrick Lang, quoted in Alterman, *When Presidents Lie*, 299. In early 2006, ex-CIA official Paul Pillar, who coordinated intelligence in the Middle East until 2005, concluded that "official intelligence was not relied on in making even the most significant national security decisions, that intelligence was misused publicly to justify decisions already made, . . . and that the intelligence community's own work was politicized." Walter Pincus, "Ex-CIA Official Faults Use of Data on Iraq," *Washington Post*, February 10, 2006, A1.

51. "The Secret Downing Street Memo," *Sunday Times*, May 1, 2005, at www.timesonline.co.uk/article/0,,2087-1593607,00.html.

52. Paul O'Neill, in Ron Suskind, *The Price of Loyalty: George W. Bush, the White House, and the Education of Paul O'Neill* (New York: Simon & Schuster, 2003), 86.

53. Michael Elliot and James Carney, "First Stop, Iraq," *CNN.com*, March 24, 2003, at www.cnn.com/2003/ALLPOLITICS/03/24/timep.saddam.tm/.

54. Barton Gellman and Dafna Linzer, "A 'Concerted Effort' to Discredit Bush Critic," *Washington Post*, April 9, 2006, A1.

55. Steve Clemons, "Cheney Team's Plame Leak Sabotaged America's Iran-Watching Intelligence Effort," *Huffington Post*, February 13, 2006, at www.huffingtonpost.com/steve-clemons/cheney-teams-plame-leak-_b_15579.html.

56. Jim VandeHei and Mike Allen, "Bush Raises Threshold for Firing Aides in Leak Probe," *Washington Post*, July 19, 2005, A1.

57. R. Jeffrey Smith, "Bush Authorized Secrets' Release, Libby Testified," *Washington Post*, April 7, 2006; A1.

58. Editorial, "A Bad Leak," *New York Times*, April 16, 2006.

59. "President Reiterates Goal on Home Ownership," June 18, 2002, at www.white house.gov/news/releases/2002/06/20020618-1.html.

60. "President Bush Welcomes Canadian Prime Minister Martin to White House," April 30, 2004, at www.whitehouse.gov/news/releases/2004/04/20040430-2.html.

61. "Fallujah Death Toll for Week More Than 600," *USA Today*, April 11, 2004, at www.usatoday.com/news/world/iraq/2004-04-11-fallujah-casualties_x.htm.

62. Will Dunham, "Guantanamo Detainees Revealed," *Sunday Times* (Sydney), March 4, 2006, at www.sundaytimes.news.com.au.

63. Seymour Hersh, *Chain of Command: The Road from 9/11 to Abu Ghraib.* (New York: HarperCollins, 2004), 2.

64. Andrew Romano, "How Terror Led America toward Torture," *Newsweek,* November 21, 2005, 31.

65. Eric Schmitt and Carolyn Marshall, "In Secret Unit's Black Room: A Grim Portrait of U.S. Abuse," *New York Times*, March 19, 2006, A1.

66. Antonio Taguba, "Article 15-6 Investigation of the 800th Military Police Brigade," April 4, 2004.

67. "Report: Pentagon Warned on Torture, Abuse," *USA Today*, February 19, 2006, at www.usatoday.com/news/washington/2006-02-19-pentagon-report_x.htm. See Jane Mayer, "The Memo: How an Internal Effort to Ban the Abuse and Torture of Detainees Was Thwarted," *New Yorker*, February 27, 2006; Anthony Lewis, "The Torture Administration," *Nation*, 281, no. 22 (2005): 14.

68. Michael Isikoff, "Memos Reveal War Crimes Warnings," *Newsweek*, May 19, 2004 at www.msnbc.msn.com/id/4999734/site/newsweek/.

69. Douglas Jehl and David Johnston, "Rule Change Lets CIA Freely Send Suspects Abroad to Jails," *New York Times*, March 6, 2005, 1, 1; "Bush Says No POW Status for Detainees," *CNN.com*, January 28, 2002, at archives.cnn.com/2002/US/01/28/ret .wh.detainees/.

70. Jess Bravin, "Pentagon Report Set Framework for Use of Torture," *Wall Street Journal*, June 7, 2004. A Justice Department memo of August 2002 also narrowly defined torture as limited to abuses causing physical pain "equivalent in intensity to the pain accompanying serious organ failure, impairment of bodily function, or even death." Evan Thomas and Michael Hirsh, "The Debate over Torture," *Newsweek*, November 21, 2005, 30.

71. Tom Curry, "Did Gonzales Authorize Torture?" *MSNBC.com*, January 6, 2005, at msnbc.msn.com/id/6790622/.

72. Dana Priest and Robin Wright, "Cheney Fights for Detainee Policy," *Washington Post*, November 7, 2005, A1.

73. Hersh, *Chain of Command,* 16.

74. Dana Priest, "CIA Holds Terror Suspects in Secret Prisons," *Washington Post*, November 2, 2005, A1.

75. Hersh, *Chain of Command,* 361.

76. Dana Milbank, "Making Hay out of Straw Men," *Washington Post*, June 1, 2004, A21.

77. William T. Cavanaugh, "Taking Exception: When Torture Becomes Thinkable," *Christian Century*, January 25, 2005.

78. Elaine Scarry, *The Body in Pain: The Making and Unmaking of the World* (New York: Oxford University Press, 1987), 28.

79. Scarry, *Body in Pain*, 27.

80. Josh White and Carol D. Leonnig, "U.S. Cites Exception in Torture Ban," *Washington Post*, March 3, 2006, A4.

81. "U.S. Detention Facilities Hold More Than 11,000 in Iraq and Afghanistan," *Human Rights First*, at www.humanrightsfirst.org/media/2005_alerts/usls_0330_det.htm.

82. Lewis, "Torture Administration," 14.

83. Howard Zinn, foreword to Nancy Chang, *Silencing Political Dissent: How Post-September 11 Anti-Terrorism Measures Threaten Our Civil Liberties* (New York: Seven Stories, 2002), 11–12.

84. "Conservative Voices against the USA Patriot Act Part I," *ACLU.org*, at www.aclu.org/SafeandFree/SafeandFree.cfm?ID=12632&c=206. It's difficult to believe, but the proposed PATRIOT Act II would go even farther. This far more invasive measure would allow the government to access a citizen's credit reports without subpoena and snoop on anyone's internet usage without a warrant; collect DNA from anyone without a court order, creating a mammoth database of citizen DNA information; secretly detain U.S. citizens on suspicion of terrorist activities; and allow citizenship to be revoked if persons contributed material support to organizations deemed by the government, even retroactively, to be terrorist. In sum, if the first PATRIOT Act significantly reversed the balance between government transparency and citizens' privacy, the second PATRIOT Act threatens to obliterate the latter altogether. See Dahlia Lithwick and Julia Turner, "A Guide to the Patriot Act," *Slate.com*, September 8, 2003, at www.slate.com/id/2087984/.

85. "ACLU Releases First Concrete Evidence of Domestic Spying for Anti-War Views," *Rawstory*, March 14, 2006, at rawstory.com/news/2006/ACLU_releases_first_concrete_evidence_of_0314.html. See also Jimmy Carter, *Our Endangered Values: America's Moral Crisis* (New York: Simon & Schuster, 2005), 119.

86. Lisa Myers, Douglas Pasternak, and Rich Gardela, "Is the Pentagon Spying on Americans? Secret Database Obtained by NBC News Tracks 'Suspicious' Domestic Groups," December 14, 2005, at msnbc.msn.com/id/10454316/.

87. Charlie Savage, "Bush Shuns Patriot Act Requirement," *Boston Globe*, March 24, 2006, at www.boston.com/news/nation/washington/articles/2006/03/24/bush_shuns_patriot_act_requirement/.

88. Elaine Scarry, "Resolving to Resist: Local Governments Are Refusing to Comply with the Patriot Act," *Boston Review*, March 8, 2004, at www.bostonreview.net/BR29.1/scarry.html.

89. Dan Egan. "Ashcroft Invokes Religion in US War on Terrorism," *Washington Post*, February 20, 2002, A2.

90. James Bamford, "The Agency That Could Become Big Brother," *New York Times* December 25, 2005, at www.nytimes.com.

91. Bamford, "Agency That Could Become Big Brother." According to Doug Thompson and Teresa Hampton, "When Congress cut the funding, the Pentagon . . . simply moved the program into a 'black bag' account. . . . Black bag programs don't require Congressional approval and are exempt from traditional oversight." "Where Big

Brother Snoops on America 24/7," *Capitol Hill Blue*, June 7, 2004, at www.capitolhill
blue.com/artman/publish/article_4648A.shtml.

92. Bamford, "Agency That Could Become Big Brother."

93. Leslie Cauley, "NSA Has Massive Data-Base of Americans' Phone Calls," *USA Today*, May 11, 2006, A1.

94. "Bush Defends NSA Spying Program," *CNN.com*, January 1, 2006, at www
.cnn.com/2006/POLITICS/01/01/nsa.spying/.

95. Kathleen Hennessey, "Ex-President Carter: Eavesdropping Illegal," *ABC News*, February 6, 2006, at abcnews.go.com/US/wireStory?id=1587734&CMP=OTC-RSS-Feeds0312.

96. Tom Shorrock, "Watching What You Say," *Nation*, March 20, 2006, 14.

97. "The Death of the Intelligence Panel," *New York Times*, March 9, 2006, A22.

98. "Dan Eggan, "White House Trains Efforts on Media Leaks," *Washington Post*, March 5, 2006, A1.

99. Everett Edward Mann Jr., "The Public Right to Know Government Information: Its Affirmation and Abridgement," Ph.D. Dissertation, Claremont Graduate School, 1984, 216.

100. "Trust Gap."

101. Carter, Our *Endangered Values*, 192–193.

102. Joe Conason, "Where's the Compassion?" *Nation*, September 15, 2003, at www.thenation.com/doc/20030915/conason.

103. Tim Dickinson, "The Deficit Lie," *Rolling Stone*, January 26, 2006, 28.

104. Dickinson, "Deficit Lie," 29.

105. Thomas Franks, *What's the Matter with America? The Resistible Rise of the American Right* (London: Vintage, 2005), 6–7.

106. "Iraq, by the Numbers," *Salon.com*, February 13, 2006, at www.salon.com/politics/war_room/.

107. Michel Foucault, *The History of Sexuality: An Introduction* (New York: Vintage, 1990), 86.

3

New American Century, New American Empire: Religion, Secrecy, and the Neoconservatives

One of these days, the American people are going to awaken to the fact that we have become an imperial nation, even though the public and all our institutions are hostile to the idea.

—Irving Kristol, "The Emerging American Imperium" (1997)

If a sparrow cannot fall to the ground without His notice, is it probable that an empire can rise without His aid?

—Quotation on Dick and Lynne Cheney's 2003 Christmas card

WHEN HE RAN FOR OFFICE and then entered the White House in 2000, George W. Bush by all accounts knew little about foreign policy. Indeed, when asked by a reporter to name the leaders of Chechnya, Taiwan, India, and Pakistan, Mr. Bush was only able to come up with the partial name of the Taiwanese leader and nothing at all about the others. "What is this, twenty questions?" he asked.[1] This is striking, particularly when one considers the fact that two of those nations are nuclear powers and would become key players in the "War on Terror" less than two years later.

As Jonathan Clarke and Stefan Halper have argued in *America Alone,* it was largely due to the election of the relatively vacuous and uninformed President Bush that a small group of ideologues was able to take the reins in the White House—namely, the group of intellectuals and militarists generally labeled neoconservatives.[2] Though by no means a homogenous or singular group, these men include key political figures such as Paul Wolfowitz, Dick Cheney, Donald Rumsfeld, Gary Schmitt, Abram Shulsky, and Richard Perle; intellectuals such as Irving and William Kristol, Michael Ledeen, Allan Bloom, and (until recently) Francis Fukuyama; and powerful think tanks such as the American Enterprise Institute and the Project for the New American Century. Particularly in the wake of 9/11, this group of ideologues was able to persuade the generally naïve new president to implement an extremely aggressive foreign policy agenda that had in fact been in the works for at least a decade, centered largely on Middle East oil and Saddam Hussein.

Ever since the build-up to the Iraq war, there has been much debate over the role of the neoconservatives in this administration. While some have portrayed this as the primary guiding force behind all of Bush's policies, others such as David Brooks have dismissed the attacks on the neoconservatives (many of whom are Jewish) as a form of anti-Semitic conspiracy theory.[3]

It seems to me that the role of the neoconservatives is more complex than either of these views, at once more significant and less significant than commonly imagined. By less significant, I mean that the neoconservatives are not the only driving force in the Bush administration, but just one of several competing factions that have helped shape its policies. By more significant, I mean that their influence is undeniable and that they also give us tremendous insight into the complex, interdependent role of religion and secrecy in the Bush White House. Indeed, I would argue that the neoconservatives show us that the apparent contradiction between religion and secrecy in this case is not simply a matter of hypocrisy, as many have suggested. Rather, religion and secrecy are crucial, interrelated aspects of a broader ideology and approach to politics.

On the whole, the neoconservatives are quite clear about the need for both religion and secrecy as political tools. The former is the necessary means of maintaining social cohesion, moral order, and patriotism; the latter is the basic means of conducting affairs of state, especially foreign policy. Already in the mid-1990s, Irving Kristol, often called the "godfather" of neoconservatism, had argued that the Republican Party needed to reach out to and embrace the Christian right as a political ally if it was to survive as a party.[4] And with the election of George W. Bush, that it is apparently just what they have done. Bush serves as the key structural link that helps tie these two factions together—the neoconservative ideologues and their most powerful base of support in the Christian Right.

At the same time, Bush's public image as a simple man of faith, piety, and honesty has helped to mask the more aggressive policies of the neoconservatives—policies that are, in fact, by no means "conservative" at all but quite radical and explicitly imperialistic. With Bush as its popular spokesman and image of piety, the administration has been able to mask and recode its aggressive foreign policies behind the language of "God's plan for history" and

America's mission to bring freedom as a "gift from the Almighty" to all parts of the world.

If there has been a good deal of debate over the role of the neoconservatives in the current administration, there has been even more over the influence of the controversial political philosopher Leo Strauss (1899–1973). Born in Germany and spending most of his career at the University of Chicago, Strauss too believed both in the power of religion as a means of maintaining social order and in the political necessity of secrecy. According to Strauss, the great philosophers all tended to use a kind of esoteric discourse or "writing between the lines" in order to transmit a message that is legible to those who know how to read it but lost to the majority of readers. President Bush himself would seem to be an ideal example of what Strauss called the "gentleman"—that is, the politician who serves as the public face of virtue and piety, even as the "philosophers" or intellectuals are really running the political show.[5] Much of Bush's public discourse also involves a subtle kind of "writing between the lines," in Strauss's sense. His frequent rhetoric of "freedom" as God's plan for history and America's historic mission is not simply a coded reference to evangelical Christian theology, but also a reference to the neoconservative ideals of the "end of history" and an "emerging American imperium."

However, while Strauss's influence is clearly important, it has often been exaggerated and given way to quasiconspiratorial thinking. At the same time, the emphasis on Strauss has led us to ignore another, arguably more important influence: Albert Wohlstetter (1913–1997), another University of Chicago theorist, who had far more direct impact on U.S. foreign policy. As a model for the character of Dr. Strangelove, Wohlstetter was an architect of U.S. Cold War defense policy and is cited by Wolfowitz and others as the primary intellectual influence among the neoconservatives. Much of the neoconservative agenda is a disturbing fusion of Strauss's esoteric philosophy with Wohlstetter's Cold War militarism—all of which is at once obscured by obsessive secrecy and clothed with powerful religious rhetoric.

As we move through Bush's second term, however, this neoconservative dream seems to be rapidly disintegrating. In the face of the increasingly bloody quagmire of Iraq and the horror of torture, even key neoconservative theorists are waking to the brutal reality of its failure.

The American Moment in World History:
The Origins of Neoconservatism

This is the American moment in world history.

—Allan Bloom, *The Closing of the American Mind*

We're all neocons now.

—MSNBC's Chris Matthews (April 9, 2003)

According to Irving Kristol, who first used the term in a positive sense, neoconservatism does not represent so much a coherent movement or party as a kind of "persuasion," or a moral and political attitude.[6] As Halper and Clarke suggest, the neoconservative persuasion can perhaps best be characterized by three basic features: first, "a belief, derived from religious conviction, that the human condition is defined as a choice between good and evil and that the true measure of political character is found in the willingness by the former to confront the latter"; second, "an assertion that the fundamental determinant of the relationship between states rests on military power and the willingness to use it"; and third, a "focus on the Middle East and global Islam as the principal theater for American overseas power."[7]

With the collapse of the Soviet Union and the end of the Cold War, as Irving's son William Kristol and Robert Kagan have argued, America now has a unique opportunity; indeed, it has a kind of *moral obligation* to use its awesome military power to spread its interests and values to every corner of the world. By the 1990s, "the United States held a position unmatched since Rome," as its "military power dwarfed that of any other nation"; we therefore have an opportunity for "preserving and reinforcing America's benevolent global hegemony, which undergirded what George H. W. Bush rightly called a 'new world order.'"[8]

Thus, one of the most important texts for neoconservative ideology is Fukuyama's widely read work, *The End of History and the Last Man*, which posits that history has a direction and that American-style democracy and free-market capitalism represent the final stage of human development with few flaws. Although Fukuyama himself has recently disavowed the neoconservative agenda as a failure, he was one of the key architects of that ideology, and his "end of history" rhetoric still informs much of Mr. Bush's public discourse.[9]

However, most of the neoconservatives also agree that the spread of America's benevolent hegemony is not likely to be a smooth or nonviolent one; on the contrary, they are quite clear that it will require a massive U.S. military and the necessary use of force. The United States must, therefore, maintain a military that is so massive, so technologically advanced—and so expensive—that no other power could possible rival it. As Anne Norton summarizes the neoconservative ideal, they hope "to establish a new world order to rival Rome. The new world order will . . . be established not with the consent of the governed but through force. Military power is essential to robust foreign policy, to forging Pax Americana."[10]

Most of the neoconservatives will also openly acknowledge that this aggressive vision of America's role in the world is a significant departure from earlier forms of "conservatism." As Irving Kristol tells us, neoconservatives "politely overlook" older conservative politicians.[11] Indeed, as Michael Ledeen put it, this is not a conservative but rather a *revolutionary* ideology: "I don't think of myself as 'conservative' at all. . . . Leo Strauss once said that it was hard to understand how the word 'virtue,' which once meant the manliness of men, came to mean the virginity of women. In like manner I am perplexed at how revolutionaries are now called "conservatives."[12]

In this bold plan for American global dominance, both religion and secrecy play a crucial role. But in order to understand how religion and secrecy play out here, we first need to delve into some of the intellectual influences behind the neoconservative persuasion, the most important of which are the University of Chicago political theorists, Strauss and Wohlstetter.

The Art of Writing between the Lines: Leo Strauss and the Necessity of Secrecy

Strauss's view . . . suggests that deception is the norm in political life.

—Gary J. Schmitt and Abram N. Shulsky, "The World of Intelligence"

Leo Strauss is a complex and controversial figure, and there is much debate as to his role and influence in current U.S. politics. Some, such as Paul Wolfowitz and Francis Fukuyama, have tried to downplay Strauss's influence, dismissing the idea as the product of "fevered minds" and conspiracy theorists.[13] However, as Halper and Clarke persuasively argue, Strauss is undeniably an inspiration for many of the neoconservatives and for much of their ideology: "by affiliation or derivation, Strauss's ideas occupied a space in the education of many students and intellectuals who subsequently progressed to the highest levels of Washington's political elite."[14] Irving Kristol, for example, clearly cites Strauss as one of his two great influences and a primary inspiration for much of the neoconservative movement in Washington:

> Leo Strauss . . . was from a different planet. . . . Helpless in all practical matters, the author of very difficult and complex texts, studious and meditative, a rationalist who pressed reason to its ultimate limits, he was no kind of "intellectual"—a class he held in, at best, tolerant contempt. . . . His students—those happy few who sat at his feet—became "Straussians." . . . These students of Strauss, in turn, have produced another generation of political theorists, many of whom have relocated to Washington D.C. since the academic world of . . . "political science" has become ever more hostile to Strauss.[15]

Strauss is a notoriously difficult author, whose work has given rise to a wide array of interpretations—even among his own students. This is not surprising, since Strauss wrote in the same kind of cryptic, doubly coded, almost Kabbalistic "esoteric writing" that he believed characterized the works of the ancient philosophers. Some believe that he deliberately taught different ideas to different students, according to different levels of knowledge and capacity.[16] Thus it is perhaps futile to try to discern what Strauss "really meant" in his works; but we can, I think, look at the ways in which he has been interpreted and implemented by the later generations of "Straussians," particularly those neoconservatives who have read him and tried to put his ideas into practice.

One of Strauss's most influential ideas is the role of secrecy as both a rhetorical strategy and a political necessity. As he argued in his classic but controversial work, *Persecution and the Art of Writing*, the ancient philosophers used a special mode of writing, an esoteric writing that is intelligible only to the educated few who are trained in the art of reading between the lines. To the majority of mankind, their works appear relatively innocuous and benign. But to the trained reader or philosopher, their works contain a deeper and more profound message. The reason for this esoteric mode of writing, Strauss tells us, is that the truths of philosophy are potentially *dangerous*. Society rests upon simple beliefs, conventional opinions, and "noble lies" for its stability. The truths the philosopher knows, however, call those noble lies radically into question. Revealing these truths openly might even place the philosopher's life in danger. Therefore, the wise writer knows how to produce an "exoteric text" that contains an "esoteric" meaning, a text "in which the truth about all crucial things is presented exclusively between the lines."[17] Such literature is addressed, not to all readers, but only to the trustworthy and intelligent:

> Philosophy or science, the highest activity of man, is the attempt to replace opinion about "all things" with knowledge of "all things"; but opinion is the element of society; philosophy or science is therefore the attempt to dissolve the element in which society breaths, and thus it endangers society. Hence philosophy . . . must remain the preserve of a small minority. . . . Philosophers . . . are driven to employ a peculiar manner of writing which would enable them to reveal what they regard as the truth to the few, without endangering the unqualified commitment of the many to the opinions on which society rests. They will distinguish between the true teaching as the esoteric teaching and the socially useful teaching as the exoteric teaching; whereas the exoteric teaching is meant to be accessible to every reader, the esoteric teaching discloses itself only to the very careful and well-trained readers after long and concentrated study.[18]

Although the philosophers are able to transcend the conventional beliefs that govern ordinary men, they do also recognize the *importance* of these conventions for the good of society. Perhaps more than anything else, they know that strong religious belief is integral for the health and well-being of a society. Because the higher philosophic ideals of "contemplation and theory" are accessible "only to the few who are wise," special precautions are needed for the governance of the populace; beliefs such as the immortality of the soul and rewards or punishments after death provide society with a transcendent authority for its laws and values, making social duty a kind of moral aspiration: "civil government . . . is not in itself sufficient for orderly corporate life within society. Religion is a regulator of order in social life. . . . It is . . . a code of law prescribed for the many by higher intelligences."[19]

Modern liberal society, in Strauss's eyes, had entered a state of profound "crisis," largely because it had lost its religious and moral foundation; without this regulator of social life, we can only breed a generation that is nihilistic, hopeless, and without any ethical framework. From Strauss's perspective, coming out of pre-Nazi Germany, the seeming prosperity of postwar America hid behind it "a deeper angst," and he warned that "America would take a course similar to the totalitarian states if it could not shore up its moral center."[20] Weimar Germany, he believed, had fallen prey to the delusion of Nazism precisely because of its weak and "perverted" brand of liberalism. And modern liberal America was in danger of falling prey to the same kind of totalitarian regime.

Thus what America needs today, if it is to save itself from the abyss of relativism and moral decay, are guiding religious myths and narratives. As Adam Curtis suggests in his BBC documentary, "The Power of Nightmares," Strauss believed in the necessity of such narratives as noble lies or pious fictions to maintain the well-being of society: "They might not be true, but they were necessary illusions. One of these was religion; the other was the myth of the nation. And in America, that was the idea that the country had a unique destiny to battle the forces of evil throughout the world."[21] Thus it is ironic and yet somehow fitting that Strauss's favorite TV show was the series *Gunsmoke*, which provided just the right mix of good guys in white hats versus bad guys in blacks hats and traditional American values. As Stanley Rosen, a pupil of Strauss, recalls,

> Strauss was a great fan of American television. *Gunsmoke* was his great favorite, and he would hurry home from the seminar . . . and have a quick dinner so he could be at his seat before the television set when *Gunsmoke* came on. And he felt that this was good, this show. This had a salutary effect on the American public, because it showed the conflict between good and evil in a way that would be immediately intelligible to everyone.[22]

Following Plato, Strauss suggests that the ideal society would be one in which the wise men or philosophers rule over the majority who are less wise.

Yet because their unique insight into truth is potentially "dangerous" to the conventional opinions that support society, they are not necessarily the best politicians. Rather, the ideal ruler would be what Strauss calls the "gentleman," a figure who embodies the virtues of piety and faith that the populace admires:

> The best regime is based on the teaching that human beings are unequal from the point of view of their perfection. The wise are better suited to rule over others. The realization of this regime depends on the "chance" appearance of princes friendly to philosophy. . . . The best possible regime includes the rule of law under which the state entrusts its administration to "gentlemen." The gentleman is sufficiently wealthy . . . and public-spirited to be involved in noble pursuits.[23]

Yet while the gentleman accepts the comforting narratives and noble values offered by religion, the philosopher knows these to be useful and necessary but ultimately empty illusions:

> The esoteric philosophy is about the secret kingship of the philosopher. If the philosopher is identified with the *Imam* or the descendent of the prophet Muhammad, that is only a concession to public opinion; it is a "noble lie," a "pious fraud," a matter of "considering one's social responsibilities." Nor is it altogether false, since the role that the philosopher must occupy in the real city is not unlike that of the prophet who has the ear of the god-fearing king. The difference is that the philosopher is a prophet without a god. But that is *his* secret.[24]

Together, the philosopher and the gentleman represent two different but complementary standards of excellence: "the virtue of the citizen best embodied in the moral excellence of the gentleman (the ruler or founder) and the excellence of the philosopher or the wise man."[25] As Deutsch suggests in his study of Strauss's impact on American politics, a modern-day gentleman would be most effective serving in the highest offices of government, particularly in the executive branch: "Service in the three branches of government, especially the presidency, would provide opportunities for the "gentleman" to gain reputations for wisdom, patriotism, and the love of justice."[26]

With the striking rise of the neoconservatives in American foreign policy, followed by the election of George W. Bush, it would seem that Strauss's ideal of the wise "philosophers" working together with the noble "gentleman" has indeed come to fruition. As Irving Kristol observes, much of the neoconservative "persuasion" is indebted to Strauss, and particularly to his critique of modern society and its loss of moral compass: "in the United States . . . the writings of Leo Strauss have been extraordinarily influential. Strauss's critique of the destructive elements within modern liberalism . . . has altered the very tone of public discourse in the United states. . . . To bring contemporary liberalism into disrepute . . . is no small achievement."[27]

Like Strauss, many neoconservatives are quite clear about the basic need for secrecy and dissimulation in politics. Certain information should not be publicly available but restricted only to those who have the wisdom and skills to use that knowledge responsibly. This is one of the basic points of a seminal article written by Gary J. Schmitt (president of the Project for the New American Century) and Abram N. Shulsky (director of the Pentagon's Office of Special Plans) entitled "The World of Intelligence." Following Strauss, Schmitt and Shulsky suggest that secrecy and lying are not just part of, but also integral to, all political life. The idea of transparency is instead an unrealistic delusion:

> Strauss's view certainly alerts one to the possibility that political life may be closely linked to deception. Indeed, it suggests that deception is the norm in political life, and the hope, to say nothing of the expectation, of establishing a politics that can dispense with it is the exception.[28]

As New York University philosopher Stephen Holmes explains this Straussian approach to statecraft, the true policy makers or "philosophers"—in this case the neoconservative ideologues such as Shulsky, Schmitt, Perle, and Wolfowitz—must learn the value of noble lies. And they must know how to lie not just to their enemies but *to their own politicians*, as well: "They believe that your enemy is deceiving you, and you have to pretend to agree, but secretly you follow your own views. . . . [P]hilosophers need to tell noble lies not only to the people at large but also to powerful politicians."[29] For, ultimately, the ruler or "gentleman" is less important than the philosophers who advise him. As Robert Pippin, chairman of the Committee on Social Thought at the University of Chicago, comments: "Strauss believed that good statesmen . . . must rely on an inner circle. The person who whispers in the ear of the King is more important than the King."[30]

However, most of the neoconservatives also agree with Strauss that religion and powerful myths and symbols are vital to the moral well-being of a nation. Religious faith is, in a sense, the most important noble lie of all. As Irving Kristol argues, strong religious faith, with a belief in the transcendent basis of moral law, is crucial to the health of the country and the strength of the economy: "The three pillars of modern conservatism are religion, nationalism, and economic growth. Of these religion is easily the most important, because it is the only power that . . . can shape people's characters and regulate their motivation."[31] Most important, religious faith is crucial for national strength and civic spirit. For it provides the spiritual basis of a kind of nationalist "civil religion" in which the populace is taught to revere its leaders and government: "Moral codes evolve from the moral experience of communities and can claim authority over behavior to the degree that individuals are reared to look respectfully, even reverentially, on the moral traditions of their forefathers. It is the function of religion to instill such respect and reverence."[32] Like Strauss, Kristol blames the loss of strong religious faith for the crisis, for the relativism and immorality of modern liberal society: "Nothing, absolutely nothing, is more dehumanizing, more certain to generate a crisis, than experiencing one's life as a meaningless event in a meaningless world."[33] The result is the nihilism and moral collapse of contemporary America, which he sees as a "steady decline in our democratic values, sinking to new levels of vulgarity."[34]

As Anne Norton suggests in her study of Strauss and the neoconservatives, this emphasis on religion is part of their broader ideal of fostering American patriotism and military strength. Religion is the most powerful means of encouraging the "moral strength" that inspires men to fight and die for their country, and so it is a crucial part of the neoconservative vision of America's role in the world:

> They, though not always religious themselves, ally themselves with religion and religious crusades. They encourage family values and the praise of older forms of family life, where women occupy themselves with children, cooking, and the church, and men take on the burdens of manliness. They see in war and the preparation for war the restoration of private virtue and public spirit. They delight in the profusion of flags. . . . Above all, Irving Kristol writes, neoconservatism calls for a revival of patriotism, a strong military, and an expansionist foreign policy.[35]

In this sense, despite their obvious ideological and socioeconomic differences, the neoconservatives and the New Christian Right share a striking sort of affinity (or at least strategic connection). Indeed, in 1995 Kristol had argued that the Republican Party needed to reach out and embrace the strong religious core of the American population—despite its tendency toward undemocratic attitudes—if it was to triumph over the liberal malaise of Clinton's America: "the Republican Party must embrace the religious if they are to survive. Religious people always create problems since their ardor tends to outrun the limits of politics in a constitutional democracy. But if the Republican Party is to survive, it must work on accommodating these people."[36]

With the election of George W. Bush, with his powerful base of support in the New Christian Right, that is apparently just what the neoconservatives and the Republican Party as a whole have done. Indeed, Bush would serve as the ideal sort of Straussian "gentleman"—a public face of compassion and piety that would appeal to this powerful base of popular support, while at the same time allowing the "philosophers" to largely direct American foreign policy.

Dr. Strangelove's America: Wohlstetter, Wolfowitz, and the Politics of Terror

How We Learned to Stop Worrying and Love Pax Americana.

—Paul Wolfowitz, "Statesmanship in the New Century"

While Strauss's influence on the neoconservatives is fairly well known, the role of Albert Wohlstetter is much less understood but in many ways far more important. Indeed, both Wolfowitz and Fukuyama largely reject the idea of Strauss's influence on the current administration, arguing that Wohlstetter was a "much more relevant figure," particularly for its foreign policy and military strategy.[37] Although also a professor at the University of Chicago, Wohlstetter was a completely different sort of intellectual. While Strauss was largely withdrawn into the realms of ancient philosophy and abstract speculation, Wohlstetter was far more engaged with the messy game of *realpolitik*. At the same time that he taught at Chicago, Wohlstetter also worked for the Rand Corporation and served as a consultant to the Pentagon on defense strategy. As such, he provided a sort of "Straussian cadet line," initiating Strauss's students of esoteric philosophy into the "real" world of global politics and national security. As Norton recalls, "Wohlstetter offered the Straussians an ally in the field of international relations. He marked the possibility that one might move out of the academy and acquire other forms of influence."[38] This "cadet line" included figures such as Paul Wolfowitz, Thomas Pangle, and Abram Shulsky. As such, Wohlstetter was a key bridge between the elite, esoteric realm of Chicago and the pragmatic, Cold War realm of D.C.:

> Wohlstetter belonged to another world: the world of the policy-making coasts: the world of Washington and Rand. He flew between Chicago and Washington, between Chicago and various think-tanks, often forgetting to teach a class. . . . He didn't live, as most of the professors did, in Hyde Park. . . . He lived at the edge of Lincoln Park in an elegant and lavish apartment, where we drank champagne and ate strawberries. This wasn't the life of the mind. This was the life of the privileged and powerful.[39]

As one of the models for the character of Dr. Strangelove, Wohlstetter was a central figure in the development U.S. Cold War policy. In his 1958 essay "The Delicate Balance of Terror," Wohlstetter laid out the principle that deterrence depends on the invulnerability of each side's retaliatory capacity, that is, its ability to survive an initial strike. This, in turn, was the logic driving the arms race, as each side competed to maintain an undeniable second-strike capability.[40] Perhaps most importantly, however, Wohlstetter was the key figure in the rethinking of the Cold War policy of "mutual assured destruction" (MAD), or the idea that the two superpowers would be discouraged from a nuclear war because both sides would be annihilated. In Wohlstetter's view, such a doctrine was ineffective, since it effectively neutralized both sides' arsenals; instead, he proposed a doctrine of "a "graduated deterrence," that is, 'the acceptance of limited wars . . . together with 'smart' precision-guided weapons capable of hitting the enemy's military apparatus.'[41] In this respect, Wohlstetter was also well known as an advocate of the limited use of nuclear weapons. After all, if we can't use weapons that would result in annihilation, we should consider the use of smaller weapons for tactical aims. As Norton recalls, Wohlstetter does not appear to have been particularly concerned about the possibility of an actual, full-scale nuclear holocaust, instead teaching his students to call "the dire warnings about nuclear annihilation 'pacific terribalism.'"[42]

Wohlstetter's approach to modern warfare had a formative impact on many neoconservative theorists and policy makers, including disciples such as Wolfowitz and Perle. As Halper and Clarke note, Wohlstetter's belief in the tactical use of nuclear weapons and the constant drive to develop new, smarter, more precise weapons has been a fundamental part of the neoconservative vision of America's global military superiority:

> Wohlstetter also had tremendous significance for neo-conservatives because of his strategic approach and personal contribution to the development of America's ability to wage high-technology wars. The imaginative employment of military technology became a central plank in neo-conservative thinking on how increased capabilities in precision targeting expanded the scope of military intervention around the world.[43]

Wolfowitz is a strong believer in Wohlstetter's vision of American military and geopolitical superiority. As he wrote in his essay "Statesmanship in a New Century" (2000), "the core of American foreign policy is in some sense the universalization of American principles" and the spread of our benevolent "Pax Americana" to the world. But this demands that we maintain our "military pre-eminence" and "continue to lead with respect to new weapon systems based on rapidly evolving technologies." And this in turn requires a willingness to spend massive amounts of money on defense funding. For Wolfowitz, maintaining our military and technological superiority is at once a kind of moral obligation to the global spread of freedom and an opportunity to spread U.S. interests to all parts of the world. And like his mentor, Wolfowitz has also argued that the Pax Americana can be best secured by the use of one type of arms in particular—tactical nuclear weapons.[44]

Like Strauss, however, Wohlstetter was also a believer in the political necessity of secrecy. After all, a nation can only maintain its strategic advantage in the delicate balance of terror if it can conceal its military capabilities from the enemy. Unfortunately, he lamented, totalitarian states such as the Soviet Union were much better at keeping secrets than an open society such as the United States: "A totalitarian country can preserve secrecy about the capabilities and disposition of his forces much better than a Western democracy."[45] It would seem that, with the ascent of the Bush II administration, the neoconservatives set out to impose a much stricter and more pervasive form of secrecy—a kind of secrecy that is perhaps quite advantageous from a military standpoint, but quite disturbing from a democratic standpoint.

Building the New American Century:
The Neoconservatives and the Invasion of Iraq

> The road to Jerusalem goes through Baghdad. The road to Tehran goes through Baghdad. The road to Damascus goes through Baghdad. . . . [I]f you change the regime through force in Baghdad, American military power will cast a long diplomatic shadow, and it will be America's decade in the Middle East.
>
> —Raymond Tanter (2002)

By now, the neoconservatives' role in the preemptive invasion of Iraq is fairly well known (indeed, most of their plans for Iraq and its oil resources can be read in articles going back to the early 1990s available on the Project for the New American Century Web page).[46] Already in 1992, toward the end of the Bush I White House, then undersecretary of defense Wolfowitz and secretary of defense Cheney came up with a bold new plan to rethink U.S. military policy, which was circulated in the top-secret Defense Policy Guidance Report. So disturbing was this report that it was leaked to the *New York Times* by a Pentagon official, who believed this strategy debate should be carried out in the public domain. Indeed, it was described by some as nothing less than an "imperialist manifesto" and a plan for the United States to "rule the world," without acting through the UN and by using preemptive attacks on potential threats.[47] As the report bluntly stated, "In the Middle East and Southwest Asia, our overall objective is to remain the predominant outside power in the region and preserve U.S. and western access to the region's oil."[48]

Although this plan was quickly shot down after its leak, it resurfaced in a new form in 1997, with the founding of the Project for the New American Century (PNAC) by Irving Kristol's son, William. As William Kristol and Robert Kagan had already argued in *Foreign Affairs* in 1996, America now has an opportunity to exercise a "benevolent hegemony" over the world while promoting democracy and free markets—an opportunity it would be foolish to let slip away.⁴⁹ Kristol and Kagan's PNAC soon emerged as the leading think tank and a who's who of the neoconservative establishment, advocating a powerful new vision of America's role as global leader through its military strength and moral principles. According to a seminal PNAC document written in 2000, *Rebuilding America's Defenses*: "The United States is the world's only superpower, combining preeminent military power, global technological leadership, and the world's largest economy. . . . America's grand strategy should aim to preserve and extend this advantageous position as far into the future as possible."⁵⁰ As Norton observes, the PNAC thus set out with a plan for what its name promises: "a design for a century . . . that is to be not merely dominated by America but thoroughly American throughout. The aim is to make the world in America's image as once . . . the Romans sought to remake their world."⁵¹

The ousting of Saddam and the rebuilding of Iraq (and by implication, the Middle East) was a key part of this program for American leadership. In the words of Raymond Tanter—a member of Reagan's National Security Council and now a visiting fellow at the Washington Institute for Near East Policy— "the road to Jerusalem goes through Baghdad"; and the use of force to oust Saddam would inaugurate "America's decade in the Middle East."⁵² This became the mantra of neoconservative foreign policy. In 1998, eighteen associates of the PNAC, including Richard Armitage, William Bennet, Francis Fukuyama, Robert Kagan, William Kristol, Richard Perle, Donald Rumsfeld, and Paul Wolfowitz, wrote a letter to President Clinton. In it they warned of the need to secure the "significant portion of the world's oil supply" in Iraq, advising the president that the only acceptable strategy is to "undertake military action" and remove "Saddam Hussein and his regime from power."⁵³ It is worth noting that ten of the eighteen signers later became members of the Bush administration.

Although Clinton chose not to take its advice, the PNAC did not give up its bold vision for America's benevolent global hegemony. In September 2000, the PNAC issued a report entitled "Rebuilding America's Defenses: Strategy, Forces, and Resources for a New Century." Its authors lament the lack of effort to "preserve American military preeminence in the coming decades" and criticize Clinton for squandering his opportunity to make the United States the sole, indomitable superpower. The removal of Saddam and the U.S. occupation of Iraq would provide both the crucial justification and the ideal precondition for this larger global agenda. Achieving this goal of undeniable U.S. power, the authors suggest, would require a radical transformation in public opinion and government policy. But they also caution that "the process of transformation, even if it brings revolutionary change, is likely to be a long one, absent some catastrophic and catalyzing event—like a New Pearl Harbor."⁵⁴

The Gentleman: The "Triple-Coding" of
Neoconservative Rhetoric in Bush's Public Discourse

> I believe there's a clash of ideologies and I think—I just know—that America must be firm in our resolve and confident in our belief that freedom is the mightiest gift to everybody in the world and that free societies will be peaceful societies.

> —George W. Bush (2004)

Not long after the publication of the PNAC document, two things occurred that handed the neoconservatives their "catastrophic and catalyzing events" on a silver platter. The first was the election of George W. Bush to the White House. The second was the terrorist attack of 9/11.

With a man who knew and cared little about foreign affairs now in the White House, the neoconservatives finally had the chance to try to put some of their aggressive and ideologically driven plans into action. As Irving Kristol himself observed, George W. was a rather fortuitous gift to the neoconservatives, in ways that the president himself did not fully grasp: "by one of those accidents historians ponder, our current president and his administration turn out to be quite at home in this new political environment, although it is clear they did not anticipate this role any more than their party as a whole did."[55]

Indeed, Mr. Bush is in many ways the ideal exemplar of Strauss's gentleman—the public face of virtue, piety, and compassion who embodies the values that appeal to the common people, despite his general lack of knowledge of foreign affairs or the details of statecraft. As in Strauss's ideal system, the real power appears to lie primarily with the philosophers around the gentleman—ideologues such as Rumsfeld, Cheney, Wolfowitz, Shulsky, and Perle, who have a much keener sense of political strategy and a bold vision of America's geopolitical power. In the wake of 9/11, in fact, a small cluster of policy advisers formed a highly secretive group within the Pentagon's Office of Special Plans. They called themselves, half ironically, "the Cabal." As Seymour Hersh reported in 2003, this Cabal—consisting largely of Straussians and disciples of Wohlstetter—was the primary driving force behind the manipulation of intelligence used to justify the preemptive invasion: "their operation, which was conceived by Paul Wolfowitz . . . brought about a crucial change of direction in the American intelligence community. These advisers and analysts, who began their work in the days after September 11, 2001, have produced a skein of intelligence reviews that have helped to shape public opinion and American policy toward Iraq."[56] In true Straussian fashion, the intelligence—or rather "noble lies"—provided by this group gave the president his "evidence" that an invasion of Iraq was both necessary and just.

While George W. Bush is surely no reader of Leo Strauss, or probably even of Francis Fukuyama, a close analysis of his public discourse reveals a number of powerful neoconservative themes and Fukuyamian rhetoric. This became particularly evident in the wake of 9/11, as he began to cast the entire world in terms of a vast struggle between the forces of freedom and tyranny, liberty and terror. As we saw in chapter 1, Bush's speeches contain a subtle kind of double coding, using careful references to specific biblical passages that are likely to be missed by most readers but heard by an evangelical audience. At the same time, however, they also contain another layer of coding, perhaps a triple coding, with specific references to neoconservative ideals. Bush's frequent use of the language of "freedom" as the goal of history and America's destiny is not just a kind of millenarian religious vision; it is also a clear reference to Fukuyama's "End of History" idealism, which also sees American-style democracy and free markets as the teleological goal of history. Thus, as Bush put it in his remarks at the National Day of Prayer and Remembrance in 2001,

> Our responsibility to history is already clear: to answer these attacks and rid the world of evil. . . . This conflict was begun on the timing and terms of others. It will end in a way, and at an hour, of our choosing. . . . God's signs are not always the ones we look for. We learn in tragedy that his purposes are not always our own. . . . In every generation, the world has produced enemies of human freedom. They have attacked America, because we are freedom's home and defender. And the commitment of our fathers is now the calling of our time. On this national day of prayer and remembrance, we ask almighty God to watch over our nation. . . . As we have been assured, neither death nor life, nor angels nor principalities nor powers, nor things present nor things to come, nor height nor depth, can separate us from God's love. . . . May He always guide our country.[57]

Even more explicit rhetoric reappeared a little over three years later, in Bush's 2005 inaugural address. With his newfound "political capital," the reelected president described America's role in the inevitable advance of liberty guided by the "Author of Liberty":

> Freedom is the permanent hope of mankind, the hunger in dark places, the longing of the soul. When our Founders declared a new order of the ages; when soldiers died in wave upon wave for a union based on liberty . . . they were acting on an ancient hope that is meant to be fulfilled. History has an ebb and flow of justice, but history also has a visible direction, set by liberty and the Author of Liberty.[58]

As various observers have noted, this speech could practically have been copied directly from a page of Fukuyama's book. Bush's words, Chris Suellentrop comments, "could have been written by Francis Fukuyama, who theorized . . . that worldwide democracy is inevitable because of man's natural striving for dignity and liberty. . . . [H]ere was Bush proclaiming that God and freedom are on the same side, and that the End of History is in sight."⁵⁹ Bush has, in effect, combined the Christian rhetoric of God's divine plan for humankind with the neoconservative idealism of America's role in the spread of freedom as the end of history.

But at the same time, in addition to this sort of warmed-over Fukuyama rhetoric, Bush has also invoked a sort of "cash of civilizations" language that seems to be a direct reference to Samuel Huntington's influential book, *The Clash of Civilizations and the Remaking of the World Order*. Huntington, we should note, offers a rather different perspective on global events does than Fukuyama; rather than a steady progression toward an "end of history" with American-style democracy and free markets for all, Huntington predicts an increasingly violent clash between fundamentally different ideologies and cultures. The most important of these clashes, he suggested, would be between Western-style secular democracy and Islam, in all its forms: "The underlying problem for the West is not Islamic fundamentalism. It is Islam, a different civilization whose people are convinced of the superiority of their culture and are obsessed with the inferiority of their power. The problem for Islam is not the CIA or the U.S. Department of Defense. It is the West, a different civilization whose people are convinced of the universality of their culture and believe that their superior . . . power imposes on them the obligation to extend that culture throughout the world."⁶⁰

Bush seems to have incorporated Huntington's clash of civilizations rhetoric, but also combined it with Fukuyama's end of history idealism. As he put it in his conversation with Christian writers and editors in 2004, the world today is witnessing a "clash of ideologies," a struggle between America's ideal of freedom and the tyranny most clearly embodied in radical Islam. In this clash, America must stand strong in its faith that freedom is the goal of history and God's plan for the world. In other words, there *is* a clash of civilizations, but *we will win it* and thereby usher in the "end of history," which is God's gift of freedom to all humankind:

> I believe there's a clash of ideologies and I think . . . that America must be firm in our resolve and confident in our belief that freedom is the mightiest gift to everybody in the world. . . .
>
> [W]e will use every asset to prevent an enemy from attacking us again. . . . I believe they want to do it because I know they want to sow discord, distrust, and fear at home so that we begin to withdraw from parts of the world where they would like to have enormous influence to spread their Taliban-like vision—the corruption of religion—to suit their purposes. . . .
>
> The long-run solution to terror is freedom. That's what we believe in America. We believe that everybody yearns to be free.⁶¹

Again, in his usual sort of vague and not entirely coherent way, Bush can combine Fukuyama's end of history with Huntington's clash of civilizations, clothing it all in a kind of generic rhetoric of freedom, faith, and an abstract ideal of America's historic mission in the world.

However, statements such as these also reveal Bush as the ideal sort of Straussian gentleman. He is able to present what are clearly neoconservative political plans for America's global hegemony and military power, while clothing them in the more palatable language of God's will as the "Author of Liberty." Such discourse is ingeniously constructed, skillfully double and even triple coded: it offers his Christian evangelical audience the promise of God's plan for humankind and the approaching millennium, even as it offers a neoconservative audience the ideal of an imminent end of history. Apparently, this discourse worked reasonably well, or at least well enough to persuade most Americans to accept, largely without criticism, the preemptive invasion of Iraq. As the president put it in his 2003 state of the union address, in which he made the strongest case for war against Iraq, Americans must be willing to fight and die in battle, for they will be dying for "freedom," which is both "*the future of every nation*" and "*God's gift to humanity.*"[62]

Whether or not George W. Bush's decision to invade Iraq was divinely inspired, it does seem to have fulfilled the neoconservative's long-held plans on both the domestic and the international fronts. As David Harvey argues in *The New Imperialism*, the attacks of 9/11 and Bush's response to them have provided the ideal rationale for imposing the neoconservatives' larger agenda of "establishment of and respect for order, both at home and upon the world stage."[63] On the domestic front, 9/11 has provided the excuse to impose extremely invasive new measures such as the PATRIOT Act. On the international front, it has provided the ideal motivation—and spiritual justification—for the neoconservatives' plans for Iraq dating back to the early '90s. In this sense, Harvey suggests, the neoconservative strategy for occupying Iraq has behind it a much larger and more disturbing global agenda. With Iraq as its base of operation, and Saudi Arabia, Syria, and Iran close at hand, the United States would be uniquely placed to dominate the flow of oil from the Middle East and, by extension, the flow of capital throughout the world in an age still fueled by oil and petrodollars:

> With the occupation of Iraq and the possible reform of Saudi Arabia and some sort of submission on the part of Syria and Iran to superior American military power and presence, the US will have secured a vital strategic bridgehead . . . on the Eurasian land mass that just happens to be the centre of production of oil that currently runs . . . not only the global economy but also every large military machine. . . . The US will then be in a military and geostrategic position to control the whole globe militarily and, through oil, economically. . . . The neo-

conservatives are, it seems, committed to nothing short of a plan for total domination of the globe.[64]

In this sense, the Iraq war was not simply "about oil," as many critics have argued (although it was indeed partly about oil); it was about a much bolder vision of the United States' unchallenged global superiority for the New American Century.

Religion, Secrecy, and Empire: America's Ambivalent Global Power

We need to err on the side of being strong. And if people want to say we're an imperial power, fine.

—William Kristol, interview on Fox News (2003)

Democracy is inimical to imperial mobilization.

—Zbigniew Brzezinski, *The Grand Chessboard*

Historically, Americans have been wary of the concept of imperialism. As Niall Ferguson observes, most Americans, including members of the Bush administration, have adamantly denied harboring any sort of colonial or imperial ambitions;[65] in fact, however, the United States has emerged as a new imperial power since the end of World War II: "Most historians agree that, if anything, American economic power after 1945 exceeded that of Britain after 1815, a comparable watershed of power following the final defeat of Napoleonic France."[66] In the last few years, however, that trend has begun to change significantly. A decade ago, Charles Maier notes, the very concept of empire had aroused "righteous indignation" because the United States was "an empire that dared not speak its name. But these days, on the part of friends and critics alike, the bashfulness has ended."[67] In the words of Michael Ignatieff, America's brand of "empire lite" is the lesser of evils in the world today and a necessary "burden" that we have a duty to bear: "the case for empire is that it has become, in a place like Iraq, the last hope of democracy and stability alike."[68]

However, the most vocal proponents of America's benevolent imperialism have been neoconservative theorists writing in the late 1990s, embracing what Kristol has called the "emerging American imperium" and what Wolfowitz has called the "Pax Americana."[69] Indeed, the Straussians on the whole tend to exhibit an "enthusiasm for empire and a determination to exploit American imperial hegemony."[70] Yet in their minds, an American empire is both an opportunity and a kind of moral obligation, comparable to that faced by Rome two thousand years ago and by the British two centuries ago. As Max Boot wrote in his essay, "The Case for an American Empire" in the key neoconservative journal, *The Weekly Standard*, "Afghanistan and other troubled lands today cry out for the sort of enlightened foreign administration once provided by self-confident Englishmen in jodhpurs and pith helmets."[71] Like the British before us, then, we have an obligation to accept the "burden" of empire.

Historically, as we noted above, empires typically go hand in hand with powerful religious ideologies that support and legitimate them. The most expansive forms of political power require the most expansive and often extremist forms of religious faith to buttress them. And this is as true for imperial Rome as for the new Pax Americana, where we now have a resurgence of the Christian right to support our own brand of empire. Far from a new phenomenon, the use of religion to buttress imperial ambitions is a very old idea. As former CIA analyst Ray McGovern comments, the neoconservatives' use of religion to justify their policies is simply the latest example of the "hijacking of 'Him' for the needs of empire":

> In 312 before the great battle at the Milvian Bridge at Rome . . . Constantine, saw a cross in the sky with the words "In Hoc Signo Vinces" ("In This Sign You Will Conquer"). Constantine had a cross inscribed on his soldiers' armor. The new "Christians" won the battle and lost Jesus' message of nonviolence. Several centuries later, "Deus Vult" ("God wills it") was the inscription chosen by St. Peter's successors as they dispatched crusaders to war in the Holy Land. And "Gott Mit Uns" decorated Nazi belt buckles. So "He" was hijacked long ago, with countless imperial and other brutalities carried out in "His" name.[72]

As Phillips observes in his discussion of imperial Rome, Hapsburg Spain, and Great Britain, extremist religion, imperial power, and reactionary politics are often closely interdependent; and these three interconnected forces have reemerged with the imperialist dream of the New American Century: "Now, in the twenty-first century political framework, readjusting to new threats, [the United States] showed glimmerings of an empire determined to strike back, even though the latter-day legions wore Kevlar instead of Roman breastplates."[73] However, the current American style of imperialism does seem to be unique in certain respects: indeed, as we will see in more detail in chapter 6, it has behind it a kind of millenarian, messianic, perhaps even apocalyptic fervor that distinguishes it from many previous historical empires.

Secrecy and the strict control of information also tend to go hand in hand with imperial powers. As Georg Simmel long ago pointed out, "secrecy has always been among the requirements of their regime."[74] More recently, Chalmers Johnson has argued that the unique new form of global empire built by the United States in the twentieth century was made possible in large part by the obsessive secrecy that surrounds our military institutions; indeed, we now have a global network of military bases, special forces, and covert operations spread to every corner of the planet, most of which is unknown to the American public. This sort of imperial secrecy has not only expanded dramatically but also has now become the rule in the wake of 9/11, after which "government at every level began to restrict information available to the public. . . . Our newspapers began to read like official gazettes, television news simply gave up and followed the orders of its corporate owners."[75] And yet, as we will see in the following chapters, this sort of messianic and secretive imperialism is not only inherently opposed to, but fundamentally destructive for, any model of open democracy and transparent government.

Thus it is perhaps time that American citizens began learning the art of "reading between the lines," in Strauss's sense. That is, we need to be able to critically examine the pious rhetoric used by the administration and discern the deeper motivations that lie behind it. As the Indian novelist and social critic Arundhati Roy suggests in her *Ordinary Person's Guide to Empire*, we need to look through the neoconservative rhetoric of "freedom" and "liberty." Such rhetoric often conceals agendas that have far more to do with spreading America's imperial might and economic interests than with bringing actual democracy to other lands:

> Phrases like "free speech," the "free market," and "the free world" have little, if anything to do with freedom. . . . [A]mong the myriad freedoms claimed by the U.S. government are the freedom to murder, annihilate, and dominate other people. The freedom to finance and sponsor despots and dictators across the world. The freedom to train, arm, and shelter terrorists. The freedom to topple democratically elected governments. . . . And most terrible of all, the freedom to commit these crimes against humanity in the name of "righteousness."[76]

As we will see in chapter 6, there are many indications that the neoconservative dream of benevolent empire has already begun to crumble, as more and more Americans begin to see through this pious rhetoric of "freedom," and as the promise of "liberty" gives way to the reality of endless bloodshed and massive debt. Even some leading neoconservative theorists, such as Francis Fukuyama, have recently declared the project a disastrous failure. But before we can begin to understand either the full complexity or the apparent failure of the neoconservative project, we first need to look at one of its most radical and influential theorists, Michael Ledeen.

Notes

1. "Bush Fails Reporter's Pop Quiz on International Leaders," *CNN.com*, November 5, 1999, at www.cnn.com/ALLPOLITICS/stories/1999/11/05/bush.popquiz/.

2. Stefan Halper and Jonathan Clarke, *America Alone: The Neo-Conservatives and the Global Order* (New York: Cambridge University Press, 2004).

3. David Brooks, "The Era of Distortion," *New York Times*, January 6, 2004, at www.nytimes.com.

4. Irving Kristol, *Neoconservatism: The Autobiography of an Idea* (New York: Free Press, 1995), 365.

5. See Urban, "Religion and Secrecy in the Bush Administration: The Gentleman, the Prince, and the Simulacrum," *Esoterica* 7 (2005): 1–36.

6. Irving Kristol, "The Neoconservative Persuasion: What It Was and What It Is," *Weekly Standard*, August 25, 2003. www.weeklystandard.com/Content/Public/Articles/000/000/003/000tzmlw.asp.

7. Halper and Clarke, *America Alone*, 11.

8. William Kristol and Robert Kagan, *Present Dangers: Crisis and Opportunity in American Foreign Policy* (San Francisco: Encounter, 2000), 5–6.

9. Francis Fukuyama, *The End of History and the Last Man* (New York: Free Press, 1992). See Roger Burbach and Jim Tarbell, *Imperial Overstretch: George W. Bush and the Hubris of Empire* (New York: Zed, 2004), 83.

10. Anne Norton, *Leo Strauss and the Politics of American Empire* (New Haven: Yale University Press, 2004),179.

11. Norton, *Leo Strauss*, 177.

12. Larisa Alexandrovnam, "A Conversation with Machiavelli's Ghost," February 28, 2006, at rawstory.com/news/2006/Conversation_with_Controversial_Neoconservative_0228.html.

13. "Deputy Secretary Interviewed by Sam Tannenhaus," *Department of Defense*, May 9, 2003, at www.defenselink.mil/transcripts/2003/tr20030509-depsecdef0223.htm. See also Francis Fukuyama, *America at the Crossroads: Democracy, Power, and the Neoconservative Legacy* (New Haven: Yale University Press, 2006), 31.

14. Halper and Clarke, *America Alone*, 67.

15. Kristol, *Neoconservatism*, 7.

16. Shadia Drury, *Leo Strauss and the American Right* (New York: Palgrave Macmillan, 1999), 59. For different views of his students, see Harry F. Jaffa, "The Legacy of Leo Strauss," *Claremont Review* 3, no. 3 (1984): 14–21, and Thomas Pangle's response in *Claremont Review* 4, no.1 (1985): 18–20.

17. Leo Strauss, *Persecution and the Art of Writing* (Glencoe, IL: Free Press, 1952), 25.

18. Leo Strauss, *What Is Political Philosophy?* (Westport, CT: Greenwood, 1973), 221–222.

19. Leo Strauss, *Spinoza's Critique of Religion* (New York: Schocken, 1965), 47. See Kenneth Deutsch, "Leo Strauss, the Straussians, and the American Regime," in *Leo Strauss, the Straussians, and the American Regime*, ed. Kenneth L. Deutsch and John A. Murley (Lanham, MD: Roman & Littlefield, 1999), 59.

20. Ted V. McAllister, *Revolt against Modernity: Leo Strauss, Eric Voegelin, and the Search for a Postliberal Order* (Lawrence: University Press of Kansas, 1996), 33. See Leo Strauss, *Liberalism Ancient and Modern* (Ithaca: Cornell University Press, 1989), 22, 64.

21. Adam Curtis, BBC Documentary, "The Power of Nightmares, I: Baby It's Cold Outside," originally aired on BBC 2, October 20, 2004.

22. Stanley Rosen, in Curtis, "Power of Nightmares."

23. Deutsch, "Leo Strauss," 54–55. See Strauss, *Persecution*, 15.

24. Shadia B. Drury, *The Political Ideas of Leo Strauss* (New York: Macmillan, 1988), 31. See Strauss, *Persecution*, 17.

25. Deutsch, "Leo Strauss," 55.

26. Deutsch, "Leo Strauss," 55.

27. Irving Kristol, *Neoconservatism*, 379–380.

28. Gary J. Schmitt and Abram N. Shulsky, "The World of Intelligence (By Which We Do Not Mean *Nous*)," in Deutsch and Murley, eds., *Leo Strauss*, 411.

29. Eric Alterman, *When Presidents Lie: A History of Official Deception and Its Consequences* (New York: Viking, 2004), 307; see Seymour Hersh, "Selective Intelligence," *New Yorker*, May 12, 2003, at www.newyorker.com/fact/content/?030512fa_fact.

30. Alterman, *When Presidents Lie*, p. 306.

31. Irving Kristol, *Neoconservatism*, 365.

32. Irving Kristol, "The Future of American Jewery," in *The Neoconservative Imagination: Essays in Honor of Irving Kristol*, ed. Christopher DeMuth and William Kristol (Washington, DC: AEI, 1995), 201.

33. Irving Kristol, "The Capitalist Future," in *The Neoconservative Imagination*, 201.

34. Irving Kristol, "Neoconservative Persuasion."

35. Norton, *Leo Strauss*, 178–79.

36. Irving Kristol, *Neoconservatism*, 368.

37. "Deputy Secretary Wolfowitz Interview with Sam Tannenhaus," *Vanity Fair*, May 9, 2003, at www.defenselink.mil/transcripts/2003/tr20030509-depsecdef0223.html; Fukuyama, *America at the Crossroads*, 31–35.

38. Norton, *Leo Strauss*, 8. See Alain Franchon and Daniel Vernet, "The Strategist and the Philosopher," trans. Mark K. Jensen (originally published as "Le stratège et le philosophe," *Le Monde*, April 15, 2003), at www.informationclearinghouse.info/article2978.htm.

39. Norton, *Leo Strauss*, 184–185.

40. Albert Wohlstetter, "The Delicate Balance of Terror," in *The Art of War in World History: From Antiquity to the Nuclear Age*, ed. Gerard Chaliand (Berkeley: University of California Press, 1994), 1004–1006.

41. Franchon and Vernet, "Strategist and the Philosopher."

42. Norton, *Leo Strauss*, 182.

43. Halper and Clark, *America Alone*, 63.

44. Paul Wolfowitz, "Statesmanship in a New Century," in *Present Dangers: Crisis and Opportunity in American Foreign and Defense Policy*, ed. Robert Kagan and William Kristol (San Francisco: Encounter, 2000), 334–335; Norton, *Leo Strauss*, 192.

45. Wohlstetter, "Delicate Balance of Terror," 1006.

46. See "Publications and Reports," *Project for the New American Century*, at www.newamericancentury.org/publicationsreports.htm.

47. David Armstrong, "Dick Cheney's Song of America: Drafting a Plan for Global Dominance," *Harper's*, October 2002, 76–83; John Nichols, *Dick, the Man Who Is President* (New York: New Press, 2004), 102.

48. Nichols, *Dick*, 102.

49. William Kristol and Robert Kagan, "Toward a Neo-Reagnite Foreign Policy," *Foreign Affairs* (July/August 1996), at www.foreignaffairs.org.

50. "Rebuilding America's Defenses: Strategy, Forces and Resources for a New Century," *Project for the New American Century*, 2000, at www.newamericancentury.org/RebuildingAmericasDefenses.pdf.

51. Norton, *Leo Strauss*, 186.

52. Jeffrey Donovan, "Mideast Policy: Does the Road to Jerusalem Run through Baghdad?" *Truthnews.com*, 2002, at truthnews.com/world/2002063343.htm.

53. The letter to Clinton of January 26, 1998, was signed, among others, by Elliott Abrams, Richard L. Armitage, Francis Fukuyama, William Kristol, Richard Perle, Donald Rumsfeld, and Paul Wolfowitz. See *Project for the New American Century*, at www.newamericancentury.org/iraqclintonletter.htm.

54. "Rebuilding America's Defenses."

55. Irving Kristol, "Neoconservative Persuasion."

56. Hersh, "Selective Intelligence."

57. "President's Remarks at National Day of Prayer and Remembrance," September 14, 2001, at www.whitehouse.gov/news/releases/2001/09/20010914-2.html.

58. "Bush Sworn in to Second Term," January 20, 2005, www.whitehouse.gov/news/releases/2005/01/20050120-1.html.

59. Chris Suellentrop, "Freedom's Just Another Word," *Slate.com*, January 20, 2005, at www.slate.com/id/2112480/.

60. Samuel Huntington, *The Clash of Civilizations and the Remaking of World Order* (New York: Simon and Schuster, 1998), 217.

61. Sheryl Henderson Blunt, "Bush Calls for Culture Change," *Christianity Today*, May 24, 2004, at www.christianitytoday.com/ct/2004/121/51.0.html.

62. George W. Bush, State of the Union Address, January 28, 2003, in *We Will Prevail: President George W. Bush on War, Terrorism, and Freedom* (New York: Continuum, 2003), 220–221; my italics.

63. David Harvey, *The New Imperialism* (New York: Oxford University Press, 2003), 190.

64. Harvey, *New Imperialism*, 198–199. As Paul Roberts comments, "though the war was 'about oil,' that was true in a way that most of Bush's critics failed to grasp. It wasn't simply that an Iraq without Saddam would enrich Bush's energy industry allies. . . . Nor was the connection merely that war in Iraq would bolster America's military and economic presence in the region. . . . Rather, it was that liberating Iraq and its oil was key to the neoconservatives' vision for the future of American power—and for the new geopolitics of oil." Roberts, *The End of Oil: On the Edge of a Perilous New World* (New York: Houghton Mifflin, 2004), 111–112.

65. As Rumsfeld argued in an interview with Al Jazeera in 2003: "We've never been a colonial power. We don't take our force and go around the world and try to take other people's real estate. . . . That's how an empire-building Soviet Union behaved but that's not how the United States behaves." Rumsfeld, quoted in Niall Ferguson, *Colossus: The Price of America's Empire* (New York: Penguin, 2004), 1.

66. Ferguson, *Colossus*, 9. See Andrew Bacevich, *American Empire: The Realities and Consequences of U.S. Diplomacy* (Cambridge: Harvard University Press, 2002).

67. Charles Maier, "An American Empire?" *Harvard Magazine* (November–December 2002): 28–30.

68. Michael Ignatieff, "The Burden," *New York Times Magazine*, January 5, 2003, 54.

69. Wolfowitz, "Statesmanship in the New Century," 309.

70. Norton, *Leo Strauss*, 186.

71. Max Boot, "The Case for American Empire," *Weekly Standard*, October 15, 2001.

72. McGovern, "Hijacking God for Empire," *Buzzflash.com*, December 29, 2003, at www.buzzflash.com/contributors/03/12/con03385.html.

73. Kevin Phillips, *American Dynasty: Aristocracy, Fortune, and the Politics of Deceit in the House of Bush* (New York: Viking, 2004), 60; see Phillips, *American Theocracy: The Peril and Politics of Radical Religion, Oil, and Borrowed Money in the 21st Century* (New York: Viking, 2006), 220–221.

74. Georg Simmel, "The Secret and the Secret Society," in *The Sociology of Georg Simmel*, edited by Kurt H. Wolff (New York: Free Press, 1950), 365.

75. Chalmers Johnson, *Sorrows of Empire: Militarism, Secrecy, and the End of the Republic* (New York: Metropolitan, 2004), 13.

76. Arundhati Roy, *An Ordinary Person's Guide to Empire* (Cambridge, MA: South End, 2004), 53–54.

4

Machiavelli Meets the Religious Right: Michael Ledeen and the Politics of Mass Manipulation

---

The course of this conflict is not known, yet its outcome is certain. Freedom and fear, justice and cruelty, have always been at war, and we know that God is not neutral between them.

—George W. Bush, address to a joint session of Congress (2001)

The politics of mass manipulation, the politics of myth and symbol—have become the norm in the modern world.

—Michael Ledeen, *D'Annunzio: The First Duce*

ONE OF THE MOST INFLUENTIAL FIGURES in the neoconservative movement— but also a figure little known to most Americans—is the historian and political theorist Michael Ledeen. Currently a resident scholar in the "Freedom Chair" at the American Enterprise Institute, Ledeen has been called by some the "driving philosophical force behind the neoconservative movement and the military actions it has spawned"; indeed, "Ledeen's ideas are repeated daily by such figures as Richard Cheney, Donald Rumsfeld, and Paul Wolfowitz.... He basically believes that violence in the service of the spread of democracy is America's manifest destiny. Consequently, he has become the philosophical legitimator of the American occupation of Iraq."[1] According to *The Washington Post*, Ledeen has been regularly consulted by Karl Rove, who said to him, "anytime you have a good idea, tell me," and more than once, "Ledeen has seen his ideas, faxed to Rove, become official policy or rhetoric."[2] At the same time, Ledeen has also been a key link between the neoconservative ideologues and their base of popular support in the Christian right; since the 1980s, for example, he has made numerous appearances on Pat Robertson's *700 Club*, promoting a strong neoconservative political agenda.

While the neoconservative movement as a whole represents a highly idealistic and indeed imperialistic vision of America's role in the post–Cold War world, Ledeen represents an even more aggressive and ruthless current among the neoconservatives—what we might call the neo-Machiavellian current. As Niccolò Machiavelli observed several centuries ago, religion and secrecy can both serve as extremely powerful political tools, and in many cases weapons, that can be wielded to manipulate public opinion, deflect public scrutiny, and destroy one's political enemies. It is from Machiavelli's harsh realism that Ledeen draws his primary philosophical inspiration.

Leo Strauss had also been a scholar of Machiavelli and in fact wrote one of the most difficult and widely debated interpretations of Machiavelli's work. Indeed, Strauss's work on Machiavelli appears to be written in the same sort of esoteric, deliberately misleading code that he believes characterizes the great ancient philosophers. Although Strauss begins his book by stating the "obvious" fact that Machiavelli was a philosopher of evil who marks the end of the ancient philosophic tradition, it is by no means entirely clear what he means by this. Some have suggested that what Strauss finds most objectionable in Machiavelli is not so much *what* he says, but rather the fact that he says it *openly*, in clear, straightforward prose, without the esoteric strategies used by the ancients; and his criticism of Machiavelli's "evil" is coupled with a "deep admiration for his genius."[3] As Strauss puts it, "Machiavelli proclaims openly and triumphantly a corrupting doctrine which ancient writers had taught covertly. . . . He says in his own name shocking things which ancient writers had said through the mouths of their characters."[4] Yet regardless of Strauss's interpretation, Machiavelli has clearly had an impact on much of the neoconservative movement. Thus, Irving Kristol also wrote an influential essay on Machiavelli's philosophy, which he calls a "strong medicine," noting that "Machiavelli *can* be a dangerous teacher; but . . . he may be a useful one."[5]

Recently, of course, it has become commonplace to describe various members of the Bush administration as "Machiavellian" in their political tactics. Cheney, for example, has been portrayed as a kind of Cardinal Richelieu and the "hand behind the throne," secretly manipulating his young dauphin from behind the scenes. In an interview with *USA Today*, Cheney was asked directly whether the comparisons of his behind-the-scenes politics with Machiavelli troubled him at all. His half-joking response to the question is telling: "Am I the evil genius in the corner that nobody ever sees come out of his hole? It's a nice way to operate, actually."[6] Likewise, Karl Rove is infamous for his Machiavellian campaign tactics, including, as we've already seen, the manipulation of both religion and secret information as political weapons.[7] Indeed, the term "Rove-ian" has today become almost synonymous with "Machiavellian" to describe vicious political strategizing.

Yet the most explicit appeal to Machiavelli as not just a metaphor but in fact a model for contemporary politics has come from Michael Ledeen. In his two most recent books, Ledeen has argued forcefully that Machiavelli's "iron rules" are as relevant today as they were in the sixteenth century—indeed, even more so now in our new "war against the terror masters."[8] Ledeen takes the neo-conservatives' powerful mixture of imperialistic foreign policy, obsessive secrecy, and religious discourse to an even further extreme with an even more ambitious plan for reshaping the Middle East. Following Machiavelli, Ledeen is clear about the need for the ruler to engage in secrecy, deception, and even the occasional "entry into evil" in order to protect his political interests. But he also follows Machiavelli's suggestion that religion—or at least the public *display* of piety—is one of the most useful ways to win popular support and generate nationalist spirit. Thus Ledeen's model for the ideal leader would be a kind of "armed prophet," a man who can wield both spiritual charisma and military force, which he sees best embodied in the figure of Moses. Like Moses leading the Israelites, a good ruler should be willing to impose a kind of "dictatorial" rule if it is in the best interests of his people.[9]

As we see in some of the administration's recent activities—such as defending torture as a necessary weapon in the war on terror or authorizing secret spying on U.S. citizens without warrant—it seems that Bush and Cheney have indeed adopted a neo-Machiavellian policy of the sort Ledeen has recommended.

The Politics of Mass Manipulation: Ledeen's Neo-Machiavellian Philosophy

> Peace is not the normal condition of mankind, and moments of peace are invariably the result of war. . . .
>
> The only important thing is winning. Machiavelli tells us that if we win, everyone will judge our methods to have been appropriate. . . .
>
> If we have to do unpleasant things, it is best to do them all at once.
>
> —Michael Ledeen, *War against the Terror Masters*

Michael Ledeen is a curious mixture of scholar, political theorist, and covert operative. Receiving his Ph.D. in history from the University of Wisconsin, Madison, Ledeen spent much of his early career studying Italian fascism, a subject that he says fascinated him from an early age.[10] His 1972 book, *Universal Fascism*, describes the early phase of European fascism as a powerful revolutionary force, one of the great political movements of the twentieth century, that was only later co-opted by the bureaucratic fascism of Mussolini. In his 1977 book, *D'Annunzio: The First Duce*, Ledeen then turned to Gabriele D'Annunzio, whom he credits not only as the forefather of fascism but also as the creator of modern politics. Above all, in Ledeen's opinion, D'Annunzio's powerful use of religious imagery for a secular political cause was the origin of "the politics of mass manipulation, the politics of myth and symbol" that now drives the modern world. It was D'Annunzio, Ledeen suggests, who first saw the power of wedding religious symbolism with nationalist politics, which would become one of the defining themes of the last century:

> D'Annunzio offers the possibility of viewing the fusion of "religious" and "political" themes. . . . The radicalization of the masses in the twentieth century . . . could not have succeeded without the blending of the "sacred" with the "profane." The timeless symbols that have always inspired men and women to risk their lives for higher ideals had necessarily to be transferred from a religious context into a secular liturgy if modern political leaders were to achieve the tremendous control over their followers' emotions that they have acquired.[11]

Since the 1980s, however, Ledeen has also been a shadowy figure working behind the political scenes. As a consultant to the National Security Council head, Robert MacFarlane, Ledeen played a key role in the Iran-Contra affair, introducing NSC aide Oliver North to the Iranian arms dealer Manucher Ghorbanifar (an episode that he describes in his own insider account of Iran-Contra, *Perilous Statecraft*).[12] More recently, Ledeen has been cited by many observers as a possible (and some would say probable) source for the forged documents that were used to suggest Saddam Hussein had attempted to obtain yellow-cake uranium from Niger. According to James Moore, coauthor of the incisive study of Karl Rove, *Bush's Brain*, "The blatantly fake papers . . . turned up after a December 2001 meeting in Rome involving neocon Michael Ledeen, Larry Franklin, Harold Rhodes and Niccolo Pollari, the head of Italy's intelligence agency SISMI, and Antonio Martino, the Italian defense minister."[13] In a series of articles investigating the forgery, Carlo Bonini and Giuseppe D'Avanzo of the Italian paper *La Repubblica* report that Ledeen had been sent to Rome at the request of the Pentagon's Office of Special Plans to gather intelligence that would support military intervention in Iraq. Shortly after Ledeen's return to Washington in 2002, Vice President Cheney began to urge the CIA to look further into the "possible acquisition of Niger uranium," stating that a crucial piece of intelligence was held by a "foreign intelligence agency."[14]

Ledeen's covert operations are in keeping with his broader political philosophy, which is drawn explicitly from Machiavelli's "iron rules." In 1999, he published *Machiavelli on Modern Leadership: Why Machiavelli's Iron Rules Are as Timely and Important Today as Five Centuries Ago*, which was then circulated among members of Congress attending a political strategy meeting shortly after its release. Ledeen makes an unapologetic call for a return to Machiavelli's harsh but realistic advice, which he sees as the only means to save the United States from its decline into moral malaise and political ruin. The Clinton administration in particular represents the decay of strong American values and the surest sign that we need to return to Machiavelli's harsh political realism: indeed, "the corruption has spread far and wide," and "we will soon find ourselves in the same desperate crisis that drove Machiavelli to call for a new dictator to set things aright. . . . [W]e need Machiavellian wisdom and leadership."[15]

Machiavelli, of course, made no bones about the importance of dissimulation and false appearances in politics—a ruthless game that, as he had learned from his own harsh experience, requires guile, secrecy, and the willingness to deceive. Born in the Republic of Florence in 1469, Machiavelli spent his political career in the service of Piero Soderini's government until it was destroyed by the Medici in 1512. Suspected of conspiracy against the Medici, Machiavelli was arrested and tortured, and then he retired to his farm in the country. Still tormented by a desire to return to the metropolis and to politics, he drafted his most famous work on statecraft, *The Prince*, in 1513.[16] As he advises the Prince, it is absolutely necessary that a strong ruler *appear* to be virtuous, just, and compassionate; without such an appearance the populace would never be loyal to him. But it is no less critical that he be able to *act* in ways that are cruel, dishonest, and vicious. If he has a strong reputation for compassion, he can retain the loyalty of his citizens even when he is committing the cruelest of deeds:

> A prince must want to have a reputation for compassion rather than for cruelty; none the less, he must be careful that he does not make bad use of compassion. . . . So a prince must not worry if he incurs reproach for his cruelty so long as he keeps his subjects united and loyal.[17]

Therefore, an ability to lie is a great asset to the Prince. He must understand the ease with which most people are duped and the ways in which the simple-minded can be misled by the one who is clever: "one must know how to colour one's actions and to be a great liar and deceiver. Men are so simple, and so much creatures of circumstance, that the deceiver will always find someone ready to be deceived."[18]

Following Machiavelli, Ledeen is quite clear about the fact that secrecy, deception, and even treason are often necessary in the messy game of politics and war: "In Machiavelli's world—the real world as described in the truthful history books—treason and deceit are commonplace."[19] For Machiavelli had rejected the sort of naïve idealism that sees human beings as good or benevolent creatures, stating the obvious fact that humans are inherently violent creatures and that war is our natural state. It is America's failure to accept this basic fact that has been one of our nation's greatest weaknesses: One "reason we are never ready for war is our radical egalitarianism and our belief in the perfectibility of man. . . . [W]e are reluctant to accept Machiavelli's dictum that man is more inclined to do evil than to do good."[20] Consequently, Americans have naïvely clung to the ideals of openness and transparency in government, not realizing that the key to successful statecraft, foreign policy, and military strategy is precisely secrecy: "foreign policy was our Achilles heel. Foreign policy requires patience and secrecy, while we are impulsive doers and cherish the openness of our society."[21]

Still more important, however, Machiavelli was aware that strong rulers must occasionally engage in acts that may seem immoral, illegal, even "evil" in order to achieve a higher cause. In Ledeen's opinion, Machiavelli "is simply stating the facts: if you lead, there will be occasions when you will have to do unpleasant, even evil, things or be destroyed."[22] And the times when leaders must enter into evil are precisely those times when the higher good of the nation is threatened, or when some sort of revolutionary change is needed to bring society to a higher level:

> There are several circumstances in which good leaders are likely to have to enter into evil; whenever the very existence of the nation is threatened; when the state is first created or revolutionary change is to be accomplished; . . . and when the society becomes corrupt and must be restored to virtue.[23]

Already during the "liberal malaise" of the Clinton era, Ledeen believed that America had reached the kind of severe social and political crisis that would call for this kind of entry into evil. He was in fact one of the more virulent figures demanding Clinton's impeachment, warning that, now, "Only violent and extremely unpleasant methods can bring us back to virtue."[24] But if the social "corruption" of the Clinton era called for "unpleasant measures" to restore our national virtue, then the attacks of September 11, 2001, would require more extreme measures still; in Ledeen's view, 9/11 more than any other event demands that our leaders now "enter into evil."

The Politics of Myth and Symbol: The Political Expedience of Faith

> To those seeing and hearing him, [the Prince] should appear a man of compassion, a man of good faith, a man of integrity, a kind and a religious man. And there is nothing so important as to seem to have this last quality. Men in general judge by their eyes rather than their hands. . . . Everyone

sees what you appear to be, few experience what you really are. . . . The common people are always impressed by appearances and results.

—Niccolò Machiavelli, *The Prince*

The winning formula is threefold: good laws, good arms, good religion.

—Michael Ledeen, *Machiavelli on Modern Leadership*

Perhaps most of all, Ledeen admires Machiavelli's frank recognition of the power of religion as a key political tool. Several centuries before D'Annunzio, Machiavelli had observed the utility of faith and piety for effective rule. Indeed, the most important quality that a Prince must possess is that of religious faith—or rather, the *appearance* of religious faith—for the *appearance* of piety is extremely useful for generating patriotism and nationalist fervor among the common people, even though the *practice* of religious morality or compassion could be a real liability for the Prince, who must often act in quite irreligious and uncompassionate ways:

> A prince, therefore, need not necessarily have all the good qualities I mentioned above, but he should certainly appear to have them. I would even go so far as to say that if he has these qualities and always behaves accordingly he will find them harmful; if he only appears to have them they will render him service. He should appear to be compassionate, faithful to his word, kind, guileless, and devout. . . . But his disposition should be such that, if he needs to be the opposite, he knows how. . . . [A] prince, and especially a new prince, cannot observe all those things which give men a reputation for virtue, because in order to maintain his state, he is often forced to act in defiance of good faith, of charity, of kindness, of religion.[25]

Religion, deception, and politics all come together in the harsh reality of war. For war is the single most important fact for a ruler: to rule means to wage war, and the strength of a ruler lies in his ability to wage war successfully. Thus, the Prince "must have no other object or thought, nor acquire skill in anything, except war, its organization, and its discipline. The art of war is all that is expected of a ruler; and it is so useful that besides enabling hereditary princes to maintain their rule it frequently enables ordinary citizens to become rulers."[26] Both deception and religion are critical in times of war. The former is the key to strategy and the means to outwit one's enemies; the latter is the key to generating troop loyalty and persuading one's citizens to die for a higher cause:

> Religion, too, and the oath soldiers took when they were enlisted, greatly contributed to making them do their duty in ancient times; for upon any default, they were threatened not only with human punishments, but the vengeance of the gods. They also had several other religious ceremonies that had a very good

effect on all their enterprises, and would have still in any place where religion is held in due reverence.[27]

Ledeen admires Machiavelli's utilitarian approach to religion and, in fact, suggests that strong faith is critical to a strong and healthy nation. Without it, the nation becomes weak and degenerate (much as the liberal malaise of the Clinton era had, in his opinion, weakened and sickened America in the 1990s): "a good state must rest on a religious foundation. To remain good, a state must above every other thing keep the ceremonies of their religion incorrupt and keep them always in their veneration, because one can have no greater indicator of the wreck of a land than to see the divine cult scorned."[28] But what Ledeen has in mind here is not a religion of peace and love and harmony on earth; rather, following Machiavelli, Ledeen has in mind a strong, virile kind of religion that would generate the kind of nationalism and patriotism needed to die for the love of one's country: "Along with good soldiers and good laws, the best state . . . requires good religion . . . [and] fear of God underlies respect for men. . . . [Machiavelli] considers the Roman Catholic Church too corrupt and too soft. He wants a tougher, more virile version of the faith, which will inspire men to fight for the glory of their country."[29]

Here we can see Ledeen's open admiration for Machiavelli begin to mingle with his less explicit but often barely concealed admiration for twentieth-century figures such as D'Annunzio and the early fascists. Like Machiavelli before him, D'Annunzio realized the political power of religion as a means of generating nationalist sentiment: "D'Annunzio was a master of the crowd . . . and he blended religion and politics in a way that had not been seen since the Jacobin Terror during the French Revolution."[30] For Ledeen, this is also a powerful means of reawakening nationalist spirit for our own more cynical age in the twenty-first century. As Jeet Heer and Dave Wagner note, "Ledeen displayed an activist's interest in deploying sacred nationalist mythology for contemporary political purposes. For Ledeen, early twentieth-century European mass politics . . . could serve as a wellspring for reinvigorating contemporary middle-class nationalism, particularly in the United States."[31] As we've seen in the massive outpouring of flags, "God Bless Americas," and our president's repeated references to the Almighty in the wake of 9/11, this kind of religious nationalism is indeed still a powerful force in the twenty-first-century United States.

The Armed Prophet: Creative Destruction and the Necessity of Evil

[Moses] knows that somewhere in the shards of the shattered tablets it says "Thou shalt not murder." He readily admits that the means are evil, but he insists that they are the only ones that work in such dire circumstances.

—Michael Ledeen, *Machiavelli on Modern Leadership*

The kind of religion Ledeen is talking about, then, is clearly not that of Jesus or the Sermon on the Mount. Following Machiavelli, Ledeen contrasts two different kinds of religious leaders: the "unarmed prophet" and the "armed prophet." While the former knows the good but cannot fight to save it, the latter knows the good and knows how to preserve it, even if necessary by "evil" means. The prime example of the unarmed prophet is Girolamo Savonorola, the Dominican reformer who was executed in Florence in 1498. Conversely, the prime example of the armed prophet is Moses. For it was Moses who first brought God's Law in the Ten Commandments and then—in a part of the Bible most Christians would rather forget—ordered the slaughter of all those idolaters who worshipped the golden calf instead:

> He said unto them, "Thus saith the Lord, the God of Israel: Put ye every man his sword upon his thigh, and go to and fro from gate to gate throughout the camp, and slay every man his brother, and every man his companion and every man his neighbor," . . . and there fell of the people that day about three thousand.[32]

Ledeen follows Machiavelli's conclusion, then, that "whoever reads the Bible sensibly will see that Moses was forced, were his laws and institutions to go forward, to kill numberless men"; thus it is the armed prophet, the one who is willing to kill to uphold the law, who provides the most effective model for leadership. For the realist knows that "leaders will sometimes have to violate religious strictures to prevail against merciless enemies and competitors."[33]

Ledeen's neo-Machiavellian teachings have had a notable influence, not just in neoconservative circles, but more broadly through his appearances in Christian venues such as the *700 Club*. There is much evidence to suggest that Ledeen's advice and his aggressive vision of foreign policy has been followed by the neoconservatives in the Bush administration, particularly in its preemptive invasion of Iraq.[34] A more disturbing fact, however, is that Ledeen has been urging the administration to go further still, by taking the next step in asserting its power in the Middle East and using military force in Iran. As he stated in a 2004 interview with Pat Robertson on the *700 Club*,

> Iran is the center of the terror network, . . . it's the most dangerous of all the terror countries, and you really marvel that it's taken us this long to get on board with what the president has wanted to do all along.[35]

Robertson's response to Ledeen's call for war on Iran was a glowing affirmation: "we hope and pray that we'll get some normal Americans in the State Department soon," thanking him for appearing once again on his show. "Thank you, Pat," Ledeen replied, "it's always a treat."

There is good indication that many in the administration have in fact listened to and seriously considered Ledeen's revolutionary plans for Iran. According to *The New Yorker*, Ledeen "told a group of Iranian expatriates in Los

Angeles not long ago, 'I have contacts in Iran, fighting the regime. They need funds. Give me twenty million, and you'll have your revolution.' He [said] that in 2001 and 2002, when he pressed the case for Iran with friends in the administration, he had support from some officials in the Pentagon and in the office of the Vice-President Dick Cheney."[36] (Interestingly enough, in February 2006, Secretary of State Condoleezza Rice made a supplemental budget request for $75 million to help "confront the aggressive policies of the Iranian regime" and "work to support the aspirations of the Iranian people for freedom and democracy in their country").[37] By mid-2006, the drums for an Iran war were beating strong among the ranks of the neoconservatives, and Ledeen was leading the charge.[38]

Ledeen is well aware that a revolutionary upheaval in Iran could be devastatingly violent, perhaps catastrophic, for the entire region. Indeed, he predicts that we are heading for a far larger conflagration in the region, heralding "a much broader war, which will in all likelihood transform the Middle East for at least a generation, and reshape the politics of many older countries around the world."[39] Yet, for Ledeen, this is all part of America's role in history. As he explains in *War against the Terror Masters*, we are by nature a revolutionary nation, destined to bring the transformative power of "creative destruction" to the entire world:

> Creative destruction is our middle name, both within our own society and abroad. We tear down the old order every day, from business to science, literature, art, architecture, and cinema to politics and the law. Our enemies have always hated this whirlwind of energy and creativity, which menaces their traditions. . . . Seeing America undo traditional societies, they fear us. . . . They cannot feel secure so long as we are there. . . . They must attack us in order to survive, just as we must destroy them to advance our historic mission.[40]

At times, Ledeen tells us, America's creatively destructive power must be exercised with brute force; we must demonstrate to the world that we mean business, that we have the guns to back us up and that we will destroy any and all who stand in our way. As he put it, in frighteningly brown-shirted terms, "Every ten years or so, the United States needs to pick up some crappy little country and throw it against the wall, just to show the world we mean business."[41]

Yet this American brand of creative destruction and sanctioned violence is also, for Ledeen, the means to bring true "freedom" to the Middle East and to all nations. Indeed, he is quite explicit that, despite his admiration for Machiavelli, he has always emphasized "*the centrality of human freedom*."[42] Rejecting the label of "conservative," he calls himself a "democratic revolutionary,"[43] asserting that we are born to be free and that America's mission is to bring this gift of freedom to all oppressive regimes. And it is this innate thirst for freedom, he believes, that will help topple the regime in Iran, spreading freedom throughout the entire Middle East and ultimately reforming the world as we now know it:

> We will have to pursue the war against terror far beyond the boundaries of the Middle East, into the heart of Western Europe. And there, as in the Middle East, our greatest weapons are political: the demonstrated desire for freedom of the peoples of the countries that oppose us.[44]

It is not difficult to see the influence of Michael Ledeen in the current policies of the Bush administration. Indeed, Mr. Bush is in many ways the ideal embodiment of Ledeen's "armed prophet," who, like Moses, knows the good but is willing to use violence in order to preserve it. As we saw in chapter 1, the narrative that Mr. Bush and his biographers have constructed about his life is itself modeled on the story of Moses, the man called by God to lead his people at a time of great need. Like Ledeen's armed prophet, Mr. Bush is not afraid to use both strong religious rhetoric and military force in order to pursue what he believes to be the higher good. Echoing Ledeen's language, Bush has repeatedly invoked "freedom" as both "God's gift to humanity" and America's historic mission in the world. Yet going still further, he has also described freedom as a powerful and at times violent force, one that destroys those who oppose it. As he declared in his 2005 inaugural address, in words that could have been written by Ledeen himself,

> We have lit a fire as well—a fire in the minds of men. It warms those who feel its power, it burns those who fight its progress, and one day this untamed fire of freedom will reach the darkest corners of our world.[45]

Finally, if we take a brief look at the activities of this administration over the past five years, it would also seem that Bush and Cheney have accepted Ledeen's belief that a strong leader must at times engage in extreme and unpleasant acts—to "work the dark side," as the vice president put it. From the hundreds of uncharged, untried detainees at Guantanamo Bay, to the bewildering flurry of dissimulation surrounding the preemptive invasion of Iraq, to the appalling prisoner abuse at Abu Ghraib, to the CIA's global network of secret prisons, to Cheney's defense of torture as a necessary method in the war on terror, to the NSA's spying on U.S. citizens without warrant, this administration has apparently adopted the strategy of necessary deception and the occasional "entry into evil."

A Temporary Dictatorship?

> Machiavelli's favorite hero . . . Moses exercised dictatorial power, but that
> awesome power was used to create freedom.
>
> —Michael Ledeen, *Machiavelli on Modern Leadership*

> There is no Form of Government but what may be a Blessing to the People
> if well administered; and I believe farther that this is likely to be well ad-
> ministered for a Course of Years, and can only end in Despotism as other
> Forms have done before it, when the People shall become so corrupted as
> to need Despotic Government, being incapable of any other.
>
> —Benjamin Franklin, speech at the Constitutional Convention

Most Americans—and surely all of us who have seen Michael Moore's *Fahrenheit 911*—are familiar with Mr. Bush's infamous statement made during a
meeting with congressional leaders on Capital Hill in late 2000: "If this were a
dictatorship, it'd be a heck of a lot easier, just so long as I'm the dictator."[46]
Probably far fewer Americans are familiar with Ledeen's statement that what
we most need today is in fact a new kind of dictator, indeed, a new Moses. According to Ledeen's neo-Machiavellian logic, what we need today is a form of
"temporary dictatorship" in order to help us resist that greater evil of a slide
into corruption, liberal malaise, and decadence: "Paradoxically, preserving liberty may require the rule of a single leader—a dictator—willing to use those
dreaded 'extraordinary measures,' which few know how, or are willing, to employ."[47] Such extreme measures are now the only way to preserve the long-
term goal of true "freedom":

> A brief period of iron rule is a choice of the lesser of two evils: if the corruption
> continued, a real tyranny would be just a matter of time . . . whereas freedom can
> be preserved if a good man can be found to put the state back in order. Just as it
> is sometimes necessary temporarily to resort to evil actions to achieve worthy
> objectives, so a period of dictatorship is sometimes the only hope for freedom.[48]

Like most Americans, I initially took Mr. Bush's 2000 statement to be simply
another failed attempt at humor by a man who is well-known for his bungled
sentences and torturing of the English language. Surely a man who was unable
to name the president of Pakistan could not manage a political concept as
complex as dictatorship. Yet today, in 2006, as we receive an almost daily series
of revelations about the Bush administration's various activities—the NSA's
warrantless spy program, Cheney's defense of torture as a method in the war
on terror, the CIA's global network of secret prisons, the vengeful outing of

CIA operative Valerie Plame, the continuing lies about the reasons for the invasion of Iraq, and so forth—it is now less clear that Mr. Bush was joking when he spoke of dictatorship. As Jonathan Alter of *Newsweek* notes, it appears that Bush believes he has "license to act like a dictator."[49] Jonathan Schell of *The Nation* put it even more strongly: "There is a name for a system of government that wages aggressive war, deceives its citizens, violates their rights, abuses power and breaks the law, rejects judicial and legislative checks on itself, claims power without limit, tortures prisoners and acts in secret. It is dictatorship. The administration of George W. Bush is not a dictatorship, but it does manifest the characteristics of one in embryonic form."[50] Indeed, it seems possible that Mr. Bush's offhand remark about the benefits of dictatorship may have been one of the rare occasions on which he actually told us the truth.

As we saw in chapter 2, this president has quietly claimed the authority to disobey even the minor safeguards written into the PATRIOT Act, issuing a signing statement that asserts his ability to ignore any provisions that conflict with his own interpretation of the Constitution. According to *The Boston Globe*, Mr. Bush issued similar, largely unpublicized signing statements that assert his ability to "disobey *more than 750* laws enacted since he took office"; he thus claims the power to ignore military rules and regulations, affirmative action provisions, safeguards against political interference in federally funded research, and even McCain's torture ban. Whether or not we choose to call it "dictatorship," this is an unprecedented assertion of executive power and an arrogant defiance of the entire system of checks and balances. As law professor Phillip Cooper describes it, this is in fact a "very carefully thought-out, systematic process of expanding presidential power at the expense of the other branches of government."[51]

I am not suggesting, of course, that Mr. Bush has been reading Machiavelli or secretly conspiring with Michael Ledeen behind the scenes; rather, I think they are both expressions of a broader push toward a far more autonomous, secretive, unaccountable, and aggressive ideal of executive power—one that has a kind of religious faith in its own omnipotence and infallibility. What we are witnessing now is not simply a stronger model of the presidency with what Cheney calls "robust executive authority,"[52] but an imperialized presidency[53] that claims the need for unchecked executive power, warrantless government surveillance, unaccountable secrecy, unprovoked use of force, and the occasional entry into evil.

There is, of course, a profound paradox here. How can one embrace both an ideal of "revolutionary democracy" and Machiavelli's dictatorial "iron rules"? How can one publicly denounce torture (as Ledeen, Bush, Rumsfeld, and others have) and yet claim the need to "work the dark side" and "enter into evil"? How can a government purport to be spreading "freedom" and democracy around the globe, even as it embraces a form of imperialism and violation of civil liberties at home? How can it claim to embody the good, even as it repeatedly asserts the need to enter into evil? In an interview in March 2006, for example, Ledeen publicly rejected the use of torture as an "abhorrent" act;[54] yet it is not difficult to see how his written work, with its explicit call for extreme measures and the use of "evil means," could be used to justify and even encourage such as acts. Ledeen himself is well aware of this paradox, the seeming contradiction between extolling democracy while calling for "iron rules." It is, as he puts it, "the usual Machiavellian paradox: Compulsion . . . makes men noble, and enables them to remain free, while abundant choice is dangerous, leads to chaos, and leaves men at the mercy of their enemies."[55] In other words, iron rules and compulsion give us the moral strength to truly deserve freedom, while too much freedom without such discipline only leads to weakness and degeneracy.

Ledeen's call for a kind of temporary dictatorship, the use of deception and secrecy in the war on terror, and a necessary "entry into evil" appears to have been accepted by a surprisingly large percentage of the American public.[56] Even in the face of an increasingly invasive government and warrantless surveillance, even with the knowledge that our leaders condone torture and preemptive war, much of the country seems to accept that a certain entry into evil is a necessary part of our war on terror. It is important to keep reminding ourselves, then, that Ledeen's neo-Machiavellian ideology has little in common with the ideals of those who wrote our Constitution. Indeed, it would seem to be the exact opposite of those ideals. Jefferson, Franklin, Madison, Adams, and the rest were all too aware of the temptations of empire and dictatorial power, and they warned repeatedly that this fragile democracy should at all costs resist the lust for power that would destroy the ideals upon which it was founded. As John Quincy Adams put it, warning against the temptation to impose our military strength on other nations:

> Wherever the standard of freedom and independence has been or shall be unfurled, there will [America's] heart, her benedictions and her prayers be. But she goes not abroad, in search of monsters to destroy. She is the well-wisher to the freedom and independence of all. She is the champion and vindicator only of her own. . . . She well knows that by once enlisting under other banners than her own, were they even the banners of foreign independence, she would involve herself, beyond the power of extrication, in all the wars of interest and intrigue, of individual avarice, envy, ambition, which assume the colors and usurp the standard of freedom. . . . She might become the dictatress of the world; she would no longer be the ruler of her own spirit.[57]

Ledeen would no doubt argue that Adams's eighteenth-century, Enlightenment idealism is no longer relevant in a twenty-first-century world of "war against the terror masters." And a great many conservative politicians and religious leaders appear to agree with him. Thus American citizens now face an important decision for the next decade: do they want to embrace an aggressive, neo-Machiavellian logic of "creative destruction," benevolent dictatorship, and perpetual war, or do they want to struggle to restore an older ideal of limited government power, protection of personal privacy, and resistance to wars of imperial aggression?

On the surface, this might seem like an absurd rhetorical question. Unfortunately, as we will see in the following chapter, this administration also has a powerful and increasingly propagandistic spin machine at its disposal, as well as an embarrassingly uncritical and often complicit corporate media. Together, they have successfully prevented many Americans from even realizing the Machiavellian logic that drives this administration and from understanding that there are in fact alternatives to its destructive imperial ambitions.

Notes

1. William O. Beeman, "Who Is Michael Ledeen?" *Alternet*, May 8, 2003, at www .alternet.org/story.html?StoryID=15860. On Ledeen as the "guru of the Neoconservatives," see James Bamford, "Iran: The Next War," *Rolling Stone*, July 24, 2006, at www.rollingstone.com/politics/story/10962352/iran_the_next_war.

2. Thomas B. Edsall and Dana Milbank, "White House's Roving Eye for Politics," *Washington Post*, March 19, 2003, A-1.

3. Shadia B. Drury, *The Political Ideas of Leo Strauss* (New York: Macmillan, 1988), 115.

4. Leo Strauss, *Thoughts on Machiavelli* (Chicago: University of Chicago Press, 1958), 10.

5. Irving Kristol, *Neoconservatism: The Autobiography of an Idea* (New York: Free Press, 1995), 157. "Nothing that Machiavelli said about affairs of state was really novel to his readers. They knew . . . that politics is a dirty business; that a ruler may better secure his power by slaughtering innocents, breaking his solemn oaths, betraying his friends than by not doing so. . . . Where Machiavelli was original was first, in brazenly announcing these things, and second, in implying . . . that wicked princes did not rot in hell for the sufficient reason that no such place existed" (155).

6. Tom Engelhardt, "Flushing Cheney," MotherJones.com, February 2, 2004, at www.motherjones.com/news/dailymojo/2004/02/02_500.html. See Anne Geyer, "Dick Cheney: American Richelieu," *American Conservative*, February 2, 2004, at www.amconmag.com/2004_02_02/index1.html.

7. See Kaplan, *With God on Their Side: How Christian Fundamentalists Trampled Science, Policy, and Democracy in George Bush's White House* (New York: New Press,

2004), 77; James Moore and Wayne Slater, *Bush's Brain: How Karl Rove Made George W. Bush Presidential* (Hoboken, NJ: Wiley & Sons, 2003).

8. Michael Ledeen, *Machiavelli on Modern Leadership: Why Machiavelli's Iron Rules Are as Timely and Important Today as Five Centuries Ago* (New York: St. Martin's, 1999); Ledeen, *War against the Terror Masters* (New York: St. Martin's, 2002).

9. Ledeen, *Machiavelli*, 174.

10. John Laughland, "Flirting with Fascism: Neocon Theorist Michael Ledeen Draws More from Italian Fascism Than from the American Right," *American Conservative*, June 30, 2003, at www.amconmag.com/06_30_03/print/featureprint.html.

11. Michael Ledeen, *D'Annunzio: The First Duce* (New Brunswick, NJ: Transaction, 2002), 202. See Ledeen, *Universal Fascism: The Theory and Practice of the Fascist International, 1928–1936* (New York: Fertig, 1972).

12. Michael Ledeen, *Perilous Statecraft: An Insider's Account of the Iran-Contra Affair* (New York: Scribner, 1988). See Jim Lobe, "Veteran Neocon Advisor Moves on Iran," *Asia Times*, June 26, 2003, at www.atimes.com/atimes/Middle_East/EF26Ak03.html, and Lawrence E. Walsh, "Final Report of the Independent Counsel for Iran/Contra Matters," August 4, 1993, at www.fas.org/irp/offdocs/walsh/part_i.htm.

13. James Moore, "Fitzgerald's Historic Opportunity," *TomPaine.com*, October 21, 2005, at www.tompain.com/articles/20051021/fizgeralds_historic_opportunity.php.

14. Carlo Bonini and Giuseppe D'Avanzo, "Pollari ando alla Casa Bianca per offrire la sua verita sull'Iraq," *Repubblica*, October 25, 2005, at www.repubblica.it/2005/j/sezioni/esteri/iraq69/bodv/bodv.html.

15. Ledeen, *Machiavelli*, 188.

16. Anthony Grafton, introduction to Niccolò Machiavelli, *The Prince*, trans. George Bull (New York: Penguin, 2003), xx.

17. Machiavelli, *Prince*, 53.

18. Machiavelli, *Prince*, 57.

19. Ledeen, *Machiavelli*, 61.

20. Ledeen, *War against the Terror Masters*, xvii.

21. Ledeen, *War against the Terror Masters*, xvii.

22. Ledeen, *Machiavelli*, 106.

23. Ledeen, *Machiavelli*, 101–102.

24. Michael Ledeen, quoted in Jeet Heer and Dave Wagner, "Man of the World: Michael Ledeen's Adventures in History," *Boston Globe*, October 10, 2004, at www.boston.com/news/globe/ideas/articles/2004/10/10/man_of_the_world?pg=3.

25. Machiavelli, *Prince*, 57.

26. Machiavelli, *Prince*, 47.

27. Niccolò Machiavelli, *The Art of War*, trans. Ellis Farnesworth (New York: Bobbs-Merrill, 1965), 128.

28. Ledeen, *Machiavelli*, 109–110.

29. Ledeen, *Machiavelli*, xx.

30. Ledeen, *D'Annunzio*, x.

31. Heer and Wagner, "Man of the World."

32. *Exodus* 32:26–28, quoted in Ledeen, *Machiavelli*, 92.

33. Ledeen, *Machiavelli*, 109–110.

34. See Laughland, "Flirting with Fascism"; Edsall and Milbank, "White House's Roving Eye for Politics," A-1.

35. Pat Robertson, interview with Michael Ledeen, 2004, at cbn.com/CBNNews/News/030623e.asp?option=print. Ledeen has called repeatedly for the invasion of Iran, calling it "the mother of modern Islamic terrorism." Ledeen, *War against the Terror Masters*, 10.

36. Connie Buck, "Exiles," *New Yorker*, March 6, 2006, 50.

37. "Rice: $75 Million Sought to Spur Democracy in Iran," *CNN.com*, February 15, 2006, at edition.cnn.com/2006/POLITICS/02/15/iran.usa.reut/.

38. See Bramford, "Iran: The Next War"; Sidney Blumenthal, "The Neocons' Next War," *Salon.com*, August 3, 2006, at www.salon.com/opinion/blumenthal/2006/08/03/mideast/index_np.html.

39. Michael Ledeen, in Heer and Wagner, "Man of the World."

40. Ledeen, *War against the Terror Masters*, 212–213.

41. Lewis H. Lapham, "The Demonstration Effect," *Harper's Magazine*, June, 2003, 11.

42. Ledeen, "Dishonorable Congressman," *National Review*, September, 23, 2003, at www.nationalreview.com/ledeen/ledeen091003.asp.

43. Larisa Alexandrovnam, "A Conversation with Machiavelli's Ghost," February 28, 2006, at rawstory.com/news/2006/Conversation_with_Controversial_Neoconservative_0228.html.

44. Michael Ledeen, "A Theory," *National Review*, March 10, 2003, at www.nationalreview.com/ledeen/ledeen031003.asp.

45. George W. Bush, Second Inaugural Address, January 20, 2005, at www.whitehouse.gov/news/releases/2005/01/20050120-1.html.

46. "Transition of Power: President-Elect Bush Meets with Congressional Leaders on Capitol Hill," *CNN.com*, December 18, 2000, at transcripts.cnn.com/TRANSCRIPTS/0012/18/nd.01.html.

47. Ledeen, *Machiavelli*, 173.

48. Ledeen, *Machiavelli*, 174.

49. Jonathan Alter, "Bush's Snoopgate," *MSNBC.com*, December 21, 2005, at www.msnbc.msn.com/id/10536559/site/newsweek/.

50. Jonathan Schell, "The Hidden State Steps Forward," *Nation*, December 29, 2005, at www.thenation.com/doc/20060109/schell.

51. Charlie Savage, "Bush Challenges Hundreds of Laws," *Boston Globe*, April 30, 2006, at www.boston.com/news/nation/articles/2006/04/30/bush_challenges_hundreds_of_laws/.

52. Deb Reichmann, "Cheney Calls for Stronger Presidential Powers," *AOL News*, December 21, 2005, at aolsvc.news.aol.com/news/article.adp?id=20051221010000 9990003.

53. See "Mr. Cheney's Imperial Presidency," *New York Times*, December 23, 2005, at www.nytimes.com.

54. Alexandrovnam, "Conversation with Machiavelli's Ghost."

55. Heer and Wagner, "Man of the World."

56. According to a January 2006 Gallup poll, only a slight majority of Americans opposed the president's authorization of secret wiretapping of U.S. citizens. See Joseph Carroll, "Slim Majority of Americans Say Bush Wiretapping Was Wrong," *Gallup Poll*, January 25, 2006, at poll.gallup.com/content/Default.aspx?ci=21058&VERSION=p.

57. John Quincy Adams, quoted in *The William Appleman Williams Reader*, ed. Henry W. Berger (Chicago: Dee, 1992), 216.

5

Never Say Lie: The Corporate Media and the Projection of the Bush Image

There has never been an American war, small or large, in which access has been so limited as this one. Limiting access, limiting information to cover the backsides of those who are in charge of the war, is extremely dangerous and cannot and should not be accepted. And I am sorry to say that . . . over-whelmingly it has been accepted by the American people. And the current administration revels in that, they relish that, and they take refuge in that.

—Dan Rather, interview with BBC News (2002)

Propaganda and terror present two sides of the same coin.

—Hannah Arendt, *The Origins of Totalitarianism*

IT SEEMS DIFFICULT TO BELIEVE that the Bush administration could have gotten away with such a brazen disregard for transparency and democratic process (and often facts and truth) without the help of one other important cultural force: the American media. For the most part over the past five years, the mainstream media have helped project Bush's image as a man of religious faith and integrity, while at the same time generously ignoring most of his less admirable activities. To cite just one of the more stunning examples: in its March 10, 2003, issue—*just ten days before the preemptive invasion of Iraq*—*Newsweek* published a cover story entitled "Bush and God." The article went to great lengths to portray Mr. Bush as a man of prayer, faith, and sincere re-ligious conviction, as a president whose *every policy decision* is informed by his deep spiritual values. Indeed, *Newsweek* tells us, his faith far outweighs any merely economic or military motivations in his policy making:

> This president—this presidency—is the most resolutely "faith-based" in modern times, an enterprise founded, supported and guided by trust in the temporal and spiritual power of God. Money matters, as does military might. But the Bush administration is dedicated to the idea that there is an answer to societal problems here and to terrorism abroad: give everyone, everywhere, the freedom to find God.[1]

This was in fact the *top-selling* issue of *Newsweek* for 2003, reaching millions of American readers with this message that Bush's foreign policy is guided more by religious faith than by economic or military interests.

Remarkably, however, neither *Newsweek* nor any other mainstream media outlet was willing to look very closely into the ways in which Mr. Bush and his administration had manipulated, exaggerated, and distorted intelligence to justify the war that would come ten days later. As Eric Alterman notes, "The president was aided in his effort to deceive the nation . . . by many in the media," and, in fact, the media continued to treat Bush with a delicate hand even as his justifications for the war were proven to be fictional.[2] Even when Dana Milbank bravely collected a number of Bush's falsehoods in a front-page story for the *Washington Post* in 2002, he carefully avoided using the word "lie"; instead, he chose phrases such as "embroidering" assertions, "dubious" flights of fancy, or "taking some liberties." Incredibly, despite staggering evidence of his false statements, the words "Bush lied" have not to my knowledge appeared in any major American newspaper during the president's term.[3] In fact, economist Paul Krugman has said that the only time he was censored by *The New York Times* was when he tried to use the word "lie" to describe Bush's tax-cut policies.[4]

There is, however, much about this administration that seems fictional and often quite surreal. Indeed, it is perhaps best described using Jean Baudrillard's term "hyperreal"—that is, seemingly "more real" and more attractive than reality itself, leading us to forget the very distinction between the factual and the imaginary, the genuine and the fake.[5] "Since Machiavelli," Baudrillard observes, "politicians have . . . known that the mastery of *simulated* space is the source of power, that the political is not a *real* activity but a simulation model, whose manifestations are simply achieved effects."[6] Yet this administration, with its obsessive concealment and display of piety, has mastered this simulated space as no other before it. As Bush himself admitted at one point before beginning his political career, he is not so much a politician as a media creation: "You know, I could run for governor but I'm basically a media creation. I've never done anything. I've worked for my dad. I worked in the oil business. But that's not the kind of profile you have to have to get elected to public office."[7] In some ways, the election of a media creation would seem only the next logical step after the election of a former movie star to office. In an age of digitally enhanced movies, when films such as *The Matrix* can conjure not just characters, but entire worlds through the magic of digital simulation, why not a digitally enhanced president?

The projection of the Bush image as a man of faith and piety, I would argue, is the joint creation of two primary forces. On the one hand, there is the ingenious spin machine of Karl Rove, Frank Luntz, and other advisers, who are remarkably attuned to the desires of American voters and have crafted what seems to be an ideal sort of political persona. Rove and others in the administration appear to have adopted an ideology of "create your reality," the belief that they can actually shape reality by the sheer power of political spin and slick advertising. And they have also worked hard to keep their gentleman/president deliberately in the dark, distanced from facts and reality, in order to help him serve as the spokesman for and embodiment of the fantastic image they have created.

On the other hand, there is the mainstream media, which is today owned largely by just five major corporations and has remained stunningly uncritical of Mr. Bush's most blatant lies and obsessive secrecy. While the right-wing ranters such as Rush Limbaugh and Bill O'Reilly complain endlessly about the "liberal media bias," there is little empirical evidence for this claim; in fact, all credible analyses of the media show that the exact opposite is the case. If anything, the corporate media are driven primarily by profit, which is secured less by providing serious critical information than by dispensing simplistic, distracting infotainment. And in many cases, the interests of the corporate media blend quite nicely with the consistently procorporate policies of the Bush administration. Perhaps the most obvious example is Rupert Murdoch's Fox media empire, one of the five largest media conglomerates, which has a clear right-wing agenda and strong ties to the neoconservatives. Through its ostensibly "fair and balanced" look at the news and its many tentacles in books, magazines, and internet outlets, the Fox empire has been one of the most important forces in the shaping of Bush's image as a man of virtue, compassion, and religious faith. Meanwhile, other outlets and newscasters who dare to speak the truth to power—Dan Rather, for example—have been systematically intimidated, silenced, or destroyed.

In this sense, however, the presidency of George W. Bush is not really a strange aberration or radical departure from modern American politics. On the contrary, it is perhaps the logical, if rather disturbing, end result of a "society of the spectacle" and a culture dominated by advertising, sound bytes, "reality TV," and media spin. Bush's display of piety is apparently what many American voters and consumers want to see; and his administration's intense concern with secrecy serves to insulate those voters from the disturbing realities that might undermine his image, while at the same time enhancing the "aura of power" that surrounds their divinely chosen leader.

Create Your Own Reality: The Post-Real Presidency of George W. Bush

We're an empire now, and when we act, we create our own reality.

　　　　　　　　　　　　　—senior White House adviser, quoted by
　　　　　　　　　　　　　Ronald Suskind in *New York Times Magazine*

Their moral cynicism, their belief that everything is permitted, rests on the solid conviction that everything is possible.

　　　　　　　　—Hannah Arendt, *The Origins of Totalitarianism*

However else we might try to describe it, the Bush administration seems to be characterized by a fundamental conviction that faith, ideas, and belief can and do shape reality. This sort of idealism was already apparent in the writings of neoconservatives such as Irving Kristol, who argued that "what rules the world is ideas, because ideas define the way reality is perceived."[8] But this conviction is even more evident in the policies of the current administration, which appears to believe that ideas have the power to make reality—and, indeed, that image and spin are more important than reality.

From the outset, the genius behind the construction of Bush's public image has been Karl Rove, whose brilliant but ruthless campaign strategies earned him the title "Bush's brain." It was largely Rove who was able to take a thrice-failed businessman, refashion his image, and transform him into a remarkably popular presidential candidate. As James Moore and Wayne Slater put it: "Bush is the product. Rove is the marketer. One cannot succeed without the other."[9] A key part of Rove's marketing was to repackage Bush for several different audiences—as a procorporate, big business advocate on the one hand, and as a devout Christian and liaison to the evangelical right on the other. Rove helped present him, in short, as a kind of ambiguous ink blot, whose message of "compassionate conservatism" could be read in a variety of ways according to various corporate and religious interests. As Craig Unger comments,

The task of reinventing and marketing [Bush] fell to Karl Rove, Bush's longtime friend, confidant, and handler. . . . His solution was to create a Rorschach test candidate so that moderates, conservatives, and independents would see in Bush exactly what they wanted to see. Bush's theme of "compassionate conservatism" meant whatever one wanted it to mean. To Wall Street Republicans . . . Bush was his father's son, a . . . moderate who would be good for business. To the powerful cadres of the radical Christian right, Bush's vow to restore honor and integrity to the White House, his promise that his deepest commitment was to his faith and family, meant that he was unmistakably one of them.[10]

As such, there is much about this presidency that seems quite scripted, simulated, and hyperreal in Baudrillard's sense, concerned far more with image and spin than with substance, often blurring the distinction between the genuine and the fake. While President Reagan had played a cowboy in the movies, Mr. Bush plays one on his cowless, horseless, nonworking ranch, which was built for him just in time for the 2000 presidential campaign.[11] But surely the most stunningly hyperreal moment of this presidency was Bush's staged landing on an aircraft carrier to declare "mission accomplished" and the "end" of the apparently endless Iraq war (itself a bad sequel to the first, already hyperreal and media-constructed Gulf War under the first Bush). The ironies contained in this event are countless. Here was Mr. Bush, who appears to have skipped more than a year of the National Guard service that kept him out of Vietnam, now highlighting his expert flying experience. But he did so by flying a pathetically short distance in a plane flown by a real pilot onto a ready-made stage carefully designed to project his heroic image. As Arundhati Roy describes the bizarre surreality of this incident: "In what probably constitutes the shortest flight in history, a military jet landed on an aircraft carrier, which was so close that . . . administration officials acknowledged positioning the massive ship to provide the best TV angle for Bush's speech with the sea as his background instead of the San Diego coastline."[12] Such an event is the epitome of Baudrillard's hyperreality: a display of simulated images "which have no referent or ground in any reality except their own."[13]

But this event was only symptomatic of a far more pervasive hyperreality that characterizes this entire administration. From the very beginning, this White House has conducted public relations, press conferences, and major political events according to predetermined and highly choreographed scripts. As John Dean notes,

> Bush has a White House that works constantly on projecting the image it wants to put out. At times his presidency is literally scripted. Before Bush took office, Karl Rove studied previous presidential debuts, looking for what had worked. . . . Rove developed and tested a detailed plan for the first seven days. . . . The first week launch went off like a successful Broadway opening. Andy Card later acknowledged that it was "like a screenplay. I had a script."[14]

Indeed, for public appearances, the White House has even hired its own professional choreographer, communications specialist and former ABC producer Scott Sforza, to help craft Bush's TV image. For example, at a speech at Mount Rushmore, cameramen were given a platform that presented Bush's profile as if he were already carved into the mountain alongside Washington, Jefferson, Lincoln, and Roosevelt. As Reagan's chief image maker, Michael

Dever, points out, the Bush White House has taken the technique of presidential image making to a level of sophistication that is unrivaled in modern history: "They understand the visual as well as anybody ever has, . . . and they've taken it to an art form."[15]

Among the president's favorite scripted events are his "town-hall meetings," which assemble crowds of adoring citizens who lob him a series of softball questions, most if not all apparently prepared beforehand. At one point in a town-hall meeting in January 2005, the president actually got a bit ahead of the script and accidentally revealed that the entire event was a staged performance. During a conversation with a woman about his plan for Social Security reform, the president accidentally stated the age of the woman's mother before she told him:

> MS. STONE: I would like to introduce my mom. This is my mother, Rhoda Stone. And she is grandmother of three, and originally from Helsinki, Finland, and has been here over 40 years.
> THE PRESIDENT: Fantastic. Same age as my mother.
> MS. STONE: Just turned 80.[16]

As amusing as this incident is, it is also disturbing evidence of how artificial and scripted this entire presidency has become. What is still more troubling, however, is that these sorts of fake public discussions and "town-hall meetings" also serve to silence and marginalize any sort of actual public debate. Indeed, at many Bush campaign rallies and speeches in 2004, citizens were actually required to sign a "loyalty oath," pledging to "endorse George W. Bush for re-election" before being admitted to the event; and in at least one astonishing case in Florida in October 2004, some two thousand attendees at a Bush rally were even required to raise their right hands and recite "the Bush pledge," in which they promised to "work hard to re-elect George W. Bush."[17] Meanwhile, there have been numerous incidents of individuals being ejected from Bush events by the Secret Service because of their t-shirts; in one case in Denver, attendees were ejected simply because they had antiwar bumper stickers on their cars in the parking lot.[18] Apparently, there are to be no dissident voices in the audience that could in any way challenge, critique, or question the administration's staged performances.

In addition to its staged public appearances, the administration has spent massive amounts of money on stealth advertising campaigns, often disguised as legitimate "news," to promote its agenda. In February 2006, a Government Accountability Office (GAO) report revealed that the administration spent more than $1.6 billion of taxpayer money in public relations and media contracts in a two-and-a-half-year period. In what many in Congress decried as a form of "covert propaganda," the administration spent $1.4 billion on advertising agencies, $197 million on public relations firms, and $15 million on media organizations. Among the more remarkable expenditures: several federal departments hired firms to develop "video news releases" that promoted department initiatives, while appearing to viewers to be independent newscasts; meanwhile, the Department of Education paid commentator Armstrong Williams to promote the No Child Left Behind Act on the radio and in his columns. As Rep. George Miller commented, the administration has essentially created a "propaganda machine" that uses over a billion dollars a year to secretly promote policies that have consistently failed to benefit most Americans: "The extent of the Bush Administration's propaganda effort is unprecedented and disturbing. The fact is that after all the spin, the American people are stuck with high prescription drug prices, high gas prices, and high college costs."[19]

Still more remarkable than its staged public presentation and fake news releases, however, is the fact that even high-level cabinet meetings in this administration are often staged and "scripted." As former National Security Council member Paul O'Neill revealed, cabinet meetings work according to virtual screenplays, "where everyone but Bush has speaking parts. Bush's role is merely to nod or listen expressionlessly, aside from his occasional cryptic remarks."[20] In other words, this administration is a kind of simulated performance both within and without, a *performance even to itself.*

But it is not just critical observers who have noted the hyperreal and simulated nature of this administration; at times, the administration itself seems to embrace and endorse its own hyperreal approach to politics. The most stunning example of this self-consciously postmodern attitude is described in Ron Suskind's 2004 article, "Faith, Certainty and the Presidency of George W. Bush." Suskind quotes an unnamed senior adviser to Bush who describes this administration's unique sort of "post-reality" politics, in words that might as well have come straight out of Baudrillard:

> The aide said that guys like me were "in what we call the reality-based community," which he defined as people who "believe that solutions emerge from your judicious study of discernible reality. . . . That's not the way the world really works anymore. . . . We're an empire now, and when we act, we create our own reality. And while you're studying that reality . . . we'll act again, creating other new realities. . . . We're history's actors . . . and you, all of you, will be left to just study what we do."[21]

In Suskind's view, this hyperreal attitude lies at the very heart of the Bush presidency. It is the epitome of an ideologically driven administration that believes in its own, almost godlike power to shape reality. This attitude was also aptly satirized in Tom Tomorrow's comic, "This Modern World," in a cartoon entitled "The Republican Matrix." Echoing this senior aide's words, Tomorrow compares the current White House to the computer-simulated world of the Wachowski brothers' film:

> What is the republican Matrix? It is an illusion that engulfs us all . . . a steady barrage of images which obscure reality. It is a world born anew each day . . . in which there is nothing to be learned from the lessons of the past . . . a world where logic holds no sway . . . where reality itself is a malleable thing . . . subject to constant revision. In short it's their world.

The cartoon closes with Bush, Cheney, and Rumsfeld wearing sunglasses like the agents in *The Matrix*. "What should we do today, fellas?" Bush asks. "Any damn thing we want," answers Cheney.[22]

Meanwhile, the president himself appears to be almost as much a believer in these projected images and constructed realities as the voters who support him. Even in the face of a total absence of WMD in Iraq, a catastrophic war, and an increasingly disillusioned American public, Mr. Bush has continued to assert the same groundless claims about the invasion and seems unbothered by their lack of connection to reality. Following the invasion, after his own appointed weapon's inspector had found no evidence of WMD, Bush still insisted that he had been right all along: "Did Saddam have a weapons program? And the answer is: absolutely. And we gave him a chance to allow the inspectors in, and he wouldn't let them in." At this astonishing denial of history, even a sympathetic reporter such as CNN's Howard Kurtz was forced to admit that Bush's assertion had "no relation to reality."[23] Other observes such as *Time* magazine's Joe Klein have described the president's stunning denial of factual evidence as simply "surreal" and at once "stale and fantastic."[24] The strategy adopted by Bush, Cheney, and their spokesmen seems to be only to continue repeating the same falsehoods over and over again, in flagrant disregard of all evidence to the contrary, in the hope that an untruth repeated often enough will magically become reality—or at least begin to seem to be reality to an American public that is too distracted and bored to notice the difference. As Matt Taibbi comments, we seem to have entered the "the Obey Your Thirst/Image Is Everything era of American politics," where the president's strategy for dealing with any difficult situation is simply to stare into the cameras and repeat the same phrases over and over again until the problem disappears: "Bush and his mouthpieces continue to try to obfuscate and cloud the issue of why we're in Iraq, and they do so not only selectively but constantly, compulsively, like mental patients."[25]

However, while many critics see Bush simply as a hypocrite or a liar, it seems increasingly likely that he himself is a devout believer in the imaginary world that Rove and Cheney have created for him. According to one former Defense official quoted by Seymour Hersh, the president appears to live in an insulated bubble of religious belief and unshakable faith in the rightness of his mission, but increasingly detached from the disastrous effects that his policies are having in the real world:

> "Bush is a believer in the adage 'People may suffer and die, but the Church advances.'" He said that the President had become more detached, leaving more issues to Karl Rove and Vice-President Cheney. "They keep him in the gray world of religious idealism, where he wants to be anyway." . . . Bush's public appearances . . . are generally scheduled in front of friendly audiences, most often at military bases. Four decades ago, President Johnson, who was also confronted with an increasingly unpopular war, was limited to similar public forums. "Johnson knew he was a prisoner in the White House . . . but Bush has no idea."[26]

In many ways, this sort of unquestioning religious idealism is far more disturbing than the possibility that Bush is simply a hypocrite. Indeed, it would be more comforting to think that the president is just a liar—for at least then he might have some sense of the distinction between truth and falsehood, reality and political spin. Instead, the more unsettling possibility is that Bush has a truly messianic faith in the "reality" that his spin machine has created, that he has no interest in even considering the idea that he might be wrong. As Hersh concludes, "There are many who believe that Bush is a liar, a President who knowingly and deliberately twists facts for political gain. But lying would indicate an understanding of what is desired, what is possible, and how best to get there. A more plausible explanation is that words have no meaning for this president beyond the immediate moment, and so he believes that his mere utterance of the phrases makes them real. It is a terrifying possibility."[27]

However, as "surreal" and postmodern as this sort of idealism might seem, it is really not all that new as an historical phenomenon. As Hannah Arendt pointed out a half-century ago in her classic study on totalitarianism, this sort of arrogant belief in one's own omnipotence and reality-creating power is characteristic of most totalitarian regimes:

> Their moral cynicism, their belief that everything is permitted, rests on the solid conviction that everything is possible. It is true that these men, few in number, are not easily caught in their own specific lies . . . yet they too are deceived, deceived by their impudent conceited idea that everything can be done and their contemptuous conviction that everything that exists is merely a temporary obstacle that superior organization will certainly destroy.[28]

The current administration is in many ways a disturbing embodiment of Arendt's description of earlier twentieth-century regimes. In the Bush White

House, obsessive secrecy and unaccountable lies have been combined with a kind of messianic faith in its own power not just to shape public perception but to remake reality itself.

Propaganda, American Style: Media Consolidation and the Society of the Spectacle

As far as I'm concerned, we do not need to find any weapons of mass destruction to justify this war. . . . Mr. Bush doesn't owe the world any explanation for missing chemical weapons (even if it turns out the White House hyped this issue).

—Thomas Friedman, *New York Times*

There have been times, living in America of late, when it seemed I was back in the Communist Moscow I left a dozen years ago. Switch to cable TV and reporters breathlessly relay the latest wisdom from the usual unnamed "senior administration officials." . . . Everyone, it seems, is on-side and on-message. Just like it used to be when the hammer and sickle flew over the Kremlin.

—Robert Cornwell, *Independent*

While Rove, Lunz, Sforza, and other spin masters have worked hard to project the Bush image as man of faith and integrity, the mainstream media have largely played into and helped broadcast that image to a mass audience of American viewers. And they have also remained stunningly uncritical of the administration's obsessive secrecy and repeated lies. Already in 1988, media critics such as W. Lance Bennett had warned that the U.S. media were moving toward a kind of "propaganda American style," with the public fed simple, stereotypical ideas from politicians via an uncritical television and newspaper media.[29] With the Bush administration, as Robert Cornwell of *The Independent* observed, that sort of American-style propaganda and uncritical media have become almost taken for granted.[30]

Many observers, for example, have pointed out the bizarre irony that the media seemed eager to attack President Clinton relentlessly for his paltry sex scandals, even as they largely ignored Bush's unprecedented history of secrecy and dissimulation. As Molly Ivins comments,

One of the oddest aspects of the Bush presidency has been how reluctant journalists are to report that Bush lies. Reporters who jumped on Bill Clinton for disingenuous hair-splitting and piled on Al Gore for harmless exaggerations have given George W. Bush pass after pass after pass.[31]

One of the most astonishing "passes" that the media have given Bush is their inability to point out the fact that he repeatedly misled both Congress and the American people about Iraq's alleged WMD and ties to Al Qaeda. As Thomas Friedman put it in *The New York Times*, echoing Bush's own words, the president has "no need for explanation" when it comes to the Iraq war and the nonexistence of Saddam's WMD.[32] On the contrary, at least until relatively recently, the mainstream media have tended to emphasize and promote the idea that Bush is a man of strong moral conviction, driven more by his sincere religious faith than by material interests. As Peter Jennings said of Bush's address at the UN in September 2002, in which the president made a strong case for war: "Great speech on moral clarity, the kind we've come to expect from President Bush. The difference between good and evil, them and us. And as he said at one point, liberty for the Iraqi people is a great moral cause."[33]

But the full magnitude of the media's general failure to interrogate Bush's lies about Iraq really hit home to me in May 2005, as I listened in astonishment to the coverage of the "Downing Street Minutes." As we saw in chapter 2, these documents were the most blatant of the various "smoking guns" showing that the Bush administration had deceived Congress and the American public into an unjust and illegal invasion of Iraq. The media response to these revelations, however, was simply astonishing: after "six weeks in the political wilderness,"[34] the Downing Street Minutes slowly made their way into the consciousness of the mainstream media, but only with a general tone of "so what else is new?" As Dan Froomkin of the *Washington Post* put it, "Well, in some ways it's old news, isn't it?"[35] Instead, most mainstream outlets engaged in a bizarre sort of metacommentary, circling vaguely around the question of why it was that the media had largely ignored this shocking revelation.[36] But the Downing Street Minutes are only one example of a much larger, more disturbing phenomenon—a strange sort of apathy and cynicism on the part of the media and the American public alike, which seems to take this generalized secrecy for granted without critical reflection.

After the failure to investigate Bush's justification for the Iraq war, one of the most stunning examples of media silence was their almost complete failure to look into the widespread complaints of voting problems in the 2004 election. This was particularly true in the case of Ohio, my home state, where I personally witnessed massive evidence of extremely disturbing voting irregularities that consistently affected minority voters. The extensive report by Rep. John Conyers, "What Went Wrong in Ohio," found a vast array of problems from start to finish of the voting process: there were misallocations of voting machines, which led to unprecedented long lines primarily in minority and Democratic areas; restrictions of provisional ballots that resulted in the disenfranchisement of tens if not hundreds of thousands of voters, again predominantly minority voters; rejection of registration applications simply

because they were on the wrong weight paper; intimidation of primarily minority voters; use of Republican Party "challengers" in largely minority and
Democratic areas; a bizarre array of unexplained anomalies and irregularities
on voting day throughout the state that were never accounted for (such as
ninety-three thousand spoiled ballots showing no vote for president; at least
twenty-five machines transferring an unknown number of votes from Kerry
to Bush; a whole county, Warren, locking out observers from the vote count
based on a false claim that the FBI had warned of a "terrorist threat"; counties
showing significantly more votes than voters in their precincts; and finally,
striking discrepancies between exit polls and the official vote counts, which
happened to be consistently in Bush's favor.[37] Perhaps the most disturbing
thing about these voting "irregularities" is that they disproportionately affected minority voters, mainly African Americans, who vote overwhelmingly
Democratic. The 2005 Democratic National Committee report, *Democracy at
Risk*, found that *twice as many* African Americans in Ohio reported problems
at the polls as whites, and African Americans waited an average of *fifty-two
minutes* to vote, as opposed to *eighteen minutes* for whites.[38]

Yet despite this mass of information regarding the severe—and disturbingly
racialized—electoral problems in Ohio and elsewhere, the mainstream media
gave the 2004 election almost zero attention. With the sole exception of
MSNBC's Keith Olbermann, who bravely followed the "conspiracy theories"
of voting fraud for several months after the election, almost no one in the
mainstream media addressed the issue in any serious way. Indeed, although a
reporter from the *Washington Post*—a key part of the alleged "liberal media
bias"—called me for a phone interview on voting problems in Ohio, neither
he nor any other reporter from any major paper ever bothered to make the
short trip out to do serious investigative reporting on the subject. This absence of media attention is all the more incredible when we consider the fact
that we now know that a full and fair count in the 2000 election, following the
requirements of Florida's own state constitution, would have resulted in Gore,
not Bush, being elected the forty-third president of the United States (and we
also know that subsequent investigations revealed widespread disenfranchisement of Florida voters during that election, particularly of African American
voters).[39]

This unwillingness on the part of the media to look critically at the Bush
administration is the result of several factors. The first is simply the administration's intense secrecy and unwillingness to share information with the
press, as the job of the press secretary is now largely simply to discourage and
shut out the media. As Seymour Hersh comments, "This is scary. I have never
had less of a pulse" of what's going on in government.[40] A second factor, however, is a real timidity on the part of the media and a paralyzing fear of ap-

pearing unpatriotic or "liberally biased." Above all, following the shock wake of 9/11, a new spirit of hyperpatriotic civil religiosity spread throughout the country, including the media, in which criticism of the president was tantamount to sacrilege. As Dan Rather put it, "there was a time in South Africa that people would put flaming tires around the people's necks if they dissented. . . . [T]he fear is that you will be 'necklaced' here, you will have a flaming tire of lack of patriotism put around your neck. Now it is that fear that keeps journalists from asking the toughest of tough questions." He went on to suggest that this is in part a form of "self-censorship": "One finds oneself saying: I know the right question, but you know what? This is not exactly the right time to ask it."[41] Mr. Rather, of course, would suffer directly from the sin of criticizing the administration, losing his job because of one minor error in his report on Bush's Vietnam service.

The result of all this is that the media are largely afraid to criticize the president and instead largely reinforce his image of morality, integrity, and faith. As Stacks concludes:

> This constant quest for a large audience breeds a real timidity on the part of . . . the press, even in the face of a virtual information lockout by the Bush administration. Bush is popular, or least has been since September 11, and the press is following the polls. It voiced only mild criticism of the president's policies, even as he prepared a military adventure unlike any in the nation's history.[42]

However, the final and perhaps most important factor in the silencing of the media has been the rapid and dramatic process of corporate consolidation. Already in 1983, Ben H. Bagdikian had raised alarms about the disturbing level of media consolidation, warning that fifty corporations then dominated most of the mass media. Twenty years later, his numbers look practically utopian when compared to our own generation, where basically five or six conglomerates now control most of the mass media: Time Warner, Disney, Bertelsmann, Fox, Viacom, and General Electric.[43] Increasingly, then, the media are driven less by the ideal of providing serious, critical investigation to inform the public than by the same interest that drives every other corporate power—namely, profit. And, today, profit is best secured by providing comforting, entertaining, and distracting images that keep viewers' short attentions and continue to sell products. In the words of Phil Donahue, the former host of MSNBC's highest-rated show who was fired by the network in 2003 for bringing on antiwar voices, "We have more [TV] outlets now, but most of them sell the Bowflex machine. The rest of them are Jesus and jewelry. There really isn't diversity in the media anymore. Dissent? Forget about it."[44]

In many ways, the media are arguably doing far more to hurt than help American citizens—distracting and confusing them by repeating the same partisan spin projected by the politicians, rather than engaging in serious critical discourse about politics. As Jon Stewart put it in his exchange with Tucker Carlson on CNN's *Crossfire*, "See, the thing is, we need your help. Right now, you're helping the politicians and the corporations. . . . You're part of their strategies. You are partisan, what do you call it, hacks."[45] Increasingly, the media today have shifted largely away from political substance and toward political theater. It so happens, however, that this sort of distracting, vapid, uncritical news fits very well with the Bush administration's agenda, which is to keep its activities secret, unexamined, and outside of serious public debate. As Hacker and Pierson comment, "Since the news media are in the entertainment business, the temptation to cover government like sports is hard to avoid. Yet it dovetails perfectly with the efforts of political elites to structure policymaking in ways that shed as little light as possible on their most extreme initiatives."[46] Going still further, however, it also seems clear that the Bush administration is *the most blatantly procorporate administration we've ever had,* consistently favoring tax cuts, economic policies, and subsidies that favor corporate interests over public interests. Thus, it is no surprise that a corporate-controlled media would be disinclined to criticize such an administration.

In direct contradiction to the right-wing complaints about a "liberal bias in the media," moreover, virtually all credible media analysts conclude that the opposite is in fact the case. According to the national media watch group, Fairness and Accuracy in Reporting (FAIR), the mainstream media have shown a significant conservative and right-wing bias for at least the past decade. In 1997, FAIR found that the top two conservative think tanks, Heritage Foundation and the American Enterprise Institute, were cited 1,813 and 1,323 times, respectively, as opposed to the top two progressive think tanks, the Urban Institute and the Economic Policy Institute, which were cited only 610 and 576 times.[47] This bias has remained consistent for the past nine years. A 2005 report by FAIR, which ranked think tanks by their right, center, and left orientations, found that conservative or right-leaning think tanks received 50 percent of media citations, centrists received 33 percent of citations, and left-leaning or progressives received a mere 16 percent. That same report also noted that media outlets—including ostensibly "liberal" outlets—consistently cite Republicans more often than Democrats, by ratios ranging from three to two on National Public Radio, to three to one on nightly network news, to a staggering five to one on Fox News's *Special Report.* In sum, the complaints about a "liberal bias" in the media are not only groundless but an absurd inversion of the factual evidence.[48]

The intensive corporate consolidation becomes even more disturbing when we realize that most of these companies have their tentacles in many other corporate and military interests. Thus General Electric (GE), the owner of

NBC, CBN, MSNBC, Bravo, Universal Pictures, and many other outlets, also happens to be a major weapons manufacturer. It seems difficult to believe that the representation of a U.S. war on these stations would be unbiased. On the contrary, as Amy and David Goodman point out in their discussion of media coverage during the first Gulf War, "GE made most of the parts for many of the weapons in the Persian Gulf War. It was no surprise, then, that much of the coverage on those networks looked like a military hardware show." In the case of the current U.S. invasion of Iraq, meanwhile, the corporate media has become more or less a kind of "conveyor-belt for the government's lies."[49]

At this point, then, the hyperreality of the Bush administration begins to intersect with, and at times become indistinguishable from, the hyperreal world projected by the corporate media. As Alterman suggests, the combined forces of audience- and sponsor-driven corporate media and the administration's obsessive secrecy have created an increasingly superficial, vapid, and almost "virtual" brand of journalism—a form of news in which "reality" and "facts" are nowhere near as important as audience numbers and advertiser dollars:

> The current historical moment in journalism is hardly a happy one. . . . Corporate conglomerates increasingly view journalism as "soft ware" valuable only insofar as it contributes to the bottom line. In the mad pursuit for audience and advertisers, the quality of the news itself becomes degraded. . . . Meanwhile, they face an administration with a commitment to secrecy unmatched in modern American history.[50]

At the same time, however, these corporate powers have also exerted a certain degree of active pressure to *silence* any serious criticism of the administration. Dan Rather's case was the most obvious but by no means the only one. In an interview with C-SPAN in 2006, Keith Olbermann said quite frankly that his corporate masters had actively discouraged any negative perspectives on this president: "There are people I know in the hierarchy of NBC, the company, and GE, the company, who do not like to see the current presidential administration criticized at all."[51]

This intense process of media consolidation is indeed a disturbing thing. Most Americans would likely agree that a free press with diverse opinions and perspectives is critical to a free and open democracy; and most historians agree that a restricted and corporate-controlled press has often gone hand in hand with the most repressive and ruthless totalitarian regimes. As Robert F. Kennedy Jr. soberly reminds us, the corporate control of the media was one of the very first things that heralded the rise of fascism in mid-twentieth-century Europe: "the first thing Hitler did was consolidate the media, allowing the big friendly media groups to swallow the little guys."[52] When that sort of media consolidation is combined with the intense secrecy that we see in the Bush administration, the American public is almost completely shut out of the political process, left with no means to make informed decisions; democracy itself, meanwhile, is in serious danger of being reduced to a kind of reality-TV-show parody of itself, a simulacrum of actual political freedom.

A Fair and Balanced Look at the Propaganda: The Fox Media Empire

> For me, the news that really rocks
> Confirms my beliefs held by our flocks.
> My mind remains quite closed, with locks.
> So set the channel, please, to Fox.
>
> —Calvin Trillin, "On the Revelation that Dick Cheney requires the Television
>   to be Pre-set to Fox News in Any Hotel Room He Is about to Occupy"

One of the most important—and blatantly biased—media conglomerates for the dissemination of the Bush administration's desired image has been the Fox media empire, owned by Rupert Murdoch. With the advent of Fox, we might say, we have fully entered Baudrillard's realm of hyperreality, in which the line between news and fiction, information and propaganda, begins to dissolve altogether: "the TV newscast . . . creates the news if only to be able to narrate it,"[53] as the era of manufacturing consent gives way to the era of manufacturing news. The kind of news Fox manufactures, moreover, is closely tied to the image this administration would like to project.

Murdoch and the neoconservatives share many common political interests and have a relationship going back to the 1990s. Through the vast network of Fox media outlets in television, magazines, and books, neoconservative ideas and their version of issues such as Iraq and Al Qaeda have been able to reach a remarkably large audience. As Halper and Clarke observe, "With Murdoch's financial assistance, the modern neo-conservative voice came to be heard in magazines, newspapers and TV news networks. . . . As a neo-conservative ally, projecting and conveying its perspectives through the lens of US media, [Murdoch] added a critical dimension to the neo-conservative effort."[54] The neoconservative influence is particularly clear in the case of the Fox News Channel, whose brand of ratings-driven, right-leaning journalism fits nicely with the neoconservatives' foreign policies. Indeed, "when the neo-conservatives advanced their carefully crafted political discourse, designed to meld the War on Terrorism into a case for war against Iraq, this media culture was invaluable."[55] At one point during the Iraq war, William Kristol was even moved to thank Fox News and Murdoch personally for their support of Bush's foreign policies: "Many people at Fox news have been supportive of Bush's foreign policy. They deserve a bit of mention. And Murdoch personally."[56]

It would seem there was good reason for Kristol and the neoconservatives to be grateful to Fox. According to a study done by the Program on International Policy Attitudes between January and September 2003, Americans who relied on Fox News as their main source of information tended to have a disturbing number of misperceptions about Iraq and the war on terror. Fox viewers were far more likely than viewers of any other news source to believe that Saddam had ties to Al Qaeda and that the United States had in fact found WMD in Iraq:

> In testing the frequency of three specific mistaken impressions—that evidence of links between Iraq and al Qaeda had been found, that weapons of mass destruction had been discovered in Iraq, and that world public opinion approved of America's going to war—results showed that Fox News watchers were three times more likely to hold all three. The audiences of NPR/PBS, however, consistently demonstrated a majority who did not hold any of the three views. Some 80 percent of Fox viewers . . . held one or more of the three perceptions.[57]

During the 2004 election campaign, Fox's brand of fabricated news was at times directly used as a form of political advertising and propaganda for the Republican Party. The documentary *Outfoxed*, in fact, showed that the Fox News director regularly hands down instructions on how to spin the news in a Republican direction to his editors and reporters. One such memo advised reporters how to cover Mr. Bush, suggesting that his "political courage and tactical cunning are worth noting in our reporting throughout the day," while another suggested that John Kerry was "starting to feel the heat for his flip-flopping voting record."[58]

In sum, despite its claim to represent a "fair and balanced look at the news," Fox News has consistently and shamelessly pushed such an obviously right-wing and pro-Bush agenda as to make it more or less a branch of the Republican Party. Indeed, Bill O'Reilly's "no spin zone" and Fox's "fair and balanced" news disseminate information to the American public about as honestly as Pravda (which means "truth" in Russian) did in the Soviet Union. As Mark Crispin Miller observes, in the dream world of Fox News, "deficits don't matter, CO_2 is not a pollutant, we're making good progress in Iraq, and war is peace . . . and if you see things differently, you are the enemy."[59] Thus comedian Jon Stewart was moved to compare Fox's brand of manufactured journalism to his own *Daily Show*, calling it "that *other* fake news show."

Fox is not, of course, the only media conglomerate sympathetic to neoconservative views. In addition, there is the omnipresent Clear Channel network, the largest radio owner in the country, with over 1,200 stations, whose CEO contributed hundreds of thousands of dollars to Bush's election campaign (in fact, Clear Channel even organized its own pro-war "rallies for America" to counter the anti–Iraq war protests, and then used its radio stations to cover the events as if they were "breaking news").[60] And then there are also conservative talk radio icons such as the omnipresent Rush Limbaugh and Christian televangelists such as Robertson and Falwell, who help promote a radically far-right agenda to a massive audience of millions of AM radio listeners and Christian TV viewers. As Halper and Clarke conclude, "the cable networks, the conservative talk radio shows, and the conservative print outlets were all in place to carry the abstract war into the governing philosophy of American foreign policy by inundating people with the discursive reality created by neoconservatives."[61]

The disturbing fact, however, is that this "discursive reality" constructed by the neoconservatives bears less and less resemblance to the "empirical reality" that the rest of us are now observing in Iraq and here at home. Indeed, the on-the-ground evidence makes the neoconservative ideal seem more and more like a kind of bizarre board-game fantasy than any sort of realistic policy that could be implemented in the mortal human realm. And yet, through the magic of TV and radio, through the magic of advertising and digital simulation, this ideological dream was able to reach a vast audience of consumers, while at the same time persuading them that this was a necessary part of America's divine mission in the world.

Through the Looking Glass: The Fusion of Political, Corporate, and Media Power

> This War wasn't political at all, the politics all theatre, all just to keep the people distracted. . . . [S]ecretly, it was being dictated instead by the needs of technology.
>
> —Thomas Pynchon, *Gravity's Rainbow*

In the past five years, the fictional reality projected by the Bush administration and the fictional reality projected by the corporate media have intersected increasingly and at times have become almost indistinguishable. As we saw in chapter 1, the Bush administration represents a disturbing fusion of religious authority and political power, with a very troubling dissolution of the boundaries between church and state. At the same time, however, it also represents a disturbing fusion of other sorts of power—a consolidation of political, corporate, and media power that is unprecedented in U.S. history. With the rise of the Bush II administration, our political leaders are now largely former CEOs (many from the energy industries) such as Cheney, Rumsfeld, Rice, and Bush himself, as corporate power and political power have been increasingly fused into one. At the same time, with the administration's staged public performances, fake news releases, and media displays such as Fox News, politics and media also seem increasingly indistinguishable. As Arundhati Roy suggests, it is perhaps a mistake to think that the corporate media simply "support" or "echo" the administration's political agenda; increasingly, the two are one and the same, both part of the same military-industrial-corporate complex: "It is the nexus, the confluence, the convergence, the union, the chosen medium of those who have power and money. . . . This mutual dependence spawns a sort of corporate nationalism. . . . It has become the unwavering anthem of the mass media."[62] Indeed, even war itself becomes a bizarre melding of fake news, propaganda, and entertainment, as staged and scripted as everything else in this administration (with the sole exception of the dead bodies that are never actually seen on TV): "As America's show business gets more and more violent and war-like, and America's war gets more and more like show business, some interesting cross-overs are taking place. The designer who built the $250,000 set in Qatar from which General Tommy Franks stage-managed news coverage of Operation Shock and Awe also built sets for Disney, MGM, and 'Good Morning America.'"[63]

Mr. Bush himself lies at the key intersection of these various corporate, political, religious, and media interests. In many ways, George W. does seem a kind of vacuous "media construction," a man with little going on in his own head, who has been constructed, digitally enhanced, and deployed by various others working off camera and behind the scenes. What makes Bush so effective in conjoining these overlapping interests is precisely his own status as a kind of "floating signifier"—or perhaps what Roland Barthes calls a "degree zero signifier"[64]—that is, a Rorschach blot that can be interpreted and manipulated by various factions for their own political interests. Again, religion and secrecy are the keys to Bush's "floating signification." The constantly projected image of Bush's piety is a very powerful way to persuade millions of Americans, as we see in his earnestly praying face on the cover of *Newsweek*'s best-selling "Bush and God" issue in 2003; and yet the true content of Mr. Bush's faith—like everything else about his administration—remains hidden, unknown, unverifiable, and undisclosed, a degree zero signifier that could mean almost anything to anyone.

In Bush's "through the looking glass" world, the "reality" and "facts" that the rest of us care about are not only unimportant; they seem to be an annoyance getting in the way of the hyperreal world the Bush administration wants to create for us instead. As Richard Kim put it, "Watching television momentarily transports us through the looking glass into a warped, alternate reality; the Bush Administration would have us live there."[65] Indeed, as we stagger through Bush's second term, it seems increasingly clear that this administration does not even make much of an effort to tell us the truth, but rather seems to believe that a lie told over and over again will somehow magically become reality. Michael Kinsley of *Slate.com* sums this up rather well:

> Bush II administration lies are often so laughably obvious that you wonder why they bother. Until you realize: They haven't bothered. If telling the truth was less bother, they'd do that, too. The characteristic Bush II form of dishonesty is to construct an alternative reality on some topic and to regard anyone who objects to it as a sniveling dweeb obsessed with "nuance," which the president . . . has more important things to do than worry about.[66]

When we read statements by senior White House aides who claim the imperial power to "create their own reality," we really have to wonder if we haven't already crossed over into a kind of Matrix-like simulation or Baudrillardian hyperreality. As Baudrillard argues, today's media-dominated society has blurred and ultimately lost the distinction between the reality and image, material fact and digital simulation: "boundaries between information and entertainment, images and politics, implode. . . . TV news and documentary assume more and more the form of entertainment. . . . [I]n political campaigns . . . image is more important than substance, and political campaigns become increasingly dependent on media advisors, public relations experts, and pollsters who have transformed politics into image contests."[67] Today, the simulated image no longer covers over some reality or truth hidden beneath its representation. Rather, the simulated image now serves to conceal the *real secret*, which is the far more disturbing fact that *there no longer is any reality or truth beneath the simulated image*: "The transition from signs which dissimulate something to signs which dissimulate that there is nothing marks the decisive turning point. The first implies a theology of truth and secrecy. . . . The second inaugurates an age of simulacra and simulation, in which there is no longer any God to recognize his own, nor any last judgment to separate true from false, the real from its artificial resurrection."[68] In other words, the spin, the media hype, the digitally enhanced images begin to surpass and replace reality itself. "Truth" becomes a naïve idea, as "quaint" and outdated as the Geneva Conventions, as we are left with just the tantalizing aura of power that radiates from the endless deceptions and religious displays projected on the screen.

None of this, of course, bodes well for a democracy. Indeed, it is catastrophic for any model of democracy based on open, public debate and rational critique, all of which seems naïve and romantic in this new post-truth, post-real form of politics. It is difficult to imagine a healthy democracy in which political leaders are disseminating a largely hyperreal version of events while the corporate-controlled media are not only happily ignoring but actively complicit in that hyperreality. But what is perhaps most distressing—and yet all too predictable given this situation—is that the American public seems either unaware or uninterested in any of this. As senior White House correspondent Helen Thomas lamented in 2005, following the release of the Downing Street Minutes, Americans no longer even seem to care about the credibility or accountability of their leaders: "I am not surprised at the duplicity. But I am astonished at the acceptance of this deception by voters."[69]

Almost two hundred years ago, James Madison warned that a society without access to reliable information about the doings of its government was, at best, an absurdity and, at worst, a recipe for tyranny: "A popular government without popular information or the means of acquiring it is but a prologue to a farce or a tragedy or perhaps both."[70] More recently, critics such as David Brock have suggested that the right-wing manipulation of news and information is an explicit attempt to undermine one of the basic pillars of our democratic system; indeed, "The conscious effort by the right wing to misinform the American citizenry—to collapse the distinction between journalism and propaganda—is thus an assault on democracy itself."[71] Indeed, it has far less in common with democracy than with totalitarianism (or perhaps the "necessary dictatorship" imagined by Ledeen).

As we have seen throughout this book, the control of power always tends to rely upon the control of knowledge, and the control of the media as public disseminator of knowledge is therefore critical to the monopolization of power. The rapid consolidation of the media in the hands of a few very large companies is therefore an extremely unsettling trend. But this trend is all the more frightening when combined with an administration that is not only obsessively secretive but that also has an unshakable faith in its own divinely appointed mission, one that tolerates no dissident voices at its fake town-hall meetings, but demands unquestioning belief in its own ability to create reality.

This would appear to be the fulfillment, and perhaps the most absurd exaggeration, of what Madison had warned us of two centuries ago: a tragic farce, but one with catastrophic consequences.

Notes

1. Howard Fineman, "Bush and God," *Newsweek*, March 10, 2003, 25.

2. Eric Alterman, *When Presidents Lie: A History of Official Deception and Its Consequences* (New York: Viking, 2004), 303.

3. Alterman, *When Presidents Lie*, 304; see Dana Milbank, "For Bush, Facts Are Malleable," *Washington Post*, October 22, 2002.

4. Paul Krugman, "The War in Iraq and the American Economy." Lecture at the University of California, Berkeley, September 26, 2003, at www.berkeley.edu/news/media/releases/2003/09/26_krugman.shtml.

5. Jean Baudrillard, *Simulacra and Simulations* (Ann Arbor: University of Michigan Press, 1994). As Steven Best and Douglas Kellner explain, "Hyperreality points to a blurring of distinctions between the real and the unreal in which the prefix 'hyper' signifies more real than real whereby the real is produced according to a model. . . . The hyperreal . . . is a condition whereby models replace the real, as exemplified in such phenomena as the ideal home in women's magazines, ideal as sex as portrayed in sex manuals. . . . [T]he model becomes a determinant of the real, and the boundary between hyperreality and everyday life is erased. . . . [S]imulations come to constitute reality itself." Best and Kellner, *Postmodern Theory: Critical Interrogations* (New York: Guilford, 1991), 119–120.

6. Jean Baudrillard, *Seduction*, in *Jean Baudrillard: Selected Writings*, ed. Mark Poster (Stanford, CA: Stanford University Press, 1988), 158.

7. George W. Bush to Roland Betts, in J. H. Hatfield, *Fortunate Son: George W. Bush and the Making of an American President* (New York: Soft Skull, 2002), 95.

8. Irving Kristol, *Neoconservatism: The Autobiography of an Idea* (New York: Free Press, 1995), 233.

9. James Moore and Wayne Slater, *Bush's Brain: How Karl Rove Made George W. Bush Presidential* (Hoboken, NJ: Wiley & Sons, 2003), 12.

10. Craig Unger, *House of Bush, House of Saud: The Secret Relationship between the World's Two Most Powerful Dynasties* (New York: Scribner, 2004), 192.

11. As Tim Grieve comments, "From the beginning, the presidential-getaway-as-ranch has been a construct, a way to make a millionaire from Yale look like some kind of workaday cowpoke." Grieve, "We're Not Playing Cowboy Anymore," *Slate.com*, August 17, 2005, at www.salon.com/politics/war_room/?blog=/politics/war_room/2005/08/17/ranch/index.html.

12. Arundhati Roy, *An Ordinary Person's Guide to Empire* (Cambridge, MA: South End, 2004), 148–149. See Paul Krugman, "Man on Horseback," *New York Times*, May 6, 2003, A31.

13. Poster, introduction to *Baudrillard*, 6. On the hyperreality of the first Gulf war, see Jean Baudrillard, *The Gulf War Did Not Take Place* (Bloomington: Indian University Press, 1995).

14. John Dean, *Worse Than Watergate: The Secret Presidency of George W. Bush* (New York: Little, Brown, 2004), 73. See Bob Davis, "Presidential Perceptions," *Wall Street Journal*, February 9, 2001, A12.

15. Elisabeth Bumiller, "Keepers of Bush Image Lift Stagecraft to New Heights," *New York Times*, May 16, 2003, at www.nytimes.com.

16. "President Participates in Conversation on Social Security Reform," January 11, 2005, at www.whitehouse.gov/news/releases/2005/01/20050111-4.html.

17. Chris Suellentrop, "One Nation under Bush," *Slate.com*, October 29, 2004, at www.slate.com/id/2108852; Dana Milbank, "Republicans Sign along the Dotted Line," *Washington Post*, August 1, 2004, A5.

18. Howard Pankratz, "Bush Staffers Ejected 3 at Speech," *Denver Post*, March 20, 2006, at www.denverpost.com/news/ci_3619779.

19. "Bush Admin. Spent over $1.6 Billion on Advertising and P.R. since 2003, GAO Finds," *RawStory*, February 13, 2006, at rawstory.com/news/2005/Bush_Admin._spent_over_1.6_Billion_0213.html.

20. Dean, *Worse Than Watergate*, 73n. See Ron Suskind, *The Price of Loyalty: George W. Bush, the White House, and the Education of Paul O'Neill* (New York: Simon & Schuster, 2003), 147, 160.

21. Ron Suskind, "Faith, Certainty and the Presidency of George W. Bush," *New York Times Magazine*, October 17, 2004, at www.nytimes.com.

22. Tom Tomorrow, "The Republican Matrix," *workingforchange*, at www.working forchange.com/comic.cfm?itemid=15021.

23. Alterman, *When Presidents Lie*, 303.

24. Joe Klein, "Bush's Broken Political Antenna," *Time Online Edition*, February 26, 2006, at www.time.com/time/columnist/klein/article/0,9565,1167728,00.html.

25. Matt Taibbi, "The Magical Victory Tour," *Rolling Stone*, December 15, 2005, 40, 42. "Obey Your Thirst" is the advertising slogan for Sprite soft drinks.

26. Seymour Hersh, "Up in the Air," *New Yorker*, December 5, 2005, at www.newyorker.com/fact/content/articles/051205fa_fact.

27. Seymour Hersh, *Chain of Command: The Road from 9/11 to Abu Ghraib* (New York: HarperCollins, 2004), 367.

28. Hannah Arendt, *Totalitarianism: Part Three of the Origins of Totalitarianism* (New York: Harcourt Brace, 1985), 85.

29. W. Lance Bennett, *News: The Politics of Illusion* (New York: Longman, 1988), 176.

30. Robert Cornwell, "Don't Believe All the Patriotic Fire on American TV," *Independent*, April 23, 2003.

31. Molly Ivins, *The Lies of George W. Bush*, at www.randomhouse.com/acmart/catalog/display.pperl?isbn=9781400050673.

32. Thomas Friedman, "The Meaning of a Skull," *New York Times*, April 27, 2003, section 4, 13.

33. Peter Jennings, ABC News, September 12, 2002, *Media Research Center*, at www.mrc.org/cyberalerts/2002/cyb20020913.asp.

34. Dan Froomkin, "The Memo Comes in from the Cold," *Washington Post*, June 8, 2005, at www.washingtonpost.com/wp-dyn/content/blog/2005/06/08/BL2005060801519_pf.html.

35. Dan Froomkin, "White House Talk," *WashingtonPost.com*, May 4, 2005, at www.washingtonpost.com/wp-dyn/content/discussion/2005/04/28/DI2005042800981.html.

36. See Mark Memmot, "Downing Street Memo Gets Fresh Attention," *USA Today*, June 8, 2005, 8A; Matthew Clark, "Why Has 'Downing Street Memo' Story Been a 'Dud' in US?" *Christian Science Monitor*, May 17, 2005, at www.csmonitor.com/2005/0517/dailyUpdate.html.

37. Anita Miller, ed., *What Went Wrong in Ohio: The Conyers Report on the 2004 Presidential Election* (Chicago: Academy Chicago, 2005), 1–7. See Mark Crispin Miller, *Fooled Again: How the Right Stole the 2004 Election and Why They'll Steal the Next One Too (Unless We Stop Them)* (New York: Basic, 2005); Robert F. Kennedy Jr., "Was the 2004 Election Stolen?" *Rolling Stone*, June 2006, at www.rollingstone.com/news/story/10432334/was_the_2004_election_stolen.

38. Democratic National Committee, *Democracy at Risk: The 2004 Election in Ohio*, June 2005, at www.democrats.org/a/2005/06/democracy_at_ri.php.

39. Hendrick Hertzberg, "Recounted Out," *New Yorker,* December 24, 2001; U.S. Commission on Civil Rights, *Voting Irregularities in Florida during the 2000 Presidential Election* (June 2001); Conyers, *What Went Wrong in Ohio,* 15; Kennedy, "Was the 2004 Election Stolen?"

40. Seymour Hersh, quoted in John F. Stacks, "Watchdogs on a Leash: Closing Doors on the Media," in *The War on Our Freedoms: Civil Liberties in an Age of Terrorism,* ed. Richard C. Leone and Greg Anrig Jr. (New York: Public Affairs, 2003), 240–241.

41. "Veteran CBS News Anchor Dan Rather Speaks Out," *BBC News,* May 15, 2002, at www.bbc.co.uk/pressoffice/pressreleases/stories/2002/05_may/16/dan_rather .shtml. See also David Brock, *The Republican Noise Machine: Right-Wing Media and How It Corrupts Democracy* (New York: Three Rivers, 2005), 14.

42. Stacks, "Watchdogs on a Leash," 250.

43. Ben H. Bagdikian, *The Media Monopoly* (Boston: Beacon, 2000). See Bagdikian, *The New Media Monopoly* (Boston: Beacon, 2004); Noam Chomsky, *Media Control: The Spectacular Achievements of Propaganda* (New York: Seven Stories, 2002).

44. Amy Goodman and David Goodman, "Why Media Ownership Matters," *Seattle Times,* April 3, 2005, at seattletimes.nwsource.com.

45. *CNN Crossfire,* October 15, 2004, at transcripts.cnn.com/TRANSCRIPTS/0410/ 15/cf.01.html.

46. Jacob S. Hacker and Paul Pierson, *Off Center: The Republican Revolution and the Erosion of American Democracy* (New Haven: Yale University Press, 2005), 178.

47. Brock, *Republican Noise Machine,* 53.

48. Michael Dolny, "Right, Center Think Tanks Still Most Quoted: Study of Cites Debunks 'Liberal Media' Claims," *Fairness and Accuracy in Reporting* (May/June 2005), at www.fair.org/index.php?page=2534.

49. Goodman and Goodman," Why Media Ownership Matters."

50. Eric Alterman, *What Liberal Media? The Truth about Bias and the News* (New York: Basic, 2003), 262.

51. Lloyd Grove, "Furious George Hits Gutless Dems," *New York Daily News,* March 13, 2006, at www.nydailynews.com/news/gossip/story/399189p-338232c.html.

52. Robert F. Kennedy Jr., speech in Toronto, June 21, 2003, *Lake Ontario Keeper,* August 1, 2003, at www.greenpartysask.ca.

53. Poster, introduction to *Baudrillard,* 6.

54. Stefan Halper and Jonathan Clarke, *America Alone: The Neo-Conservatives and the Global Order* (New York: Cambridge University Press, 2004), 187. See Brock, *Republican Noise Machine,* 171–176.

55. Halper and Clarke, *America Alone,* 186.

56. Joe Hagan, "Spawned in New York," *New York Observer,* April 28, 2003, 6.

57. Halper and Clarke, *America Alone,* 193, summarizing the survey "Misperceptions: The Media and the Iraq War," conducted by the Program on International Policy Attitudes and Knowledge Networks Poll, October 2, 2003.

58. Brock, *Republican Noise Machine,* 391.

59. Mark Crispin Miller, *Cruel and Unusual: Bush/Cheney's New World Order* (New York: Norton, 2004), 295.

60. Roy, *An Ordinary Person's Guide*, 156–157. See Douglas Jehl, "Across Country, Thousands Gather to Back US Troops and Policy," *New York Times*, 24 March, 2003, B15.

61. Halper and Clarke, *America Alone*, 199.

62. Roy, *An Ordinary Person's Guide*, 92.

63. Roy, *An Ordinary Person's Guide*, 157. See Frank Rich, "Iraq around the Clock," *New York Times*, March 30, 2003, section 2, 1.

64. Roland Barthes, *Writing Degree Zero* (New York: Hill & Wang, 1977).

65. Richard Kim, "Pop Torture," *Nation*, December 26, 2005, at www.thenation .com/doc/20051226/kim.

66. Michael Kinsley, "Lying in Style," *Slate.com*, April 18, 2002, at www.slate.com.

67. Best and Kellner, *Postmodern Theory*, 120.

68. Jean Baudrillard, *Simulacra and Simulations*, in Poster, ed., *Jean Baudrillard*, 170–171.

69. Matthew Clark, "Why Has 'Downing Street Memo' Been a 'Dud' in US?".

70. James Madison, letter to W. T. Barry, August 4, 1822, *The Writings of James Madison*, ed. Gaillard Hunt (New York: Putnam's Sons, 1910), 9:103.

71. Brock, *Republican Noise Machine*, 11.

6

America Left Behind: Millenarian Dreams and the Sorrows of Empire

"Is [Jesus] gonna kill a bunch of people here, like He is over there?"
"I'm afraid He is. If they're working for the Antichrist, they're in serious trouble."

—Tim LaHaye and Jerry B. Jenkins, *Glorious Appearing: End of Days*

I see things this way: The people who did this act on America . . . are evil people. . . . As a nation of good folk, we're going to hunt them down . . . and we will bring them to justice.

—George W. Bush, September 25, 2001

As a professor of comparative religion and cultural studies, I have long been fascinated by the strange intersections between religion, politics, and popular culture. One of the most striking such intersections occurred to me in the summer of 2004 as I sat down to read the twelfth and last volume of the wildly popular *Left Behind* series, by evangelical preacher Tim LaHaye and novelist Jerry Jenkins (1995–2004). For those who haven't yet had a chance to read any of LaHaye and Jenkins's series, the story is basically an evangelical interpretation of the Book of Revelation set in the context of contemporary global politics: the Rapture has taken place, the Antichrist has taken control of the UN and created a single global economy, and a small group of American-led believers battles the forces of evil in a showdown in the Holy Land. Dubbed by Jerry Falwell "the most influential books since the Bible,"[1] the *Left Behind* novels have sold tens of millions of copies, transmitting a highly conservative and often spectacularly violent interpretation of the Millennium to a massive audience of American readers.

At the same time that I was immersed in this entertaining mixture of Stephen King–esque thrills and evangelical rhetoric, I had also been researching the role of the neoconservatives and their aggressive foreign policy, which formed the basis of chapters 3 and 4 of this book. As we saw in chapter 3, the election of George W. Bush and the confusion following 9/11 allowed a small but radical group of intellectuals to seize the reins of U.S. foreign policy. Led by figures such as Wolfowitz, Cheney, Rumsfeld, Ledeen, and the members of the Project for the New American Century, the neoconservatives have been able to put into effect a long-held plan for asserting a U.S. global hegemony, in large part by dominating the Middle East and its oil resources.

The two narratives that I was reading here—the neoconservatives' aggressive foreign policy, centered on the Middle East, and the evangelical story of the imminent return of Christ in the Holy Land—struck me as weirdly similar and disturbingly parallel. The former openly advocates a "New American Century" and a "benevolent hegemony" of the globe by U.S. power, inaugurated by the invasion of Iraq, while the latter predicts a New Millennium of divine rule ushered in by apocalyptic war, first in Babylon and then in Jerusalem.

I was tempted at first to dismiss the similarity as an amusing but insignificant coincidence. Yet the more I began to examine the neoconservatives' strategies and the ties between Bush and the Christian right, the less this link seemed to be either coincidental or unimportant. I am not, of course, suggesting that there is some kind of conspiratorial plot at work between neoconservative strategists and evangelical writers such as LaHaye, or that the two are somehow working secretly together behind the scenes. Rather, I am suggesting that there is a subtle but powerful "fit," or what Max Weber calls an "elective affinity," between the two that has helped them reinforce one another in very effective ways. The otherwise vacuous figure of George W. Bush represents a crucial link or structural pivot between these two powerful factions, helping to tie them together: Bush represents the neoconservatives' radical foreign policy in a guise that is acceptable to his large base of support in the Christian right, even as he reassures his Christian base that their moral agenda (antiabortion, anti–gay marriage, faith-based initiatives) will be given powerful political support. In Bush, America as the benevolent hegemon of the neoconservatives and the American-led "Tribulation Force" of LaHaye's novels come together in a disturbing, yet surprisingly successful, way.

There is, however, a profound sort of double irony in all of this. For in its aggressive push to spread American-style democracy and free markets to all corners of the globe, the United States risks bankrupting itself with massive debt, deficit spending, and military waste, while at the same time undermining the very civil liberties that it so proudly holds up as beacons of freedom to the rest of the world.

Glorious Appearing, End of Days:
Tim LaHaye and the Council for National Policy

We're in a religious war and we need to aggressively oppose secular humanism; these people are as religiously motivated as we are, and they are filled with the devil.

—Tim LaHaye on Jerry Falwell's show, *Listen America*

In the past two decades, Tim LaHaye has emerged as not only the theological brains behind the best-selling *Left Behind* series, but also as one of the most influential figures in the American Christian right. Indeed, when the Institute for the Study of American Evangelicals decided to name the most influential evangelical leader of the past twenty-five years, they chose not Billy Graham, Pat Robertson, or Jerry Falwell but Tim LaHaye, in large part because of his work in evangelical politics.[2] For LaHaye, Christians today are engaged in a religious war, a war of good versus the evil of secular humanism, which is progressively taking over the world and evacuating society of true Christian teaching. As Amy Frykholm comments in her study of LaHaye's books, "His religious war includes antigay, antiabortion, and antipornography campaigns, as well as campaigns for prayer and creationism in schools. He believes the secularists are in a quest for world domination and that Christians have no choice but to fight back. . . . Rhetoric like LaHaye's divides the nation into two groups—the good and the evil."[3]

Not only is LaHaye an influential preacher and interpreter of prophecy and revelation, but he has also become a remarkably powerful force in domestic and now even international politics through the highly secretive Council for National Policy (CNP), founded in 1981. Though there is some debate as to who the actual founders of the CNP might have been, LaHaye was its first president and is often cited as one of its primary inspirations.[4] Called by some "the most powerful conservative group you've never heard of,"[5] the CNP is a group that is largely unknown to most Americans, and intentionally so. Indeed, one of the cardinal rules of the organization is that "The media should not know when or where we meet or who takes part in our programs, before or after a meeting"; the membership itself is "strictly confidential." As Jeremy Leaming and Rob Boston explain in their report on the CNP, "Guests can attend only with the unanimous approval of the organization's executive committee. The group's leadership is so secretive that members are told not to refer to it by name in email messages. Anyone who breaks the rules can be tossed out."[6] In fact, while claiming tax-exempt status since 1981, the CNP has consistently defied the Internal Revenue Service's requirements for a tax-exempt organization by refusing to provide forums, panels, or lectures that are open to the public. And this secrecy in turn has allowed it to conceal the political power that it has exerted for the past twenty-five years. As Sarah Posner comments, "because CNP has been so successful at maintaining its secrecy—flouting the law for more than two decades—it has managed to obscure the depth of its reach in conservative political organizations, political fundraising, the conservative media, and even the Bush administration itself."[7]

Despite the intense secrecy surrounding the CNP, the secular watchdog group the Institute for First Amendment Studies did obtain the CNP's 1998 membership roster, which gives us a sense of who has been involved with this powerful organization. Indeed, it reads like a who's who of the radical right. The list includes prominent religious leaders such as James Dobson (president of Focus on the Family), Jerry Falwell, Donald Hodel (president of the Christian Coalition), Bob Jones III (president of Bob Jones University), Beverly and Lee LaHaye (wife and son of Tim LaHaye), Pat Robertson, Ralph Reed, and Reconstructionist theologians Gary North and R. J. Rushdoony. But it also includes powerful congressmen and political figures such as Gary Bauer (undersecretary of education and domestic policy advisor for Reagan, member of the PNAC), Edwin Feulner (president of the Heritage Foundation), Senator Jesse Helms, Senator Trent Lott, Edwin Meese III (holder of the Ronald Reagan Chair in Public Policy at the Heritage Foundation), Grover Norquist (president of Americans for Tax Reform), Oliver North, and Paul Weyrich (president of the Free Congress Foundation). And, finally, the list includes powerful corporate leaders and lobbyists such as Howard Ahmanson (millionaire financier and major funder of far-right Christian organizations such as the Discovery Institute and the Chalcedon Foundation), Holland and Jeffrey Coors of the Coors brewing empire, and Richard DeVos, founder of Amway and owner of the National Basketball Association's Orlando Magic. In addition, a few of the more noteworthy former members of the CNP include the stunningly corrupt lobbyist Jack Abramoff and the Pentecostal former attorney general, John Ashcroft.[8]

Speakers at the Council's highly private meetings have included Supreme Court Justice Clarence Thomas, White House counsel Alberto Gonzales, and Timothy Goeglein, deputy director of the White House Office of Public Liaison. Thus Donald Rumsfeld has dubbed the CNP nothing less than "the heart of a great conservative movement that helped to make America strong and prosperous in the 20th century—and is now helping to ensure she remains free and secure in the 21st century," while Indiana Republican Congressman Mike

Pence called it "the most influential gathering of conservatives in America."[9] But all of this, as Posner points out, forces us to ask the question of whether it is acceptable in a democracy (or, indeed, legal) for a Supreme Court justice (Thomas), a White House counsel and now attorney general (Gonzales), and a close Bush adviser (Goeglein) to give "secret speeches or have secret meetings with a secret organization subsidized by the American taxpayer."[10]

But, most importantly, the CNP has worked to bring together the two powerful factions discussed throughout this book: the far right wing of the evangelical Christian community and the far right wing of the Republican Party. The former has worked to mobilize the popular support among American voters, while the latter has provided the political and financial support for this larger conservative agenda. "From the beginning," Posner explains, "the CNP sought to merge two strains of far-right thought: the theocratic Religious Right with the low-tax, anti-government wing of the GOP. The theory was that the Religious Right would provide the grassroots activism and the muscle. The other faction would put up the money."[11] And the agendas of the CNP represent the nexus between these two powerful conservative factions. Although the group initially focused primarily on domestic issues such as abortion and homosexuality, LaHaye's council has recently begun to turn to larger international issues, such as U.S. policy in the Middle East and the state of Israel. On both the domestic and foreign policy fronts, however, the CNP has served as a powerful—and highly secretive—forum in which conservative religious and political agendas come together.

The most controversial and still-today most secretive speech at a CNP meeting was made by none other than George W. Bush. Soon after he made the decision to run for president in 1999, Bush delivered a speech to the CNP that has never been made public, the content of which is still known only to the small group who were in attendance. While the Internet contains various speculations about what was said or promised by Mr. Bush at the meeting, "Bush the candidate refused to release the text of the speech, citing CNP's own internal policy of closed meetings. And the CNP, of course, refused to release it for the same reasons."[12] Whatever Mr. Bush said, however, it seems clear that he emerged as a key part of the nexus that helped unite the two powerful factions of the Christian right and the conservative Republicans.

Apocalypse Soon: LaHaye's Vision of the Millennial Kingdom

For the indignation of the Lord is against all nations, and His fury against all their armies; he has utterly destroyed them, He has given them over to the slaughter.

—LaHaye and Jenkins, *Glorious Appearing: The End of Days*

Published from 1995 to 2004, the *Left Behind* series has provided a key outlet for spreading LaHaye's political agenda to a massive audience of American readers. The twelve-volume story is not simply an evangelical reading of the Apocalypse, but also a Christian right perspective on contemporary global politics. LaHaye's interpretation of the final days is premillenarian (as opposed to postmillenarian or amillenarian): Christ must return to defeat the Antichrist before the great Millennium of divine rule and peace can be established.

LaHaye's narrative takes as its starting point the moment of the Rapture, when a small group of true believers is spontaneously taken up out of this world into heaven and is thereby spared the terrible tribulation of the earth's final days. We should note, however, that the idea of the Rapture is not in fact a very old one at all. It occurs nowhere in the Old or New Testaments and is a rather recent concept developed primarily by the Irish preacher John Darby in the early nineteenth century. It was really Darby who propagated the Rapture idea by creatively interpreting certain passages of Revelation and the Latin Vulgate translation of Paul's first letter to the Thessalonians.[13] LaHaye essentially translates the Darbyite idea into a fictional narrative in which the Rapture has just taken place, the chosen souls have been taken directly to heaven, and the rest of those "left behind" must struggle against the rising power of the Antichrist. A small group of former-sinners-turned-believers forms a "Tribulation Force" to fight this divine war, led by pilot Rayford Steele, his daughter Chloe, journalist Buck Williams, and pastor Bruce Barnes.

As Melani McAlister observes, evangelical narratives about the End Times are by no means anything new. Indeed, they can be traced back at least to the early 1970s and Hal Lindsay's *Late Great Planet Earth*. Many of these popular narratives also centered around the pivotal role of the Middle East—and specifically the state of Israel—as the geographic and political locus for the unfolding of God's action in history (even as the Palestinian people tend to be "wiped off the evangelical map").[14] In fact, one of the founding principles of the Moral Majority was to support the state of Israel everywhere. As Jerry Falwell put in 1978: "I believe that if we fail to protect Israel we will cease to be important to God. . . . [W]e can and must be involved in guiding America towards a biblical position regarding her stand on Israel."[15]

But the *Left Behind* series is by far the most successful—and also well-timed—apocalyptic narrative to date. Its publisher, Tyndale House, has grown from a $40-million-a-year enterprise to one earning more than $160 million a year. Above all, *Left Behind*'s vivid portrayal of an apocalyptic showdown in the Middle East achieved a striking new kind of popular power above all in the wake of the 9/11 terrorist attacks; suddenly in the post-9/11 world, these apocalyptic narratives seemed frighteningly relevant, and their sales jumped by 60 percent.[16]

Much of the narrative of *Left Behind* is clearly a commentary on the processes of globalization and America's role in a transnational era. The Antichrist, in the person of a sinister Romanian named Nicolae Carpathia, has progressively taken over the United Nations and the world's economic system, unifying all political states ("Global Community"), media ("Global Community Network,"), and religions ("Enigma Babylon One World Faith") under a Nicolae-appointed supreme pontiff. As McAlister observes, the Antichrist's one-world tyranny "embodies every conceivable form of liberal tyranny. It is simultaneously economic (the Antichrist introduces a single currency), cultural (he has a monopoly on world media) and political (his police state employs "Morale Monitors" who patrol the streets, hunting down and executing any dissidents)."[17] The millions of the Antichrist's followers are branded with a loyalty mark and even "vaccinated" with a biochip embedded with their personal information.

Eventually, the Antichrist establishes "New Babylon"—that is, Iraq—as the epicenter of the world's political and financial networks, spreading its digital tentacles into every aspect of life and commerce in the new global order. (As McAlister notes, the choice of Iraq as the center of the Antichrist's global empire predated the current Iraq war, though it does connect impressively with the United States' current military action).[18] As leader of the new Global Community, the Antichrist promises to build a united world of peace, cooperation, and prosperity for all humankind: "we have worked to draw this Global Community together under a banner of peace and harmony.... I am, always have been, a pacifist. I do not believe in war. I do not believe in weaponry.... I feel responsible for you, my brother or my sister in this global village."[19] Meanwhile, the Tribulation Force is led by (mostly white male) Americans who see through the Antichrist's lies and manage to persuade a few converts to join their brave coalition against this global menace.

In the penultimate volume of the series, *Armageddon*, New Babylon is destroyed by the Lord's ongoing series of apocalyptic dispensations, throwing the world's entire economic structure into chaos.[20] This leads the way for Christ's return in the last volume, *Glorious Appearing*, in which the Tribulation Force and the armies of the Antichrist gather around Jerusalem for the final conflict. As the apocalypse unfolds, the Jews at long last begin to return to Christ and accept Him as the true Messiah (though the millions of those branded by the Beast refuse to do so, God having "hardened their hearts"). In the spectacularly violent final battle, the returning Christ mows down the Antichrist's massive armies in the most gory fashion, splitting bodies apart and spilling entrails across the earth with the sharp two-edged sword of His Word. Indeed, as theologian Harvey Cox observes, it is impossible to read the series without getting the impression that the authors have a perverse sort of "lip-licking anticipation of all the blood" that will soon be spilled.[21] Thus the returning Christ proclaims,

> Come near, you nations, to hear; and heed, you people! Let the earth hear, and all that is in it, the world and all things that come forth from it. For the indignation of the Lord is against all nations, and His fury against all their armies; He has utterly destroyed them, He has given them over to the slaughter.[22]

And this proclamation is accompanied by a stunningly graphic account of Christ's divine destruction. In graphic (at times frankly nauseating) detail, La-Haye and Jenkins describe the violence and bloodshed unleashed by Christ's terrible Word:

> And with those very first words, tens of thousands of Unity Arms soldiers fell dead, simply dropping where they stood, their bodies ripped open, blood pooling in great masses. . . . With every word, more and more enemies of God dropped dead, torn to pieces. . . . The living screamed in terror and ran about like madness, some escaping for a time, others falling at the words of the Lord Christ. . . . For miles lay the carcasses of the Unity Army. The manic, crazed, survivors ran and staggered and drove over and through them, fleeing for their lives. "I am the Word of God. I am Jesus. I am the Root and the Offspring of David, the Bright and Morning Star."[23]

> Men and women, soldiers and horses seemed to explode where they stood. It was as if the very words of the Lord had superheated their blood, causing it to burst through their veins and skin. . . . Tens of thousands of foot soldiers dropped their weapons, grabbed their heads or their chests, fell to their knees, and writhed as they were invisibly sliced asunder. Their innards and entrails gushed to the desert floor, and as those around them turned to run, they too were slain, their blood pooling and rising in the unforgiving brightness of the glory of Christ.[24]

In the end, only a small remnant of true believers survives to populate the Millennium and inhabit the New Jerusalem. But they have been rewarded for their unwavering faith, made the new rulers in the dominion of God's millennial kingdom: "This was Him who loved us and washed us from our sins in His own blood, and has made us kings and priests to His God and Father, to Him be glory and dominion forever and ever."[25]

As Amy Frykholm observes in her study of the series, *Rapture Culture*, the *Left Behind* books contain a strong political message and a "conservative, patriarchal, even racist agenda that mirrors the agenda of the Christ Right."[26] On the domestic front, LaHaye's books advance a strong pro-life message while targeting feminism and homosexuality as instruments of the Antichrist. On the international front, the books contain a deep message of "racially charged

American chauvinism." The leaders of the Tribulation Force are white American men, such as Rayford Steele and Buck Williams, while all "others"—women, African Americans, Arabs, Asians, and non-Americans—either submit dutifully to their leadership or are destroyed. The entire series, moreover, contains an implicit kind of anti-Semitism, portraying Israel as too stubborn to recognize Jesus as Messiah, while making heroes of Jewish converts to Christianity.[27]

Finally, the *Left Behind* series also tells us that catastrophic war in the Middle East is not only unavoidable, but is in fact a necessary part of God's plan and the cosmic triumph of ultimate good versus ultimate evil. As McAlister comments, "What they say is sobering: that war is not proof of the failure of politics, but the necessary sign of God's action in history and the path to world redemption."[28] Massive bloodshed and violence in the Middle East, then, is only the surest sign that the New Millennium and Christ's true Dominion are close at hand.

From the New Millennium to the New American Century: Bush, the Neoconservatives, and Messianic Foreign Policy

> The most worrisome thing is that this guy has a messianic vision.
>
> —A senior member of the House Appropriations
> Committee, quoted in Seymour Hersh, *New Yorker*

It is difficult not to see a number of parallels between *Left Behind's* millenarian narrative and the agenda of the neoconservatives. Indeed, these novels provide a striking kind of fictional, evangelical, and astonishingly popular counterpart to the neoconservatives' rather elite and intellectual geopolitical vision.[29] As we saw in chapters 3 and 4, the neoconservatives have since the mid-1990s envisioned a coming New American Century dominated by a kind of U.S.-led benevolent hegemony; this would, in effect, be the realization of Fukuyama's "end of history," by bringing American-style democracy and free markets to all parts of the globe. Following the mantra "the road to Jerusalem goes through Baghdad," the PNAC and other neoconservative think tanks had seen the invasion of Iraq and removal of Saddam as the key to asserting American power in the Middle East and the first stage in the dawning of this New American Century of benevolent imperialism.

But what are we to make of the striking parallels between this popular series of evangelical fiction and this aggressive neoconservative strategy for American hegemony? On the one hand, we have the vision of a New Millennium established after a small American-led group fights against the global forces of the Antichrist in the Holy Land; on the other, we have the bold vision of a New American Century established after the American-led coalition defeats the Axis of Evil and asserts its benevolent hegemony in the Middle East. Both narratives center primarily on Iraq and Israel; both reflect a deep hostility to the UN; and both see violence and massive bloodshed as necessary to usher in the New World Order. But how are these two narratives related? Is it a plot hatched secretly in one of LaHaye's Council for National Policy meetings? A coded message woven subliminally into the *Left Behind* books themselves?

Probably not. Instead, I think this connection is not so much an explicit or even necessarily intentional link, but rather a subtle yet powerful kind of "elective affinity," in Weber's sense of the phrase. As Weber argued in his classic work, *The Protestant Ethic and the Spirit of Capitalism*, it is not simply the case that Protestant Christianity *caused* the rise of early modern capitalism, or vice-versa. Rather, the two shared an affinity that was mutually beneficial and reinforcing. The Protestant ethics of hard work, thrift, restraint in consumption, and asceticism fit well with an early capitalist system based on labor and accumulation of profit and allowed the latter to flourish in ways that no other religious worldview could.[30]

So too, I would suggest, there is a fit or affinity between the evangelical vision of the New Millennium and the neoconservative ideal of a New American Century. Updating Weber somewhat, we might call this affinity "the evangelical ethic and the spirit of neoimperialism." The neoconservatives and the Christian right may not be conspiring together secretly behind the scenes, but they *do need each other* to promote their respective agendas, and they overlap on certain key issues, such as their focus on the Middle East, and specifically Israel, as the epicenter of the coming New Millennium/New American Century.

In fact, in the first volume of his new fictional series, *Babylon Rising*, LaHaye makes this link between Christian apocalypticism and neoconservative ideology quite directly. In his preface, he dedicates the book to

THE HEBREW PROPHETS, who saw, under divine inspiration, forecasts of world events so necessary to know for those living in what they call "the time of the end," or what some modern historians call "the end of history," which could occur in the early part of the twenty-first century.[31]

The imminent "end of history" predicted here is, of course, a direct reference to one of the pillars of neoconservative ideology, Fukuyama's *The End of History and the Last Man*.

Finally, the neoconservatives and the leaders of the Christian right do have enough similar interests to find common ground in the prodigal son,

George W. Bush. As a relatively empty, unformed "floating signifier," Bush serves as the key link in this elective affinity, the point at which the otherwise conflicting interests of the neoconservatives and the evangelicals come together in a disturbingly powerful way. And with his powerful and repeated rhetoric of good versus evil and freedom as God's gift to humanity, Bush also uses a kind of language that encodes within it both the millenarian vision of the evangelicals and the imperialist agenda of the neoconservatives. As we saw in chapter 3, Bush's invocation of "freedom" as the goal of history and God's plan for the world subtly combines both Fukuyama's "end of history" rhetoric and the evangelicals' expectation of the coming New Millennium. As Paul S. Boyer, professor of history at the University of Wisconsin, comments, "he is not only playing upon our still-raw memories of 9/11. He is also invoking a powerful and ancient apocalyptic vocabulary that for millions of prophecy believers conveys a specific and thrilling message of an approaching end—not just of Saddam but of human history as we know it."[32]

There are many indications, moreover, that the president believes himself to have a divinely appointed mission in world history. As we saw in chapter 2, Bush, like Reagan before him, sees himself as playing a key role in the defeat of "evil." Now, however, the war against "evil" is much vaster than the war against the evil empire, expanding to a war to rid the world of evil altogether, a war to bring freedom as God's gift to all humankind. There are, we saw, clear parallels between a kind of postmillenarian vision of history and Bush's rhetoric of the progressive spread of liberty as God's divine plan and the "goal of history." However, with his insistence on the need to use military force and the "burning fire of freedom," Bush also seems to invoke a more violent, premillenarian confrontation between good and evil as the necessary sort of tribulation before God's divine plan can be realized here on earth. In much the same way that his ambiguous rhetoric blends Fukuyama's end of history language with Huntington's clash of civilizations, Bush seems to blend a postmillenarian vision of inevitable progress toward divine rule with a premillenarian vision of spectacular violence in the clash of good and evil.

This sort of messianic idealism has been noted by both critics and admirers of Mr. Bush. More skeptical observers such as Seymour Hersh have repeatedly noted the messianic faith that seems to drive much of Bush's foreign policy. As Hersh commented in an interview in April 2006, Bush appears to have a kind of "messianic sense" about "what's needed to be done in the Middle East. I think Bush is every bit as committed to this world of rapture."[33] A similar observation was made by Bruce Bartlett, a former policy adviser to Reagan and treasury official to the first Bush. As Bartlett suggests, George W.'s sense of messianic purpose is every bit as radical and fanatical as that of the Muslim extremists he has vowed to "bring to justice":

> I think a light has gone off for people who've spent time up close to Bush: that this instinct he's always talking about is this sort of weird, Messianic idea of what he thinks God has told him to do. . . . This is why George W. Bush is so clear-eyed about Al Qaeda and the Islamic fundamentalist enemy. He believes you have to kill them all. They can't be persuaded, they're extremists, driven by a dark vision. He understands them, because he's just like them.[34]

But even conservatives and admirers of the president have noted Bush's sense of divine mission and destiny. According to Norman Podhoretz, editor of the conservative Jewish journal *Commentary*, it is likely that the president really does believe that he has been appointed by God to carry out a war against the forces of darkness, a war that hearkens back to but goes even further than Reagan's triumph in the Cold War:

> One hears that Bush . . . feels that there was a purpose behind his election all along: as a born-again Christian, it is said, he believes he was chosen by God to eradicate the evil of terrorism from the world. I think it is a plausible rumor, and I would even guess that in his heart of hearts, Bush identifies more in this respect with Ronald Reagan—who rid the world of the "evil empire"—than with his own father, who never finished the job he started in taking on Saddam Hussein.[35]

Likewise, Stephen Mansfield's presidential hagiography praises Bush for his sense of divine mission and his willingness to act on faith when it comes to dealing with an "evil" such as Saddam Hussein. Rather than worry about complex nuances or subtle arguments about "just war," the president knows the difference between good and evil, and his foreign policy decisions are *"rooted in his own personal sense of destiny."* Thus "He eschews the theoretical and prefers the simple expressions that lead to action rather than the complex theories that he thinks will lead to perpetual debate. . . . [H]e preferred to call Saddam an "evil doer." This forms the case for war. Saddam is evil. He threatens good people. . . . Removing Saddam is a moral act. Case closed."[36]

While admirers of the president see his sense of divine mission and destiny as a good thing, many others find it deeply troubling. It is indeed a bit disturbing to think that the most powerful man in the world, the man with his finger on the button that could launch the world's most massive and devastating nuclear arsenal, may be guided more by a kind of divine vision than by reasoned debate or consultation with other mortal human beings. Indeed, this is in many ways much more frightening than even Reagan's belief that his was the generation that might see Armageddon. As Chip Berlet suggests, Bush is "very much into the apocalyptic and messianic thinking of militant Christian evangelicals" and accepts a worldview based on "a giant struggle between good and evil culminating in a final confrontation. People with that kind of worldview often take risks that are inappropriate and scary because they see it as carrying out God's will."[37]

Moreover, the risks that the president has already taken in Iraq have proven to be both scary and quite catastrophic—not necessarily in an apocalyptic end-times way, but in the more real sense of economic disaster and human tragedy. A case in point is the Bush administration's environmental policy, which is not only the worst in U.S. history, but quite literally one that threatens the future of the human species and life on earth as we now know it. Despite massive and almost unanimous evidence from the world's scientists that we are now facing the probability of serious, potentially cataclysmic climate change within the coming century,[38] the Bush administration has repeatedly censored, concealed, distorted, and manipulated the data of its own Environmental Protection Association. However, as Mark Crispin Miller suggests, such a laissez-faire attitude toward an imminent ecological disaster actually makes sense if one happens to believe that Jesus will be returning soon to destroy and re-create the earth anyway:

> [T]he general anti-environmentalist thrust of Christian rightist dogma has undoubtedly confirmed the Bush Republicans in the peculiar recklessness of their agenda for the planet. . . . [T]he blitheness with which Bush & Co. ignore the ever-worsening threats of global warming, air pollution, and the disappearance of endangered species . . . can only be explained as an expression of their faith. To such apocalyptic types, the prospect of a ruined earth is no big deal, as God can be alleged to go for it.[39]

For those of us who do not share the evangelical vision of an imminent apocalypse and New Millennium, however, such an attitude is incredibly disturbing, indeed quite frightening. It may make for lively fiction in a $9.99 paperback, but it makes for very chilling reality when thinking about raising our children in a world torn by war, terrorism, and environmental crisis.

Double Ironies and Sorrows of Empire: From the "End of History" to the End of the Neoconservative Dream

> [T]he War against Terror is not really about terror, and the War on Iraq not only about oil. It's about a superpower's self-destructive impulse towards supremacy, global hegemony.
>
> —Arundhati Roy, *An Ordinary Person's Guide to Empire*

Roman imperial sorrows mounted up over hundreds of years. Ours are likely to arrive with the speed of FedEx. . . . Their cumulative impact guarantees that the United States will cease to bear any resemblance to the country once outlined in our Constitution.

—Chalmers Johnson, *Sorrows of Empire*

Popular works of fiction such as the *Left Behind* series really highlight the complex but striking sort of "fit" or elective affinity between the New Christian Right and the far right of the Republican Party. Despite their many ideological and cultural differences, these two factions share many things in common: a fundamental and utopian belief in an imminent "end of history"; a deep faith in America's role as the agent of the spread of freedom and the realization of this goal of history; an equally deep suspicion of the United Nations; and a primary focus on the Middle East, particularly Iraq and Israel, as the central locus of the inevitably violent end of history. Again, it seems unlikely that Tim LaHaye and the neoconservatives are secretly plotting together behind the scenes. But clearly these two factions *do need each other,* and they do provide mutual support for one another. While the evangelicals provide the grassroots popular support for the neoconservatives' aggressive political agenda, the latter provide the political power that can push the Christian right's agenda. And Bush, with his own apparent belief in his divinely appointed, even messianic role in history, forms the critical link between these two factions. At once American Moses and Straussian gentleman, his media-projected, hyperreal image is the perfect sort of empty signifier that can bring these two otherwise very different factions together.

In all of this, however, there is a very disturbing double irony. While the neoconservative dream of a New American Century and the evangelical vision of a New Millennium have been persuasive to many Americans, both carry with them some much darker and more disturbing real-life implications. As David Harvey has argued, the aggressive foreign and domestic strategies of the neoconservatives bear a twofold danger. First, the extremely invasive domestic policies put into place after 9/11—of which the PATRIOT Act is the most obvious example—risk turning the United States into the same sort of oppressive regime that we so despised in the former Soviet Union.[40] Indeed, it is extremely ironic to recall that Leo Strauss had warned that America was in danger of sliding into a new form of fascism, just as Weimar Germany had in the 1930s; yet today, the neoconservatives seem to have ignored Strauss's warning by imposing frightening new limits on our civil liberties that would seem to propel us further and further away from an open democracy.

Second, the intense militarism and reckless deficit spending by this administration threatens to bankrupt the United States in much the same way that the Soviet Union was destroyed by its massive military expenditure during the Cold War. "If the Soviet Empire was really brought down by excessive strain on its economy through the arms race," Harvey asks, "then will the U.S., in its blind pursuit of military dominance, undermine the economic foundations of its own power?"[41] As of 2006, we face a budget deficit of over $400 billion, a trade deficit of over $800 billion, and a national debt of almost $9 trillion, the majority of which is now owed to foreign lenders such as China and Japan. Even billionaire investor Warren Buffett has expressed grave doubts about our current policy of massive debt and mounting deficits. In his 2005 Berkshire Hathaway report, he warned that "What we owe to foreigners is extremely high, and projected to double in four or five years. The net ownership of the US by other countries a decade from now will amount to roughly $11 trillion. . . . A country that is now aspiring to an 'ownership society' will not find happiness in . . . a 'sharecropper's society.' But that's precisely where our trade policies . . . are taking us."[42] Likewise, Princeton economist Paul Krugman warns that these massive debts and deficits are fundamentally unsustainable by any sane standard of measure; for most other countries, they would spell financial apocalypse: "America's twin deficits are as big, relative to the economy, as the deficits that signaled economic Armageddon in Argentina and Indonesia."[43] Yet, incredibly, the administration refuses to cut spending or raise taxes to make a dent in that deficit. While Wall Street seems to be living in much the same fantastic dreamworld as Mr. Bush, the rest of us face a looming economic precipice: "You can't eliminate 25 percent of spending without cuts into the big three: Medicare, Medicaid, and Social Security. But you can't do that. So something has to happen. Will we go bankrupt? So far the markets are in denial. . . . The United States is going to do a Wile E. Coyote run off a cliff, look down, and . . . poof!"[44]

But perhaps the final irony in the neoconservative dream is that of building an empire upon a dwindling and violently contested resource such as oil. By the time we finally secure the oil wealth in the Middle East and proclaim our benevolent hegemony, is it possible that most of the world will have already realized the finitude of the earth's oil supplies and moved on to alternative energy sources? While we squander thousands of lives and billions of dollars in the Iraqi quagmire, Europe and Japan are well aware of both the economic and the environmental consequences of remaining tied to a carbon-based economy, and they are moving far ahead of us in the development of alternative technologies such as hydrogen, wind, solar, and biomass.[45]

In sum, the "benevolent empire" of the neoconservatives risks meeting the same fate that other historical empires have met. As Kevin Phillips suggests in his study of imperial Rome, Hapsburg Spain, the Dutch republic, and Britain, great empires in decline tend to show a series of common symptoms as they reach a state of military overstretch, cultural decay, and economic collapse. These include "growing religious fervor"; "rising commitment to faith as opposed to reason and a corollary downplaying of science"; "popular anticipation of a millennial time frame"; and "hubris-driven national strategic and military overreach, often pursuing abstract international missions that the nation can no longer afford."[46] All of these symptoms appear to characterize the current American imperium, with its massive but now overstretched military, its mounting debt, its obsessive secrecy, and its millenarian fervor. If current trends continue, Chalmers Johnson warns, four "sorrows of empire" are likely to visit us in the very near future:

> First, there will be a state of perpetual war, leading to more terrorism against Americans wherever they may be and a growing reliance on weapons of mass destruction among smaller nations as they try to ward off the imperial juggernaut. Second, there will be a loss of democracy and constitutional rights as the presidency fully eclipses Congress and is itself transformed from an executive branch of government into something more like a Pentagonized presidency. Third, an already well-shredded principle of truthfulness will be increasingly replaced by a system of propaganda, disinformation, and glorification of war, power, and the military legions. Lastly, there will be bankruptcy, as we pour our economic resources into ever more grandiose military projects and shortchange the education, health, and safety of our fellow citizens.[47]

In the face of these profound ironies and a disastrous situation in Iraq, even many key Republicans and neoconservatives have begun to lose faith in the vision of the New American Century. As conservative writer William F. Buckley soberly concluded in February 2006, "One can't doubt that the American objective in Iraq has failed."[48] If the removal of Saddam had been the key to the neoconservatives' vision for transforming the Middle East and ushering in a New American Century, the catastrophic failure of the Iraq war heralds the end of that dream. Far from greeted with sweets and flowers, as Wolfowitz had imagined, we have met with a fierce and ongoing insurgency that has claimed the lives of over 3,000 U.S. soldiers and as many as 650,000 Iraqi civilians.[49] (As Al Franken recently remarked, they apparently left out the key qualifier "exploding" when they promised "sweets and flowers.") Even Francis Fukuyama has now renounced the neoconservative dream. The same man who once supported regime change and signed the 1998 PNAC letter to Clinton has now concluded that the neoconservative agenda has "evolved into something I can no longer support," and should be discarded onto history's pile of discredited ideologies.[50] Fukuyama thus compares the neoconservatives to Leninists, that is, aggressive ideologues who "believed that history can be pushed along with the right application of power and will. Leninism was a tragedy in its Bolshevik version, and it has returned as farce when practiced by the United States."[51]

But, amazingly, none of these stunning ironies or catastrophic failures seems to bother President Bush. Indeed, in his characteristically "faith-based" and often quite "surreal" manner, Bush remains largely oblivious to our massive and mounting debt, our loss of civil liberties, our failure to confront ecological catastrophe, and our increasingly dismal situation in Iraq. As he put it, in frighteningly apocalyptic terms, during the buildup to the Iraq war: "At some point, we may be the only ones left. But that's OK with me. We are America."[52]

Mr. Bush, however, does not seem to grasp the full import of his own words. The most likely scenario is not that America will be the "only one left" in some sort of apocalyptic showdown between the cosmic powers of good and evil, or between the American-led Tribulation Force and the Antichrist's United Nations. Rather, if we continue to cling to an outdated Cold War mentality based on military might and an unsustainable petroleum economy, it seems increasingly probable that America really will be "left behind" in the new global order.

Notes

1. Kevin Phillips, *American Theocracy: Aristocracy, Fortune, and the Politics of Deceit in the House of Bush* (New York: Viking, 2004), 69.

2. Jane Lampman, "Apocalyptic—and Atop the Bestseller Lists," *Christian Science Monitor*, August 29, 2002, 14.

3. Amy Frykholm, *Rapture Culture: Left Behind in Evangelical America* (New York: Oxford University Press, 2004), 175. See Tim LaHaye and David Noebel, *Mind Siege: The Battle for Truth in the New Millennium* (Nashville, TN: W. Publishing Group, 2003).

4. As Mark Crispin Miller notes, "the exact identity of the council's founders is unclear; some claim that rightist propaganda genius Richard Viguerie established it as 'the Right's quiet and heady answer to the Left's Council on Foreign Relations,' while others name the Texas billionaires Nelson Bunker Hunt, Herbert Hunt and T. Cullen Davis, and still others credit Tim LaHaye." Miller, *Cruel and Unusual: Bush/Cheney's New World Order* (New York: Norton, 2004), 262.

5. Marc J. Ambinder, "Vast, Right-Wing Cabal? The Most Powerful Conservative Group You've Never Heard Of," *ABCNews.com*, May 2, 2002, at abcnews.go.com/sections/politics/DailyNews/council_020501.html.

6. Jeremy Leaming and Rob Boston, "Behind Closed Doors: Who Is the Council for National Policy and What Are They up To? And Why Don't They Want You to Know?" *Americans United for Separation of Church and State*, October 2004, at www.au .org/site/News2?page=NewsArticle&id=6949&abbr=cs_.

7. Sarah Posner, "Secret Society," *Alternet*, March 1, 2005, at www.alternet .org/story/21372/.

8. "Council for National Policy," *SourceWatch*, at www.sourcewatch.org/ index.php?title=Council_for_National_Policy. See "Council for National Policy," *Public Eye*, at www.publiceye.org/ifas/cnp/index.html, and "Data Base of Council for National Policy," *Watch unto Prayer*, at watch.pair.com/cnpdbase.html.

9. Posner, "Secret Society."

10. Posner, "Secret Society."

11. Leaming and Boston, "Behind Closed Doors."

12. Posner, "Secret Society."

13. John Nelson Darby was an Irish lawyer-turned-preacher who traveled in the United States and Canada between 1862 and 1877. Darby built on earlier ideas of dispensationalism (the belief that history is divided into eras, or dispensations, that culminate in the thousand-year reign of Christ), by adding the idea of the Rapture. According to Darby, true believers will be taken up to heaven in a secret Rapture before the world is plunged into chaos during the period of Tribulation under the Antichrist. The scriptural basis for the "Rapture" idea comes primarily from a Latin Vulgate translation of 1 Thessalonians 4:16–17: the Lord will descend from Heaven, and His believers will be "caught up" (*rapiemur*, from the verb *rapio*, noun *raptura*) in the clouds to meet Him in the air. See Ernest Sandeen, *The Roots of Fundamentalism: British and American Millenarianism, 1800–1930* (Chicago: University of Chicago Press, 1970), 62–70; Frykholm, *Rapture Culture*, 15–18.

14. Melani McAlister, "Prophecy, Politics, and the Popular: The *Left Behind* Series and Christian Fundamentalism's New World Order," *South Atlantic Quarterly* 102, no.4 (2003): 776; McAlister, ". . . And Armageddon Tops the Bestseller List," *Washington Post*, February 2, 2003, B03.

15. Jerry Strober and Ruth Tomczak, *Jerry Falwell: Aflame for God* (Nashville, TN: Nelson, 1979), 167.

16. Frykholm, *Rapture Culture*, 22. See Nancy Gibbs, "Apocalypse Now," *Time*, July 1, 2002, 43.

17. Melani McAlister, "An Empire of Their Own," *Nation*, September 4, 2003.

18. McAlister, "Empire of Their Own."

19. Tim LaHaye and Jerry B. Jenkins, *Nicolae: The Rise of the Antichrist* (Wheaton, IL: Tyndale House, 1997), ix.

20. Tim LaHaye and Jeremy B. Jenkins, *Armageddon: The Cosmic Battle of Ages* (Wheaton, IL: Tyndale House, 2003).

21. John Cloud, "Meet the Prophet: How an Evangelist and Conservative Activist Turned Prophecy into a Fiction Juggernaut," *Time*, July 23, 2002, at www.time.com.

22. Tim LaHaye and Jerry B. Jenkins, *Glorious Appearing* (Wheaton, IL: Tyndale House, 2004), 189.

23. LaHaye and Jenkins, *Glorious Appearing*, 171–172.

24. LaHaye and Jenkins, *Glorious Appearing*, 189–190.

25. LaHaye and Jenkins, *Glorious Appearing*, 171.

26. Frykholm, *Rapture Culture*, 178.

27. Frykholm, *Rapture Culture*, 178. See Tim LaHaye and Jerry B. Jenkins, *Apollyon: The Destroyer Is Unleashed* (Wheaton, IL: Tyndale House, 1999), 110–113; LaHaye and Jenkins, *The Mark: The Beast Rules the World* (Wheaton, IL: Tyndale House, 2000), 24–28.

28. McAlister, ". . . And Armageddon," B03.

29. For a fuller discussion of the parallels, see Hugh B. Urban, "America Left Behind: Bush, the Neoconservatives, and Evangelical Christian Fiction," *Journal of Religion and Society* 8 (2006), at moses.creighton.edu/JRS/2006/2006-2.html; Paul Boyer, "When US Foreign Policy Meets Biblical Prophecy," *Alternet*, February 20, 2003, at www.alternet.org/story/15221/.

30. Max Weber, *The Protestant Ethic and the Spirit of Capitalism*, trans. Talcott Parsons (New York: Scribner, 1977).

31. Tim LaHaye and Greg Dinallo, *Babylon Rising* (New York: Bantam Dell, 2003), viii.

32. Boyer, "When US Foreign Policy Meets Biblical Prophecy."

33. "Seymour Hersh: Bush Administration Planning Possible Major Air Attack on Iran," *Democracy Now*, April 12, 2006, at www.democracynow.org/article.pl?sid=06/04/12/1359254. See also Hersh, "The Iraq Plans," *New Yorker*, April 17, 2006, 31.

34. Ronald Suskind, "Faith, Certainty and the Presidency of George W. Bush," *New York Times Magazine*, October 17, 2004, 44.

35. Norman Podhoretz, "How to Win World War IV," *Commentary* 13 (2002): 19, 11.

36. Stephen Mansfield, *Faith of George W. Bush* (New York: Tarcher, 2003), 145–46; my italics.

37. Chip Berlet, quoted in "Bush's Messiah Complex," *Progressive*, February 2003, at www.progressive.org/~progress/?q=node/1344.

38. See *Time*'s major cover story on global warming, "Earth at the Tipping Point," *Time*, April 3, 2006, 28–42.

39. Miller, *Cruel and Unusual*, 276.

40. David Harvey, *The New Imperialism* (New York: Oxford University Press, 2003), 80–81.

41. Harvey, *New Imperialism*, 80–81.

42. Warren Buffett's Berkshire Hathaway Annual Report, March 2005, in Jimmy Carter, *Our Endangered Values: America's Moral Crisis* (New York: Simon & Schuster, 2005), 193.

43. Paul Krugman, commentary on *Marketplace*, American Public Media, November 23, 2004.

44. Paul Krugman, "The War in Iraq and the American Economy," lecture at the University of California, Berkeley, September 26, 2003, at www.berkeley.edu/news/media/releases/2003/09/26_krugman.shtml.

45. See Paul Roberts, *The End of Oil: On the Edge of a Perilous New World* (New York: Houghton Mifflin, 2004); Michael Klare, *Blood and Oil: The Dangers and Consequences of America's Growing Dependency on Imported Petroleum* (New York: Holt, 2004), 180–202.

46. Phillips, *American Theocracy*, 220.

47. Chalmers Johnson, *Sorrows of Empire: Militarism, Secrecy, and the End of the Republic* (New York: Metropolitan, 2004), 295.

48. William F. Buckley, "It Didn't Work," *National Review*, February 24, 2006, at www.nationalreview.com/buckley/buckley.asp.

49. Although the White House acknowledged only 50,000 Iraqi civilian casualties as of October 2006, a peer-reviewed study by researchers at Johns Hopkins University estimated as many as 655,000 civilian deaths as a result of the U.S.-led invasion. See Richard Harris and Alex Chadwick, "Study: 655,000 Iraqi Civilians Killed in War," at www.npr.org/templates/story/story.php?storyId=6247408.

50. Alex Massie, "Neocon Architect Says: 'Pull It Down,'" *Scotsman*, February 21, 2006, at news.scotsman.com/international.cfm?id=266122006. See Francis Fukuyama, *America at the Crossroads: Democracy, Power, and the Neoconservative Legacy* (New Haven: Yale University Press, 2006).

51. Francis Fukuyama, in Massie, "Neocon Architect Says: 'Pull It Down.'"

52. Bob Woodward, *Bush at War* (New York: Simon & Schuster, 2003), 65.

Conclusion

Rescuing Openness and "Moral Values" for a Post-Bushist Democracy

The best weapon of a dictatorship is secrecy, but the best weapon of a democracy should be the weapon of openness.

—Niels Bohr

Only the American people can redirect our government's legal, religious, and political commitments.

—Jimmy Carter, *Our Endangered Values*

I WOULD LIKE TO END THIS BOOK by returning to the point I made at the very beginning—namely, that this is not, ultimately, a book about George W. Bush or the current White House. This is not about partisan politics or the agendas of liberals versus conservatives. This is really about much broader and more worrisome trends in American politics that have pushed us toward an increasingly secretive, extremely invasive form of government and a profound erosion of the wall of separation between church and state. These are trends that have been building for several decades, given powerful fuel by the Cold War struggle against "godless communism" and the creation of a massive, often paranoiac national security state.

But these trends have come to their fullest, most dangerous fruition in the Bush administration. Mr. Bush himself lies at the intersection of several different but overlapping influences, the most important of which are the Christian right, the neoconservative movement, the energy industries, and the corporate media. Together, they have created an image that combines intense religious faith with an equally intense concern with secrecy. Bush is in many ways the ideal candidate, precisely because his relatively vacuous, Rorschach-blot image can accommodate these several overlapping forces. As a kind of floating signifier, he can appear in turns as prodigal son and corporate CEO, as Straussian gentleman and Machiavellian prince, as American Moses and postmodern media construction, appealing to different factions in different contexts.

But most important, we have seen that there is a kind of fit or elective affinity between the aggressive brand of religion pushed by the New Christian Right and the aggressive foreign policies asserted by Cheney, Wolfowitz, and the neoconservatives. Both, after all, focus on the imposition of strong order on both American society and the world, and both see the Middle East as the crucial battleground for a much larger (even eschatological) battle for global dominance.

The key to the Bush administration's success—and also its increasingly obvious failure—lies in the intertwining of secrecy and religion. For both secrecy and religion, at least in the hands of this administration, are ultimately about power. On the one hand, the strategic use of concealment and the strict control of information lie at the very core of power. Secrecy is both a tactical weapon used to destroy one's opponents and a kind of aura of mystery that surrounds the privileged few who have access to valued knowledge. On the other hand, the appeal to divine authority is also the source of an unseen, unverifiable kind of power, one that can serve as an ultimate motivator and an extremely effective means of persuasion. The claim to divine calling is a kind of power that, like the president himself, has "*no need for explanation.*" For, like secrecy, it too is largely hidden, unseen, beyond the public gaze, and based solely on the president's request that we "just trust him."

Until relatively recently, this mix of religion and secrecy seemed to work surprisingly well, persuading roughly half of Americans to reelect Mr. Bush. Indeed, it is only in his second term that this image has begun to crumble and reveal its own unreality. In the wake of the pathetic response to hurricane Katrina and the ongoing disaster in Iraq, it seems that the obsessive secrecy of the Bush administration is also an elaborate smokescreen concealing its own profound incompetence. And the results of the 2006 midterm elections suggest that this smokescreen is no longer working well at all, that the mask of piety has worn quite thin, and that the ugly reality of ineptitude is poking through. Indeed, it is tempting to conclude that this administration represents a kind of massive "Wizard of Oz" syndrome—but one in which there isn't even any "wizard" behind the curtain running all the smoke and mirrors. Perhaps it's not just that the "emperor has no clothes"; perhaps there isn't any emperor at all—just the empty signifier that the media and spin masters have constructed. As sociologist Erving Goffman put it, "often the real secret behind the mystery is that there really is no mystery. The problem is to prevent the audience from learning this too."[1]

However, while such a conclusion is tempting, I believe it misses the darker truth about this administration. I do think there is something real and deeply disturbing behind Bush and Cheney's secrecy, namely, an intense lust for power, an arrogant belief in their own omnipotence, and an almost messianic faith in their ability to "make reality," regardless of fact or truth. As Mark Crispin Miller concludes, "What rules them . . . is the same brutal messianic egotism that the Enlightenment attempted to restrain, with mixed results, but most successfully, in the design of our republic."[2] Adapting Lord Acton's famous words, we might say that "secrecy tends to corrupt, and absolute secrecy corrupts absolutely."[3] The same could be said of the melding of religion and politics: the manipulation of divine authority for political advantage corrupts, and the claim to absolute divine authority (such as "God wants me to be president" or "God told me to wage war") corrupts absolutely. The fusion of these two absolute corruptions is a terrifying prospect.

I do not think it is an exaggeration to say that this administration has pushed our democracy—like our environment—to a critical tipping point. As we look toward the post-Bush presidency, we are forced to confront the choice posed by Benjamin Franklin over two hundred years ago: are we willing to "sacrifice liberty for security"? Updating Franklin a bit for the contemporary "society of the spectacle," we might also ask: Are we willing to sacrifice truth and reality itself for the comforting lies and pious images projected by the media and government? To conclude, then, I would like to reflect more broadly on the implications of Bush-style religion and secrecy for democracy as a whole; and I'd then like to offer some more suggestions as to how we might work against obsessive government secrecy and reclaim the discourse of "moral values" in a post-Bush era.

Why Bush Could Be the Best Thing That Ever Happened to America

> In times of war, one wants one's weakest enemy at the helm of his forces. And President Bush is certainly that.
>
> —Arundhati Roy, *An Ordinary Person's Guide to Empire*

When I began writing this book, I was fairly certain that George W. Bush was the very worst thing that had ever happened to America and was surely destined to go down in history as the most catastrophic president we have ever had. One thing that I realized in the course of writing this book, however, is that Mr. Bush could also, ironically, be thought of as the best thing that's ever happened to us. As the Indian novelist and political activist Arundhati Roy points out, Bush is so arrogant, so bold, and yet also so stunningly incompetent that he lays bare for the whole world to see the dark side of America's imperial ambitions. President Clinton had been so charming, politically savvy, and well-loved that he probably could have gotten away with invading Iraq and had the Iraqis thanking us for taking their oil; Bush, conversely, has adopted a brazen, in-your-face brand of American exceptionalism that lays bare the fact that what we want is not primarily "freedom as God's gift to humanity," but rather power and the resources that are the keys to power:

> Any other even averagely intelligent US president would have probably done the very same things, but would have managed to smoke up the glass and confuse the opposition. Perhaps even carry the UN with him. George Bush's tactless imprudence and his brazen belief that he can run the world with his riot squad has done the opposite. He has achieved what writers, activists, and scholars have striven to achieve for decades. . . . He has placed on full public view the working parts, the nuts and bolts of the apocalyptic apparatus of the American Empire.[4]

Two key parts of this imperial apparatus are obsessive secrecy and a profound corrosion of the wall separating church and state. The former has been a rising trend since the 1940s; the latter is part of a much broader collusion between the right wing of the Republican Party and the New Christian Right, which has quietly worked its way into the highest levels of political power. Mr. Bush is the simply most obvious exemplar of these two trends, the public face of conservative compassion for movements that are in fact far more radical. As Michael Ledeen, Irving Kristol, and other neoconservatives themselves acknowledge, this new breed of Republicans is by no means "conservative" in the traditional sense of the term: they are by their own admission *revolutionaries.* "One should," Paul Krugman suggests, "regard America's right-wing movement—which now in effect controls the administration, both houses of Congress, much of the judiciary, and a good slice of the media—as a revolutionary power. . . . It is a movement that does not accept the legitimacy of our current political system."[5]

Indeed, some such as Kevin Phillips see these trends as a new form of "American theocracy," that is, a heady mix of imperial military power with aggressive nationalism and evangelical fervor. Thus we have a Supreme Court justice, Antonin Scalia, the prime mover behind *Bush v. Gore,* who faulted democracy for its "tendency . . . to obscure the divine authority behind government." Instead, he asserts that Americans are by nature "a religious people, whose institutions presuppose a Supreme Being," and who therefore "understand, as St. Paul did, that government carries the sword as the minister of

God to execute wrath upon the evildoer."[6] And then we have a former Republican House majority leader, Tom DeLay, now indicted for criminal conspiracy, who had a plaque on his office wall declaring "This Could be the Day," referring to the Rapture.[7] Even many Republicans are disturbed by this fusion of right-wing politics with evangelical Christianity, which has led to highly religicized policies on stem-cell research, global warming, and evolution, as well as the rise of a dangerous brand of American exceptionalism. As Rep. Christopher Shays (R-Conn) concluded in 2005, "The Republican Party of Lincoln has become a party of theocracy."[8]

Yet whether or not we see this as a rising form of theocracy, the Bush administration clearly reflects a broader movement that has deeply undermined the wall separating church and state, while at the same time imposing far more powerful forms of government secrecy and surveillance. Both of these trends are inherently dangerous—indeed, disastrous—for any democratic system.

The Costs of a "Temporary Dictatorship": Bushism and the Death of Democracy

> Fascism is a historical fact and has to do with a precise period. Therefore, even if there were a new fascism, it would be something quite different.
>
> —Renzo De Felice, quoted in Michael Ledeen, *Fascism: An Informal Introduction to Its Theory and Practice*

> When fascism comes to America it will be wrapped in a flag and carrying a cross.
>
> —Sinclair Lewis

> Yes, but we will call it anti-fascism.
>
> —Huey Long, when asked if America would ever see fascism

This administration's obsessive secrecy, invasive surveillance, and quasimessianic religious rhetoric have been all carried out in the name of spreading "freedom" and "democracy"; yet they bear with them a number of profoundly undemocratic consequences. The most basic is that we have now entered a state of perpetual war, a permanent mode of military expansion and combat that has no foreseeable end. After all, a "War on Terror" can by definition have no end; for how can one defeat a tactic? "I think this is going to be a struggle that the United States is going to be involved in for the foreseeable future," as Vice President Cheney admitted. "There's not going to be an end date when we're going to say, 'There, it's all over with.'"⁹ This state of perpetual war had already begun, of course, with the dawn of the Cold War, with U.S. forces continuously at war somewhere in the world over the past five decades. As Thomas Friedman cynically put it, the "hidden hand" of the U.S.-led capitalist market requires the "hidden fist" of the U.S. military to enforce it and ensure our benevolent global hegemony: "McDonald's cannot flourish without McDonnell Douglas. . . . And the hidden fist that keeps the world safe for Silicon Valley's technologies to flourish is called the US Army, Navy, Air Force and Marine Corps."¹⁰ Yet now, in the post-9/11 context, this state of perpetual war has been given a new name and justification—indeed, a divine legitimation as part of America's appointed role as God's agent in history. Hidden fist and hidden hand are both seen as appendages of the same divine plan for destroying evil, lowering taxes, and ensuring the flow of oil to His devoted citizens.

Yet as James Madison warned, war is always a bad thing for democracies. Indeed, it is perhaps their very undoing. War by nature squelches dissent and alternative voices; it diverts resources from enhancing quality of life to destroying life; it co-opts genuine religious sentiment in order to promote a kind of false nationalism based on fear and vengeance; it promotes obsessive secrecy over openness and public debate; and it multiplies debt for most while enriching a few:

> Of all the enemies of true liberty, war is, perhaps, the most to be dreaded, because it comprises and develops the germ of every other. War is the parent of armies; from these proceed debts and taxes; and armies, and debts, and taxes are the known instruments for bringing the many under the domination of the few. In war, too, the discretionary power of the Executive is extended; its influence in dealing out offices, honors and emoluments is multiplied; and all the means of seducing the minds, are added to those of subduing the force, of the people. The same malignant aspect in republicanism may be traced in the inequality of fortunes, and the opportunities of fraud, growing out of a state of war, and in the degeneracy of manner and of morals. . . . No nation can preserve its freedom in the midst of continual warfare.¹¹

In this sense, a state of *perpetual* war—which is the very definition of something as vague as a "War on Terror"—can only mean the steady evisceration, decline, and death of democracy.

Despite its constant rhetoric of freedom and the spread of liberty, in fact, this administration appears to have little interest in the model of democracy outlined in the Constitution. As we have seen, many neoconservatives have openly embraced an ideal of "American empire," and some, such as Ledeen, have even called for a kind of "necessary dictatorship." The president, meanwhile, has made an unprecedented grab for executive power, claiming the authority to disobey over 750 laws that conflict with his (ultimate) interpretation of the Constitution. When some of these laws concern bans on torture and oversight of the PATRIOT Act, this is a bold grab for power indeed.[12]

There are many critics on the left who have attacked Mr. Bush as a fascist or protofascist. Such charges are probably a bit premature. However, it does seem to me that the current administration has used the tools of both excessive government secrecy and religious extremism in ways that are fundamentally corrosive to any concept of democracy based on transparency, respect for privacy, and separation of church and state. While this is surely not a form of "fascism" yet, there are many clear resemblances between the cultural and economic context of Italy and Germany in the years just before the rise of fascism and the context of twenty-first-century America. As former Supreme Court Justice Sandra Day O'Connor observed in March 2006, we ought to learn the dark lessons provided by the rise of autocracies in the developing world and in former Communist countries: "It takes a lot of degeneration before a country falls into dictatorship, but we should avoid these ends by avoiding these beginnings."[13] James Hansen, the NASA climate scientist who was censored by the Bush administration for his reports on global warming, voiced a similar warning: "It seems more like Nazi Germany or the Soviet Union than the United States," he said in February 2006.[14] Finally, as we saw in chapter 2, many technology experts see the NSA's secret program of spying on U.S. citizens as a dangerous step toward something that looks much like "a police state."[15]

Fascism is, of course, a serious charge and not one to be thrown around lightly without critical examination. Based on his study of the regimes of Hitler (Germany), Mussolini (Italy), Franco (Spain), Suharto (Indonesia), and several Latin American regimes, Lawrence Britt has identified fourteen primary characteristics common to fascist regimes. These include: (1) powerful and continuing nationalism; (2) disdain for the recognition of human rights; (3) identification of enemies/scapegoats as a unifying cause; (4) supremacy of the military; (5) rampant sexism; (6) controlled mass media; (7) obsession with national security; (8) intertwined religion and government; (9) protection of corporate power; (10) suppression of labor power; (11) disdain for intellectuals and the arts; (12) obsession with crime and punishment; (13) rampant cronyism and corruption; and (14) fraudulent elections.[16]

It is difficult not to see parallels between these fourteen characteristics and what has happened under the Bush administration, particularly in the wake of 9/11. Throughout this book, we have seen ample evidence of numbers 7 and 8 on this list, the obsession with national security and the intertwining of religion and government. We have also found repeated examples of numbers 1

(the intense flag-waving nationalism of post-9/11 America), 2 (torture and secret prisons), 3 (the "Axis of Evil"), 4 (the massive and escalating military
budget), 6 (the corporate-controlled, mindlessly uncritical media), and 9 and
13 (the secret Energy Task Force and the crony capitalism that pervades this
administration). Representative Conyers and others have also provided troubling evidence of number 14 (widespread electoral fraud, at least in key states
such as Ohio and Florida).[17] In short, if the United States is not today a form
of fascism, it has moved rapidly away from the ideal of an open democratic
society with a free media and an effective system of checks and balances.

As Robert F. Kennedy Jr. points out, one of the basic preconditions for the
rise of European fascism was the government protection of corporate power,
and often the complete melding of government and corporate power. In the
face of rising European fascism in the late 1930s, President Roosevelt warned
explicitly about this dangerous fusion of corporate and political interests,
which he identified as the very core of fascism: "the liberty of a democracy is
not safe if the people tolerate the growth of private power to a point where it
becomes stronger than their democratic state itself. That, in its essence, is fascism."[18] Not only critics but even proponents described fascism in these terms,
as a form of corporatized politics. As Benito Mussolini defined it, "fascism
should more appropriately be called 'corporatism' because it is the merger of
state and corporate power."[19] It was precisely *against* such corporate power
that FDR fought when he created the New Deal and social programs that benefit ordinary Americans, rather than just wealthy businesses; and it is the
legacy of the New Deal that we are now in danger of losing in the face of this
new form of government-protected corporatism:

> The first thing Hitler did was consolidate the media, allowing the big friendly
> media groups to swallow the little guys. He cut taxes to the rich and raised taxes
> for the poor and he put the CEOs of the big corporations in power of govern-
> ment ministries; he needed the corporations to help him keep control. The Eu-
> ropean fascisms during the 1930s, Spain and Italy and Germany, they all faced
> the same depression that we faced here in this country but we elected Franklin
> Roosevelt and he raised taxes for the rich and he created anti-trust laws and he
> put people to work. He created public parks and social programs to help the
> poor. We took a different road than the European fascisms but today all of those
> programs that Roosevelt put in place are being dismantled. The first thing they
> do is privatize the commons and give big corporations control of the things that
> belong to all of us.[20]

Although the United States took a different road from fascism in the 1930s
and '40s, the threat of a corporate-controlled state has never left us. We have
seen throughout this book that the Bush administration is closely allied with,

and often indistinguishable from, corporate power, particularly the oil, gas, and coal industries that are at the core of its highly secretive national energy policy. Indeed, this administration—with a president who was director of Harken Energy, a vice president who was CEO of Halliburton, a secretary of state who was on the board of Chevron, and a former commerce secretary who was CEO of Tom Brown, Inc.—could be described as a *hostile takeover of the White House by corporate power,* and specifically by the energy industries. Cheney's secret dealings with the most powerful corporations in his Energy Task Force are only the most blatant example of this merger of government and corporate power.[21] As Paul Bigioni suggests in his article, "Fascism Then, Fascism Now," the economic conditions of the United States today bear an unsettling resemblance to those of Weimar Germany, in which corporate power and government were increasingly intertwined and the state was progressively reduced to a servant of the wealthy classes. While the United States is not "fascist" now, it has created the basic *economic and cultural conditions* that could give rise to a form of fascism, as happened in Germany seventy years ago:

> In the end, the rich get richer and the poor get poorer. As in Weimar Germany, the function of the state is being reduced to that of a steward for the interests of the moneyed elite. All that would be required now for a more rapid descent into fascism are a few reasons for the average person to forget he is being ripped off. Hatred of Arabs, fundamentalist Christianity or . . . perpetual war may well be taking the place of Hitler's hatred for communists and Jews.[22]

Surely one of the most unsettling of the quasifascistic elements in America today is the use of fear as a major political tool. The stunning and spectacular image of the World Trade Towers crashing down has been manipulated ad infinitum to terrify us into silence, to persuade us to renounce civil rights and privacy, and to listen politely while the administration spouts patently absurd untruths. This too is a classic fascist tactic, as Hitler learned from the burning of the Reichstag. "It is always a simple matter to drag the people along," Hermann Goering noted. "All you have to do is tell them they are being attacked, denounce the peacemakers for lack of patriotism and exposing the country to danger. It works the same in any country."[23] It has certainly worked well in this one.

Finally, one other important characteristic of fascism that is not on Britt's fourteen-point list is pervasive secrecy. If secrecy lies at the core of power, then the most brutally powerful regimes have typically been the most secretive, often closely resembling traditional secret societies with their hierarchies of knowledge and grades of access to information. As Alexandre Koyré pointed out over sixty years ago, totalitarian movements could be called "secret societies established in broad daylight."[24] Such movements tend to be organized by the logic of secrecy, obsessive control of information, dissimulation toward all outsiders, and the aura of mystery that surrounds the inner circle of those in power. As Hannah Arendt notes in her classic work on totalitarianism,

> Secret societies also form hierarchies according to degrees of initiation, regulate the life of their members according to a secret and fictitious assumption which makes everything look as though it were something else, adopt a strategy of consistent lying to deceive the non-initiated external masses, demand unquestioning obedience from their members who are held together by allegiance to a . . . mysterious leader, who himself is surrounded . . . by a small group of initiated who in turn are surrounded by half-initiated who form a buffer area against the hostile profane world.[25]

It would be difficult to find a better description of the Bush administration. If anything, this administration has fused this sort of corporatized, hierarchical secrecy with a religious faith in both the "mysterious leader" and the aura of power that surrounds him.

In many respects, this administration seems to be a stunning fulfillment of Sinclair Lewis's brilliant and prescient novel about the rise of American-style fascism in the 1930s, *It Can't Happen Here*. Some of the parallels are so obvious one wonders if Karl Rove hadn't been using Lewis's novel as his personal playbook. With its flag-waving nationalism, cross-bearing religious fervor, and fearful hatred of the amorphous terrors lurking just beyond its borders, Lewis's 1930s America bears a troubling resemblance to our twenty-first-century context. As Lewis's protagonist Doremus Jessop remarked, "Why, there's no country in the world that can get more hysterical—yes more obsequious!—than America. . . . Why, where in all history has there ever been a people so ripe for dictatorship as ours! We're ready to start on a Children's Crusade—only of adults—right now!"[26] But in the famous words of Huey Long, who provided the model for the charismatic dictator in Lewis's novel, if fascism ever emerged in America, "we would call it anti-fascism."[27]

Perhaps, then, we need to come up with another term altogether to describe the unique mix of religious fervor, intense secrecy, and lust for power that characterizes the current administration. Maybe it is better described not as "fascist" or "theocratic," but, again, simply as "Bushist." Unlike earlier forms of totalitarianism, this is a regime that is at once strangely old and yet weirdly postmodern; it is at once "Christianist"—that is, exhibiting a form of religious extremism comparable to what the administration has dubbed "Islamist extremism"—and "Post-truthist, that is, showing a belief in its own power to create reality, in which the distinction between real and fake, true and false has become irrelevant, now replaced by the endlessly repeated images on the TV screen.

But whatever we decide to call it, the current political formation is one that seems increasingly self-destructive and stunningly unaware of its own vulnerability. As we saw in chapter 6, the dream of a New American Century driven by imperialism, militarism, and messianic faith has already shown signs of its own unsustainability. At some point, short of a second coming of Jesus or other divine intervention, our massive deficits and debt will catch up with us. As various observers have suggested, the Bush administration bears a troubling resemblance to Ken Lay's Enron (to which it had many close ties) shortly before its collapse. Indeed, Bruce Bartlett, the domestic policy advisor to Reagan and author of *Reaganomics*, sees the collapse of Enron as a metaphor for Bush's entire economic policy.[28] As in the Enron case, Americans have been deliberately kept in the dark by a consistent pattern of secrecy; and as in the Enron case, this secrecy has been used to funnel more and more money away from ordinary Americans toward the wealthiest few, even as the entire debt-ridden system seems increasingly precarious. As Hacker and Pierson conclude,

> America's political market no longer looks like the effectively functioning markets that economics textbooks laud. Rather, it increasingly resembles the sort of market that gave us the Enron scandal, in which corporate bigwigs with privileged information got rich at the expense of ordinary shareholders, workers. and consumers. . . .
>
> American government has not turned into Enron. But . . . the systematic efforts of political elites to distort public perceptions of their activities bear more than a passing resemblance. And as was true in recent financial scandals, the goal of many of these efforts is not simply to exploit limitations in knowledge in general but to exploit limitations in knowledge precisely among those who would be most likely to be angered if they were aware of what was going on.[29]

Whether or not the U.S. economy meets a similar fate as Enron remains to be seen. But the parallels between Bush's pattern of secrecy and that of his close friend "Kenny Boy" are indeed worrying. In this regard, however, the Bushist regime is by no means unique. Historically, empires inevitably fall; dictatorships ultimately implode or destroy themselves. It seems unlikely that a "temporary dictatorship" under Bush and Cheney would be exempt from this historical fate. As Arendt noted several decades ago, "Totalitarian domination, like tyranny, bears the germs of its own destruction."[30]

Reclaiming "Moral Values" from the Religious and Political Right

> Democracy, to crush fascism internally, must . . . put human beings first and dollars second. It must appeal to reason and decency and not to

violence and deceit. We must not tolerate oppressive government or industrial oligarchy in the form of monopolies and cartels.

—Vice President Henry Wallace, "The Danger of American Fascism"
(1944)

It is the vast difference between the religion *about* Jesus and the religion *of*
Jesus.

—Bill Moyers, "A Time for Heresy" (2006)

Many of the conclusions of this book are, admittedly, rather grim and sobering. Probably most Americans do not like to imagine that their government
could have as much in common with fascism as it currently does, or that Sinclair Lewis's 1935 novel might prove to be so prescient. But it is my opinion
that Americans today need to be sobered up a bit after living so long in the
media-induced intoxication of Fox News, "American Idol," and "Who Wants
to Be a Millionaire?" The Bush administration has managed to do incredible
damage to our political system in just five short years, in much the same way
that it has done massive—perhaps irreparable—damage to our environment
in a very short time. To confront and deal with such damage, therefore, requires a sort of espresso shot in the veins of real alarm, anger, and occasional
outrage.

But this book is not intended to be a cause for pessimism or despair. On the
contrary, it is meant to be an inspiration for change. And change, I believe,
needs to be undertaken on at least two levels. The first is a recovery of an ideal
of "moral values" that at once defends the separation of church and state and
promotes a deep ethical concern for all citizens, all human beings, and the environment as a whole. The second is a serious critique of excessive government secrecy and the struggle for a more open form of deliberative and communicative democracy.

If we are to move forward toward a healthier sort of post-Bushist democracy, the most basic step is to fundamentally reframe the discourse of values
and spirituality. By an incredible sort of cultural coup, the far right has managed to co-opt the language of morality, Christianity, and "family values,"
while demonizing "liberals" as godless hedonists and communists. Indeed, if
we listen to Fox News, we find that religion and moral values are consistently
associated with "conservatism," while secularism and amorality are consistently associated with "liberalism" (thus throughout the 2004 race, Fox tire-
lessly repeated the "statistical fact" that John Kerry and John Edwards were
two of the "most liberal members of Congress," as if this implied they supported pagan orgies and free drug use for children). This is indeed remarkable
when we recall that, not long ago, being a good Christian and a champion of

spiritual values was a Democratic thing, and that Carter, Gore, and Clinton are all born-again Christians; meanwhile, Reagan, despite his religious hyperbole, was not a churchgoer and G. H. W. Bush was only nominally Episcopalian.

What is even more remarkable, however, is that the political and religious right has managed to redefine "moral values" to mean basically just two things: antiabortion and anti–gay marriage. In so doing, they have obscured and marginalized a wide range of other, arguably far more pressing sorts of moral questions, such as protecting the environment and combating what is now an imminent ecological catastrophe; addressing poverty both within the United States and around the world, as well as the obscene gap between the very rich and the very poor; providing health care for all our citizens, including the ten million American children without health coverage; and stopping an illegal war that has involved all manner of hideous abuses. As Jim Wallis, an evangelical Christian and author of *God's Politics*, has argued, we need to greatly widen our definition of "values" to include these other, more urgent ethical questions: "Poverty is a religious issue. The environment is a religious issue. A war of choice fought on false pretenses is a theological issue. But Republicans have narrowed religious issues to a short list of four or five that happen to be very important to their constituency."[31] Widening our definition of morality in this way, he suggests, would be far more in keeping with an honest interpretation of Scripture, which has a great deal to say about poverty, for example, and very little to say about homosexuality. After searching the Bible for every verse that referred to wealth and poverty, Wallis found that one out of sixteen verses in the New Testament, one in ten in the Gospels, and one in seven in *Luke* referred to money or the poor; in the Hebrew scriptures, only idolatry was mentioned more times than the relationship between rich and poor. Yet only two refer to homosexuality, an issue that apparently did not concern Jesus Christ himself in the least:

> The right is very comfortable with the language of faith and values. . . . In fact, they think they own it sometimes, or almost own religion or own God.
>
> And then they narrow everything to one or two hot-button social issues, as if abortion and gay marriage are the only two moral values questions. . . .
>
> I'm an Evangelical Christian and I find 3,000 verses in the Bible on the poor, so fighting poverty is a moral value too, or protecting the environment—protecting God's creation is a moral value. The ethics of war—whether we go to war, how we go to war, whether we tell the truth about the war—are fundamental moral and religious questions.[32]

Indeed, it seems to me that the far right has exploited the two red-flag issues of gay marriage and abortion not only to co-opt the language of moral

values, but also to *divert* our attention away from these other serious moral issues and to *conceal* a wide range of activities that are arguably quite immoral.
Even as they profess compassion, the religious and political right have promoted a preemptive invasion that does not meet the criteria of "just war" in
any religion I know of; even as they purport to be conservative, they have
pushed tax cuts and economic policies that consistently favor the very richest
and harm the poorest Americans, while creating massive debt and deficits;
even as they preach family values, they have systematically dismantled environmental protections in order to help big energy industries, often at the expense of our children's health. It is difficult to think of any religion—even Tim
LaHaye's brand of lip-licking apocalypticism—that urges its believers to rape
the environment as this administration has. As President Carter reminds us,
"America is by far the world's leading polluter, and our government's abandonment of its responsibilities is just another tragic step in a series of actions
that have departed from the historic bipartisan protection of the global environment. Our proper stewardship of God's world is a personal and political
moral commitment."[33]

It seems increasingly clear that the agenda of the Bush administration and
of the far right in general has little to do with anything Jesus said; but it has a
great deal to do with what Ledeen called the "politics of myth and symbol," or
the manipulation of powerful religious symbols in order to persuade Americans to go along with economic policies that are not only against their own
self-interest but are also profoundly un-Christlike. As Bill Moyers has argued,
this sort of religious rhetoric has been used to deceive American citizens while
at the same time taking us back to a kind of pre–New Deal form of robber-
baron capitalism:

> We are dealing here with a vision sharply at odds with the majority of Ameri-
> cans. These are people who want to arrange the world for the convenience of
> themselves and the multinational corporations that pay for their elections. With
> their fundamentalist medicine men twirling the bullroarers in the woods, they
> would turn America into . . . a society run by the powerful, oblivious to the weak,
> free of accountability, thriving on crony capitalism. . . . If the corporate, political,
> and religious right have their way, we will go back to the first Gilded Age, when
> privilege controlled politics, votes were purchased, legislatures were bribed, bills
> were bought, and laws flagrantly disregarded—all as God's will. . . . These char-
> latans and demagogues know that by controlling a society's most emotionally-
> laden symbols, they can control America, too.[34]

Reclaiming "moral values" for a post-Bushist democracy, then, would mean
fundamentally reframing the discourse of "values" itself, wresting it away from

the extreme right and broadening it far beyond the narrow boundaries of homosexuality and abortion. To do so, I think we need to strike a delicate balance between upholding the separation of church and state and reinjecting a serious discussion of moral values into political discourse. Unlike gay marriage and abortion, issues such as poverty, health care, war, and the environment are not simply "Christian" values and not even just "religious" values; they are things that all of us, Christian and non-Christian, religious and secular, care deeply about.

Of course, Christianity has historically been a powerful ally in this broader struggle for social justice. The teachings of Jesus—at least the Jesus of the Sermon on the Mount—are critical resources in the battle to reclaim a genuine discourse of "moral values." After all, as Moyers rightly points out,

> It was in the name of Jesus that a Methodist ship caulker named Edward Rogers crusaded across New England for an eight-hour work day. It was in the name of Jesus that Francis William rose up against the sweatshop. . . . It was in the name of Jesus that Martin Luther King Jr. went to Memphis to march with sanitation workers who were asking only for a living wage. . . .
>
> [T]he greatest heretic of all is Jesus of Nazareth, who drove the moneychangers from the temple in Jerusalem as we must now drive the moneychangers from the temples of democracy.[35]

Others have made a powerful appeal to religion in order to reclaim an ethic of environmental responsibility. At a time when the climate really is reaching a point of critical, arguably catastrophic change, we would do better to read the actual teachings of Jesus, Buddha, or Muhammad than the apocalyptic fantasies of Tim LaHaye. As Robert F. Kennedy Jr. pointedly remarks, many on the religious and political right display a stunning hypocrisy when they declare their Christian faith, even as they support the corporate rape of the environment: "They claim to embrace Christianity while violating the manifold mandates of Christianity: that we are stewards of the land, and that we are meant to care for nature. They have embraced this Christian heresy of dominion theology, which James Watt was the first to enunciate when he told the Senate, "I don't think that there is any point in protecting the public lands because we don't how long the world is going to last before the Lord returns." Instead, Kennedy suggests, an honest reading of the Gospels or the sacred texts of any religion would remind us that the divine is most clearly felt in and through nature; it would urge us to care for nature, not exploit it and look forward to its apocalyptic destruction. The founders of the world's major religions, such as Buddha, Muhammad, and Jesus, all experienced their central epiphanies in the wilderness, surrounded by nature. For it is through nature that "God talks to us most clearly," with the greatest "texture, grace and joy." Therefore,

> When we destroy these things, we're cutting ourselves off from the very things that make us human, that give us a spiritual life. And for these people on Capitol Hill to be saying that they are following the mandate of Christ by liquidating our public assets, what they are really doing is a moral affront to the next generation.[36]

Yet this broader struggle to reclaim the language of moral values cannot be limited to an appeal to Jesus—or to Muhammad, Buddha, Krishna, or Chief Seattle, for that matter. As Thomas Jefferson persuasively argued, our ideal of religious freedom is by design opposed to domination by any one faith, but is instead "meant to comprehend within the mantle of its protection the Jew and the Gentile, the Christian and the Mahometan, the Hindoo," and every denomination.[37] President Kennedy reaffirmed this ideal 160 years later when he spoke to the Protestant Council of New York City: "The family of man is not limited to a single race or religion, to a single city or country. . . . Most of its members are not white—and most of them are not Christian."[38] As we saw above, religious discourse makes an appeal to a kind of authority that is believed to be transcendent, infinite, and suprahuman. Such an appeal is perfectly appropriate in the realm of personal belief and private life; but it becomes extremely dangerous when that authority is wielded for political purposes, such as persuading citizens how to vote, whom to execute, or when to go to war. Indeed, it was precisely *against* such political use of religion that Jefferson and others struggled, insisting instead on the *human* and *historical* nature of our political system. For that is, ultimately, the only means to safeguard against the temptations of dictatorial power. As historian William Lee Miller notes, "We were founded not by an oracle or by a God or by mythic figures . . . but by a particular group of people at a particular time and place with a particular set of rather clearly articulated ideas, about which they agreed. And one of those ideas was freedom of 'conscience' or belief."[39]

The most appropriate strategy for a post-Bushist democracy is not, I believe, simply for Democrats to start invoking the Almighty and declaring their piety as loudly as the Republicans. Both Democrats and Republicans would do well to recall President Lincoln's observation in 1862 that "It is quite possible that God's purpose is something different from the purposes of either party."[40] Instead, I think we would be far better off reasserting Jefferson's wall of separation and disentangling religion from the politicians who would manipulate and exploit it, while at the same time championing more basic sorts of "moral values." Such values would have less to do with political hot-button issues such as gay marriage than with real needs such as providing health care for the more than 40 million Americans without it; reducing the obscene gap between the superrich and the superpoor; addressing the reality of climate change before it reaches a point of no return; and, most immediately, putting an absolute stop to the detention and torture of the hundreds of untried individuals now being held in an illegal, unjust war.

The progressive rabbi Michael Lerner makes a powerful case for such a redefinition of morality. The capitalist marketplace, he argues, is itself not a value-neutral space, but in fact imposes its own, often unrecognized values. These values are primarily the bottom-line values of materialism, profit, and greed, which are not always beneficial to either human beings or the environment. In place of those destructive values, we need to argue for a "New Bottom Line," one that makes human well-being and environmental sustainability the fundamental values that govern our culture. Such values are neither uniquely Christian nor uniquely religious; but they are vital to any concept of morality: "institutions, corporations, legislation and social practices should be judged efficient, rational and productive not only to the extent that they maximize money and power . . . but also to the extent that they maximize love and kindness, . . . enhance our capacities to respond to other human beings as inherently (and not just instrumentally) valuable. . . . With these values we could counter the right and save the First Amendment."[41]

The Weapons of Openness: Combating Secrecy with Deliberative and Communicative Democracy

The advancement and diffusion of knowledge is the only guardian of true liberty.

—James Madison, letter to George Thomson

I was just standing there, looking at the teleprompter with the words they had written for me to say, and I just thought, "How can I read these words when the truth needs to be said?"

—Kanye West

But perhaps the most important "moral value" to be recovered for a post-Bushist democracy is that of openness—the value of transparency and public reason in place of obsessive secrecy, hypocrisy, and hidden corporate interest. Secrecy, I believe this book has shown, is always potentially dangerous for a democratic system of government; and in its present form of generalized secrecy and unanswerable lies that we find in the Bush administration, it is simply catastrophic. Again, updating Lord Acton a bit, we could say that "Everything secret degenerates," even the most powerful and self-righteous empire, and "nothing is safe that does not show how it can bear discussion and publicity," even the most sophisticated national security state with the most elaborate methods of surveillance.

Already in 1997, Senator Moynihan had called for a new "counterculture of openness" to combat the excessive and absurd "culture of secrecy" that infected every level of government during the Cold War.[42] In place of secrecy and paranoia, Moynihan argued for the widespread declassification of information and for government secrecy to be kept to an "absolute minimum." Moynihan's call for a counterculture of openness may seem, to many, quaint and archaic in the wake of 9/11 and the War on Terror. But a push for openness is today more important than ever, as our government exploits the threat of terror to assume unprecedented power, to clothe ever more of its activities in secrecy, and to further invade the privacy of ordinary citizens. Far from quaint, a counterculture of openness is imperative. We have an obligation, I think, to insist that certain forms of government secrecy are *simply unacceptable in any democratic society*. I would argue, for example, that the following acts of the current administration have absolutely no place in a democracy and should be categorically rejected by any thinking public:

1. concealing scientific evidence about serious, potentially catastrophic, environmental threats such as climate change;
2. making citizens sign loyalty oaths in order to attend political rallies and arresting those who voice any dissenting opinions;
3. spying on U.S. citizens without warrant and without congressional oversight;
4. manipulating intelligence to promote a war that has killed thousands of soldiers and innocent civilians, costing billions of dollars that could have been spent on real needs such as education and health care;
5. holding hundreds of individuals without trial or charge in abusive conditions indefinitely;
6. defending the use of secret prisons and secret torture as necessary measures in time of war.

A president who supports any one of these things is unfit for office. One who supports any of the last three of these is not only in need of impeachment but guilty of war crimes and should be tried as such. The fact that Mr. Bush has *not* been impeached or tried for such stunningly illegal activities—even while Clinton was impeached for a minor sex scandal—is at once outrageous and profoundly unsettling. It is evidence that our media are fundamentally inept or co-opted, while our public is frighteningly uninformed or apathetic.

To passively tolerate such blatant abuse of power is simply a failure of our democratic duties as citizens. "To announce that there must be no criticism of the president, or that we are to stand by the president, right or wrong," as Theodore Roosevelt reminds us, "is not only unpatriotic and servile, but is morally treasonable to the American public."[43]

In this sense, I largely agree with the model of "deliberative democracy" developed by theorists such as Jon Elster and Jürgen Habermas. In contrast to a market-based theory of democracy, which sees citizens as individuals competing for their own self-interest, a deliberative model sees democracy "as a process that creates a public," with citizens coming together to talk about collective problems, goals, and actions; "Democratic processes are oriented around discussing this common good rather than competing for the promotion of the private good of each."[44] Such a deliberative model of democracy, therefore, demands a form of *free and open dialogue* in which various individuals and factions are able to test and challenge assertions about the public good. As Simone Chambers argues, deliberative democracy rests on a fundamental ideal of *openness and publicity*, that is, rendering one's interests open to public scrutiny, debate, and possible revision:

> All normative theories of deliberative democracy contain something that could be called a publicity principle. The principle . . . always involves a claim about the salutary effects of going public with the reasons and arguments backing up a policy, proposal, or claim. . . . [P]ublic reason involves justification and accountability directed at a public characterized by pluralism. Public reasons are reasons that this public at large could accept.[45]

Going still further, however, Iris Marion Young has argued that a healthy democracy not only requires public deliberation and reasoned discourse about the public good, but also demands a more active form of "communicative democracy," which includes the often "rowdy, disorderly, and decentered" kinds of public action such as protests, marches, political satire, and the critical use of film and art: "processes of engaged democratic communication include street demonstrations and sit-ins, musical works, and cartoons as much as parliamentary speeches and letters to the editor."[46]

In this sense, obsessive secrecy, invasive government surveillance, and a submissive media represent the very opposite of—indeed, the death knell for—a healthy deliberative and communicative democracy. Even before 9/11, Bush and Cheney had established a form of government that was radically closed, nontransparent, and ultimately antidemocratic, beginning with their secretive Energy Task Force. This was a case of brute self-interest and anti–public spirit at its very worst, as our vice president (and former CEO of Halliburton) met secretly to discuss matters of great public concern—national energy policy, environmental regulations, corporate subsidies, and geopolitical strategy—not with representatives of the public interest but almost exclusively with the energy corporations who would benefit most from those deliberations.

But not only does obsessive secrecy of the Bush-Cheney variety effectively kill the public discourse required for a deliberative democracy; it also locks out or intimidates any critical voices in the press, and still worse, it squelches the sort of "rowdy, disorderly" activism on the part of the public that is vital to a healthy communicative democracy. As Arundhati Roy observes, "Any government's condemnation of terrorism is only credible if it shows itself to be responsive to persistent, reasonable, closely argued, non-violent dissent. And yet, what's happening is just the opposite."[47] Instead of responding openly to dissent, the administration has made its citizens sign loyalty oaths, arrested those who wear critical t-shirts, and limited "protests" to absurdly restricted areas far from its fake town-hall meetings. Indeed, this systematic suppression of dissent is not only corrosive of a healthy deliberative or communicative democracy, but it also seems *strategically designed to undermine and destroy such an ideal of democracy.*

Fortunately, however, Americans are a remarkably creative and resilient lot. Despite the administration's obsessive secrecy, despite the corporate media's stunning lack of critical analysis, a variety of new forms of resistance have emerged. The past five years have witnessed a veritable renaissance of political satire, film, and music. Thus we've had chart-topping songs such as Green Day's "American Idiot," System of a Down's "BYOB" ("bring your own bombs," with the refrain "why don't presidents fight the war/why do they always send the poor"), and Neil Young's "Let's Impeach the President"; films such as Michael Moore's hugely successful documentary, *Fahrenheit 911*; progressive talk-radio networks such as Al Franken's Air America; and hip-hop stars such as Kanye West with the courage to publicly point out that the president does not appear to care about black people.

Indeed, with the general failure of the "fourth estate" as a means of checking and critiquing the government, it would seem that a new "fifth estate" of comedy and parody has emerged. As Robert J. Thompson, director of the Center for Study of Popular Television at Syracuse University, observes, the fifth estate of parody "is doing the kind of things in jokes that CNN and CBS ought to be doing."[48] For parody has a unique ability to speak truth to power and get away with it when most "serious" media cannot.

Arguably the most effective and widely popular new form of political satire is Jon Stewart's *The Daily Show*, which offers an entertaining and remarkably intelligent form of democratic response to the current political and media crisis. Indeed, some media analysts such as Jeffrey Baym see *The Daily Show* as an exemplary model of both brilliant, critical political satire and a form of deliberative democracy. With its use of both biting political satire and thoughtful interviews with a variety of prominent political and media figures, Stewart's "fake news show" offers a far better model of deliberative democracy than the sort of combative, market-driven debate of programs such as *Crossfire* or *Hardball.*[49] Unlike most corporate media pundits, Stewart refuses to simply reiterate the half-truths, misinformation, and blatant lies emanating from the administration; instead, he presents himself as an ordinary citizen who is simply astonished by the stuff his government asks him to believe, an "outraged individual who, comparing official pronouncements with his own basic common sense, simply cannot believe what he—and all of us—are expected to swallow."[50] Stewart uses his unique position as a fake news person to do what the corporate media are no longer capable of doing, namely, of pointing out the absurd lies of those in power. Thus, after playing a news clip of Mr. Cheney, who continued to insist that Iraq had ties to Al Qaeda even after the 9/11 Commission report definitively proved that connection to be false, Stewart said simply, "Mr. Vice President, your pants are on fire."[51] Similarly, he played a clip of Rumsfeld denying the allegations of "torture" at Abu Ghraib: "Uh, I think that . . . I'm not a lawyer, my impression is that what has been charged thus far is abuse, which I believe, technically, is different from torture, and therefore I'm not gonna address the torture word." Stewart's incredulous response was just the one we all wanted to hear from the mainstream media:

> I'm also not a lawyer, so I don't know technically, if you're *human*, but as a fake news person, I can tell you, what we've been reading about in the newspapers, the pictures we've been seeing . . . it's f-cking torture.[52]

Yet, in addition to its ruthless parody of media and politicians, *The Daily Show* also offers a model of rational, sane democratic discourse with guests of both left and right persuasions that is a refreshing alternative to the *Crossfire* style of "I'm gonna kick your ass" debate. Indeed, Stewart has invited even some of the most influential neoconservatives, such as William Kristol ("the man who was wrong about Iraq before anyone else," as Stewart put it), to engage in serious discussion of real issues, without the rabid screaming that accompanies most other prime-time political shows. Despite the characterization of Americans today as the "Obey Your Thirst/Image Is Everything" generation there does seem to be a hunger for this sort of rational discussion. During a 2004 episode, Stewart interviewed former Treasury Secretary Robert Reich, who called for a return to reason in political argument: "Irrationality rules the day, but reason is in the wings." Before Stewart could respond the audience burst into applause, at which Stewart leaned toward Reich and said: "By the way, the people clamoring for reason? You hear that? You don't see that too often."[53] But the point, of course, is that American viewers *are* clamoring for reason; they *are* calling out for sane, deliberative discourse instead of the hate-filled ranting of Limbaugh or the blatant propaganda of Fox News.

But surely one of the boldest uses of satire as a weapon of openness ever recorded was Stephen Colbert's appearance at the White House Correspondents Dinner with President Bush in April 2006. A former regular on *The Daily Show* who launched his own fake news show, Colbert played the part of an ultra–right-wing, God-fearing, Fox News–type admirer of Bush; but he used that parodic character to launch a blistering critique of the president, the most powerful man in the world, sitting just two chairs away from him. Like a kind of satirical guerilla fighter or "terrorist with boring hair and rimless glasses," Colbert managed to sneak right under the nose of the Secret Service in order to speak "truthiness to power."[54] The central focus of Colbert's satire was a president who lives in a faith-based reality of his own making, with less and less connection to the physical reality the rest of us inhabit. His critique was a direct response to the sort of messianic idealism and "create your own reality" ideology of the administration:

> Now I know there are some polls out there saying this man has a 32% approval rating. But guys like us, we don't pay attention to the polls. We know that polls are just a collection of statistics that reflect what people are thinking in "reality." And reality has a well-known liberal bias. . . .
>
> I stand by this man because he stands for things. Not only for things, he stands on things. Things like aircraft carriers, and rubble, and recently flooded city squares. And that sends a strong message that no matter what happens to America she will always rebound with the most powerfully staged photo-ops in the world. . . . The greatest thing about this man is he's steady. You know where he stands. He believes the same thing Wednesday that he believed on Monday, no matter what happened Tuesday. Events can change, this man's beliefs never will.

Yet Colbert had no less searing criticism to level at the mainstream media. While professing a great respect for Fox News because of its bold disregard for facts or truth, Colbert pushed the myth of a "liberal bias in the media" to its most absurd conclusion, while at the same time shaming the media for their pathetic timidity in investigating this administration:

> I am appalled to be surrounded by the liberal media that is destroying America, with the exception of Fox News. Fox News gives you both sides of every story, the president's side and the vice president's side.
>
> But the rest of you, what are you thinking, reporting on NSA wiretapping or secret prisons in Eastern Europe? Those things are secret for a very important reason—they're super-depressing. And if that's your goal, well, misery accomplished.

Over the last five years you people were so good over tax cuts, WMD intelligence, the effect of global warming. We Americans didn't want to know, and you had the courtesy not to try to find out. Those were good times, as far as we knew.[55]

Colbert's lampoon is a brilliant example of the weapon of openness, using satire to cut directly through the layers of political spin, religious rhetoric, and vapid media coverage in order to reveal the ridiculous lies underneath. As Michael Scherer notes, what Colbert did was take on the entire right-wing noise machine and so "expose the whole official, patriotic, right-wing, press-bashing discourse as a sham, as more 'truthiness' than truth."[56] But he also displayed a stunning amount of courage (he was "ballsilicious," as Jon Stewart noted), aiming a scathing critique at the most powerful man in the world while looking him dead in the eye.

Jon Stewart and Stephen Colbert, as a fake news persons, have the freedom to call Bush and Cheney's lies "lies" and Donald Rumsfeld's torture "torture"—something the "real" news people are apparently incapable of doing. But this is something that all of us, as real citizens in an as-yet-not-entirely hyperreal democracy, must be willing to do. At this point, Jimmy Carter reminds us, it is only the American people who can "redirect our government's legal, religious, and political commitments." And many are doing just that. As Michael Moore notes in his article, "Mavericks, Renegades and Trouble Makers," it is not only rock stars and comedians who have taken it upon themselves to resist the secrecy, lies, and rhetoric of the administration; "some were just average citizens who had simply seen enough."[57]

Perhaps the bravest of the many average citizens wielding the weapon of openness is Cindy Sheehan, the mother of a soldier killed in Iraq who set up camp outside the Bush ranch in Crawford Texas. With her simple, unspectacular request that the president simply meet with her and explain why it was that her son died, Sheehan sparked a massive nationwide antiwar movement. Despite fierce attacks from the O'Reillys, Limbaughs, and Coulters, Sheehan persisted in her quiet, unpretentious demand for truth and her call to end a senseless, catastrophic war:

> I want to ask the president, why did he kill my son? . . . He said my son died in a noble cause, and I want to ask him what that noble cause is. . . . I want him to honor my son by bringing the troops home immediately. . . . I don't want him to use my son's name to justify any more killing.[58]

Sheehan's form of activism is very different from the sort of massive antiwar youth protest of Vietnam. Without a draft and without the steady barrage of televised images of body bags and atrocities that accompanied Vietnam, most

Americans seem content to sit quietly and try to forget the awfulness of what's happening so far away. But Sheehan's simple but stubborn protest is a persistent reminder of the terrible pain felt by a mother whose child died for a web of lies. As Matt Taibbi observes, this is the kind of honest, simple emotion that we need in order to cut through the layers of secrecy and false realities concocted by the White House:

> Iraq is an insane blunder by a bunch of criminal incompetents who have managed so far to avoid the lash and rack only because the machinery for avoiding reality is so advanced in this country. We don't watch the fighting, we don't see the bodies come home and we don't hear anyone screaming when a house in Baghdad burns down. . . . The only movement we're going to need to end this fiasco is a more regular exposure to consequence. It needs to feel its own pain. Cindy Sheehan didn't bring us folk songs, but she did put pain on the front pages. And along a lonely road late at night, I saw it spread.[59]

There are, sadly, now over 3,000 Cindy Sheehans mourning fallen children; if we were allowed to hear and feel their pain as well, this senseless blunder would likely end tomorrow.

Ultimately, however, this sort of brave, grassroots resistance needs to be expanded to larger sorts of collective political action. A good example is the fact that over 220 U.S. cities have chosen to defy the administration's stance on climate change, rejecting its secrecy and censorship of scientific evidence on global warming, and instead voluntarily adopting the requirements of the Kyoto protocol.[60] Despite the administration's Orwellian rhetoric, San Francisco, Oakland, Berkeley, Portland, Seattle, and many other communities have realized that climate change now poses a direct threat to their economic well-being and quality of life. The citizens of Seattle, for example, realized that warmer winters were destroying both the ski industry in the Cascade mountains and the city's own water supply, which depends heavily on mountain snowpack.[61] Defying the administration, Seattle is leading a coalition of 224 cities in a Climate Protection Agreement dedicated to achieving the basic environmental protections that the federal government has consistently refused to enact.

This is just one of many examples of communities mobilizing against the administration's secrecy. But the formula is a powerful one that could be extended to many other issues: first, ignore the pious but hollow rhetoric issuing from the administration; second, cut through its lies to gather accurate information; and third, engage in collective action for a common good, rather than for the profit of a few private corporations. If such locally driven action can be applied to environmental issues, it can also be extended to combating poverty, providing health care, stopping war and torture, or even impeaching the president—in fact, in March 2006, five small communities in Vermont took it upon themselves to do precisely that, voting in town-hall meetings to call for the impeachment of George W. Bush.[62]

Terror and Hope

It is only today that we fully realize how dangerous secrecy can become. In different but only apparently independent spheres, it has become loaded with more and more power.

—Elias Canetti, *Crowds and Power*

So do not be afraid of them. There is nothing concealed that will not be disclosed, or hidden that will not be made known.

—Matthew 10:26 (NIV)

But all of these weapons of openness demand one other vital element: overcoming fear. Indeed, they demand a Colbert-like courage to speak truthiness to power. Since 9/11, this administration has repeatedly used the nebulous threat of terror as an excuse for an unprecedented abuse of power. Fear has been used to silence dissent, squelch media criticism, and justify all of the above illegal and outrageous acts (as Jon Stewart put it, the Bush administration's basic rationale is "9/11 + x = shut the f-ck up"). Again, this is not a new strategy, but one that power-hungry political regimes have long deployed. As Arendt long ago pointed out, "propaganda . . . is one, and possibly the most important, instrument of totalitarianism for dealing with the non-totalitarian world; terror, on the contrary, is the very essence of its form of government."[63] To be sure, there are terrorists and other scary things out there to be concerned about. But they were there before 9/11 and will probably be there for some time to come. Despite the administration's constant rhetoric, 9/11 did *not* change everything, it did not invalidate our Constitution, it did not justify illegal war or torture, it did not authorize illegal wiretaps—or rather, it did not *unless we allow it to.* If anything, we have far more to fear from a government that has assumed such arrogant and excessive powers, a government that threatens to dismantle the very liberties it purports to protect. "When the government fears the people," Jefferson famously put it, "you have liberty. When the people fear the government, you have tyranny." If we allow ourselves to be so overcome by the nebulous fear of "terror" that we are willing to tolerate illegal war, torture, secret prisons, spying on U.S. citizens, criminalization of dissent, and a general loss of privacy, then we have effectively chosen tyranny over liberty.

Much like our global climate—which virtually all credible scientists agree is now at a critical tipping point with catastrophic consequences—democracy in the United States lies at a point of crisis, most clearly embodied in the dangerous excesses of the Bush administration. This crisis will not go away after the 2008 election; it will remain with us no matter which party takes power after Bush leaves office. The past five years have seen an unprecedented expansion of executive power and an unprecedented invasion of citizens' rights, all in the name of an endless war. That power will remain in the hands of the next president, whether Democrat or Republican, and it should therefore be of deep concern to voters of both parties. I doubt very much that many Republicans would like to see such power in the hands of Hillary Clinton or John Kerry, any more than Democrats or Greens would like to see it in the hands of a new Republican president. Such power will not recede unless the public demands it. To move forward toward a healthy, sustainable post-Bushist democracy will therefore demand a new culture of openness, with a new set of moral and spiritual values. In the wake of the 2006 midterm elections, the Congress has a fresh opportunity to inject this much-needed spirit of transparency, openness, oversight, and acountability into our political system, and it must begin with a full investigation of this administration's obsessive secrecy, its secret prisons, its secret torture, its secret use of intelligence, and its invasion of citizens' rights and privacy.[64]

The alternative is simply to "stay the course," to use Bush's well-worn phrase, which means to concede ever more power to an increasingly secretive executive branch, to sacrifice more freedoms, rights, and privacy to an invasive surveillance state, and to watch our economy slide further into a black hole of massive debt and deficits. The Bush administration represents perhaps the logical trajectory of the growing secrecy and religious nationalism that began during the Cold War, now fulfilling the neoconservative dream of an American empire with unsurpassed military might. But it has also pushed us to the brink of the inevitable decay, exhaustion, and collapse that has befallen every arrogant empire. Historically, empires in decline tend to become very scary places. Our current empire seems to be careening toward either bankruptcy, swallowed by its own mindless debt, or totalitarianism, destroying its own freedoms in the name of endless war.

Perhaps the only way to avoid the imminent "sorrows of empire" in a post-Bushist era, then, is to renounce the obsessive secrecy and messianic fervor that has driven other empires to self-destruction. The weapons of secrecy have proven to be self-defeating, delusional, and ultimately bankrupt. Barring an actual return of Jesus, the neoconservative dream of a New American Century has turned out to be a ridiculous and bloody disaster. The weapons of openness, however, have only begun to be deployed—and thus far with some success.

In this, there is reason for hope.

Notes

1. Erving Goffman, *The Presentation of Self in Everyday Life* (Garden City, NY: Doubleday, 1959), 46.

2. Mark Crispin Miller, *Cruel and Unusual: Bush/Cheney's New World Order* (New York: Norton, 2004), 294.

3. John M. Orman, *Presidential Secrecy and Deception: Beyond the Power to Persuade* (Westport, CT: Greenwood, 1980), 7.

4. Arundhati Roy, *An Ordinary Person's Guide to Empire* (Cambridge, MA: South End, 2004), 134.

5. Paul Krugman, *The Great Unraveling: Losing Our War in the New Century* (New York: Norton, 2003), 5.

6. Antonin Scalia, "God's Justice and Ours," *First Things* 123 (May 2002): 17–21.

7. Kevin Phillips, *American Theocracy: Aristocracy, Fortune, and the Politics of Deceit in the House of Bush* (New York: Viking, 2004), 96.

8. Robyn E. Blumner, "The Dangers of Religious Fervor in Politics," *St. Petersburg Times*, March 26, 2006, at www.sptimes.com/2006/03/26/Columns/The_dangers_of_religi.shtml.

9. "Bush Vows to Rid the World of Evil-Doers," *CNN.com*, September 16, 2001, at archives.cnn.com/2001/US/09/16/gen.bush.terrorism/.

10. Thomas Friedman, "A Manifesto for the Fast World," *New York Times Magazine*, March 28, 1999, section 6, 40.

11. James Madison, "Political Observations," April 20, 1795, in *Letters and Other Writings of James Madison* (Philadelphia: Lippincott, 1865), 4:491.

12. Charlie Savage, "Bush Challenges Hundreds of Laws," *Boston Globe*, April 30, 2006, at www.boston.com/news/nation/articles/2006/04/30/bush_challenges_hundreds_of_laws/.

13. Julian Borger, "Former Top Judge Says US Edging Near Dictatorship," *Guardian*, March 13, 2006, at www.guardian.co.uk/usa/story/0,,1729396,00.html.

14. Juliet Eilperin, "Censorship Is Alleged at NOAA," *Washington Post*, February 11, 2006, A7.

15. Tom Shorrock, "Watching What You Say," *Nation*, March 20, 2006, 14.

16. Lawrence Britt, "Fourteen Defining Characteristics of Fascism," *Free Inquiry* (Spring 2003): 20. See also Reverend Davidson Loehr, "Living under Fascism," Sermon in Austin, Texas, November 2, 2004, at www.uua.org/news/2004/voting/sermon_loehr.html.

17. See Conyers, *What Went Wrong in Ohio: The Conyers Report on the 2004 Presidential Election* (Chicago: Academy Chicago, 2005); Mark Crispin Miller, *Fooled Again: How the Right Stole the 2004 Election and Why They'll Steal the Next One Too (Unless We Stop Them)* (New York: Basic, 2005).

18. Theodore Roosevelt, "Message Proposing the 'Standard Oil' Monopoly Investigation," 1938, in Robert F. Kennedy Jr., *Crimes against Nature, Rolling Stone*, December 11, 2003, 193. Henry Wallace, FDR's vice president in his third term, made a similar argument in his article "The Dangers of American Fascism": "The American fascists are most easily recognized by their deliberate perversion of truth and fact. . . . They claim to be super-patriots, but they would destroy every liberty guaranteed by

the Constitution. They demand free enterprise, but are the spokesmen for monopoly and vested interest. Their final objective toward which all their deceit is directed is to capture political power so that, using the power of the state and the power of the market simultaneously, they may keep the common man in eternal subjection." Wallace, "The Dangers of American Fascism," *New York Times*, April 9, 1944, at newdeal.feri.org/wallace/haw23.htm.

19. Kennedy, *Crimes against Nature*, 194.

20. Robert F. Kennedy Jr., speech in Toronto, June 21, 2003, *Lake Ontario Keeper*, August 1, 2003, at www.greenpartysask.ca..

21. See Katty Kay, "Analysis: Oil and the Cabinet," *BBC News*, January 29, 2001, at news.bbc.co.uk/1/hi/world/americas/1138009.stm; David Sirota, *Hostile Takeover: How Big Money and Corruption Conquered Our Government—And How We Can Take It Back* (New York: Crown, 2006).

22. Paul Bigioni, "Fascism Then, Fascism Now," *Toronto Star*, November 27, 2005, at www.thestar.com.

23. Kennedy, *Crimes against Nature*, 194.

24. Alexandre Koyré, "The Political Function of the Modern Lie," *Contemporary Jewish Record* (June 1945), quoted in Hannah Arendt, *Totalitarianism: Part Three of the Origins of Totalitarianism* (New York: Harcourt Brace, 1985), 74.

25. Arendt, *Totalitarianism*, 74.

26. Sinclair Lewis, *It Can't Happen Here* (New York: New American Library, 2005), 16–17.

27. Bigioni, "Fascism Then, Fascism Now."

28. Bruce Bartlett, *Imposter: How George W. Bush Bankrupted America and Betrayed the Reagan Legacy* (New York: Doubleday, 2006), 102ff, 141ff.

29. Jacob S. Hacker and Paul Pierson, *Off-Center: The Republican Revolution and the Erosion of American Democracy* (New Haven: Yale University Press, 2005), 166.

30. Arendt, *Totalitarianism*, 176.

31. Jim Wallis, in Kaplan, *With God on Their Side: How Christian Fundamentalists Trampled Science, Policy, and Democracy in George Bush's White House* (New York: New Press, 2004), 4.

32. Jim Wallis, in "Jim Wallis Talks about 'God's Politics' (His Latest Best Seller) and Values . . . by Which Wallis *Doesn't* Mean Hate, Greed, and War Mongering," *Buzzflash*, February 22, 2005, at www.buzzflash.com/interviews/05/02/int05008.html.

33. Jimmy Carter, *Our Endangered Values: America's Moral Crisis* (New York: Simon & Schuster, 2005), 177.

34. Bill Moyers, "A Time for Heresy," *TomPaine.com*, March 22, 2006, at www.tompaine.com/articles/2006/03/22/a_time_for_heresy.php.

35. Moyers, "Time for Heresy."

36. Robert F. Kennedy Jr., "For the Sake of Our Children," *EarthLight*, Winter 2005, at informeddissent.org/2005/02.

37. Thomas Jefferson, *Autobiography*, in *Thomas Jefferson: Writings*, ed. Merrill D. Peterson (New York: Library of America, 1984), 40.

38. John F. Kennedy, quoted in David Chidester, *Patterns of Power: Religion and Politics in American Culture* (Englewood Cliffs, NJ: Prentice Hall, 1988), 295.

39. William Lee Miller, *The First Liberty: America's Foundation in Religious Freedom* (Washington, DC: Georgetown University Press, 2002), 3.

40. Abraham Lincoln, *The Collected Works of Abraham Lincoln*, ed. Roy Basler et al., 9 vols. (New Brunswick, NJ: Rutgers University Press, 1953–1955), 5:403–404.

41. Michael Lerner, "Bringing God into It," *Nation*, April 24, 2006, 22. See Michael Lerner, *The Left Hand of God: Taking Back Our Country from the Religious Right* (San Francisco: Harper, 2006).

42. Daniel Patrick Moynihan, quoted in Athan Theoharis, ed., *A Culture of Secrecy: The Government versus the People's Right to Know* (University Press of Kansas, 1998), 13.

43. Theodore Roosevelt, editorial, *Kansas City Star*, May 7, 1918.

44. Iris Marion Young, "Communication and the Other: Beyond Deliberative Democracy," in *Democracy and Difference: Contesting the Boundaries of the Political*, ed. Seyla Benhabib (Princeton, NJ: Princeton University Press, 1996), 121. See J. Bohmann and W. Rehg, *Deliberative Democracy: Essays on Reason and Politics* (Cambridge, MA: MIT Press, 1997).

45. Simone Chambers, "Measuring Publicity's Effect: Reconciling Empirical Research and Normative Theory," *Acta Politica* 40, no.2 (2005): 255–266.

46. Iris Marion Young, "Activist Challenges to Deliberative Democracy," in *Debating Deliberative Democracy*, ed. James S. Fishkin and Peter Laslett (Oxford: Blackwell, 2003), 119.

47. Roy, *Ordinary Person's Guide to Empire*, 6.

48. Michael Ross, "Younger Americans Get News from a New Place," September 28, 2004, at MSNBC, at www.msnbc.msn.com/id/5520569/.

49. Geoffrey Baym, "*The Daily Show* and the Reinvention of Political Journalism," paper presented at the conference "Faith, Fun, and Futuramas," Chicago, September 1, 2004.

50. Susan Douglas, "Daily Show Does Bush," *Nation*, May 5, 2003.

51. *The Daily Show*, June 21, 2004.

52. *The Daily Show*, May 6, 2004.

53. *The Daily Show*, June 14, 2004.

54. Michael Scherer, "The Truthiness Hurts," *Salon.com*, May 1, 2006, at www.salon.com/opinion/feature/2006/05/01/colbert/. "Truthiness" is Colbert's brilliant term for things that politicians and the media wish were true and often persuade us are true, while knowing full well they are not true (such as WMD in Iraq). By speaking "truthiness to power," Colbert made a remarkable use of this technique against Bush himself, by mocking the president's rhetoric and exposing the lies beneath the truthiness.

55. "Stephen Colbert at the White House Correspondent's Dinner," *About.com*, at politicalhumor.about.com/od/stephencolbert/a/colbertbush.htm.

56. Scherer, "Truthiness Hurts."

57. Michael Moore, "Mavericks, Renegades and Trouble Makers," *Rolling Stone*, December 29, 2005, 66.

58. "Soldier's Mom Digs in Near Bush Ranch," *CNN.com*, August 7, 2005, at www.cnn.com/2005/POLITICS/08/07/mom.protest/. See Karen Houppert, "Cindy Sheehan: Mother of a Movement?" *Nation*, June 12, 2006, 11–16.

59. Matt Taibbi, "Bush vs. the Mother," *Rolling Stone*, September 8, 2005, 62.

60. Gregory Dicum, "Kyoto by the Gate: Local Cities Defy Federal Government, Make Their Own Climate Policies," *San Francisco Gate,* February 16, 2005, at www.sfgate.com/cgi-bin/article.cgi?file=/gate/archive/2005/02/16/gree.DTL.

61. Eli Sanders, "Seattle Leads U.S. Cities Joining Kyoto Protocol," *International Herald Tribune,* May 15, 2005, at www.iht.com/articles/2005/05/15/news/global.php. See Andrew Basmajian, "A Green Santa Monica," *Santa Monica Daily Mirror,* May 18, 2006, at www.smmirror.com/MainPages/DisplayArticleDetails.asp?eid=3011.

62. "Five Vermont Towns Vote to Impeach Bush," Associated Press, March 7, 2006, at www.commondreams.org/headlines06/0307-11.htm.

63. Arendt, *On Totalitarianism,* 42.

64. See James Sturke, "Senate to Begin Investigations of Rendition/Torture Abuses," *Guardian Unlimited,* November 14, 2006, at www.guardian.co.uk/usa/story/0,,1947647,00.html; Carl Hulse and Thom Shanker, "Democrats, Engaging Bush, Vow Early Action on Iraq," *New York Times,* November 11, 2006.

Addendum

THIS BOOK WAS IN ITS FINAL STAGES just as the 2006 midterm election results came in. Therefore, a few final words are in order. Most analysts agree that the 2006 election was in large part a referendum on the president and his policies, perhaps above all the invasion and occupation of Iraq. The shift in the political balance of power in both the House and the Senate is a strong indication that the majority of Americans are no longer content with this president's "just trust me" attitude and are increasingly disturbed by his obsessively secretive, invasive, and unaccountable form of executive power. It suggests a widespread desire for far more oversight and transparency in government across the board, but particularly in the handling of a catastrophically expensive, bloody, and mismanaged war.

It now remains to be seen whether the new Congress has the political will and the courage to fulfill its constitutional obligation: namely, to oversee, investigate, and reign in this administration's imperialistic grab for executive power.

Select Bibliography

Alterman, Eric. *What Liberal Media?* New York: Basic, 2003.

——. *When Presidents Lie: A History of Official Deception and Its Consequences.* New York: Viking, 2004.

Ambinder, Marc J. "Vast, Right-Wing Cabal? The Most Powerful Conservative Group You've Never Heard Of." *ABCNews.com*, May 2, 2002. At abcnews.go.com/sections/politics/DailyNews/council_020501.html.

Arendt, Hannah. *Totalitarianism: Part Three of the Origins of Totalitarianism.* San Diego: Harcourt Brace Jovanovich, 1985.

Bacevich, Andrew. *American Empire: The Realities and Consequences of U.S. Diplomacy.* Cambridge, MA: Harvard University Press, 2002.

Bamford, James. *Body of Secrets: The Anatomy of the Ultra-Secret National Security Agency.* New York: Anchor, 2002.

Bartlett, Bruce. *Imposter: How George W. Bush Bankrupted America and Betrayed the Reagan Legacy.* New York: Doubleday, 2006.

Boal, Iain, T. J. Clark, Joseph Matthews, and Michael Watts. *Afflicted Powers: Capital and Spectacle in a New Age of Art.* New York: Verso, 2005.

Bok, Sisella. *Secrets: On the Ethics of Concealment and Revelation.* New York: Vintage, 1989.

Bolle, Kees, ed. *Secrecy and Religions.* Leiden, Netherlands: Brill, 1987.

Brock, David. *The Republican Noise Machine: Right-Wing Media and How It Corrupts Democracy.* New York: Three Rivers, 2005.

Bush, George W. *A Charge to Keep.* New York: Morrow, 1999.

——. Foreword to Marvin Olasky, *Compassionate Conservatism: What It Is, What It Does, and How It Can Transform America.* New York: Simon & Schuster, 2000.

——. "Bush Delivers Graduation Speech at West Point." June 1, 2002. At www.whitehouse.gov/news/releases/2002/06/20020601-3.html.

———. *We Will Prevail: President George W. Bush on War, Terrorism, and Freedom.* New York: Continuum, 2003.

———. "President Bush Reaffirms Resolve to War on Terror." March 19, 2004. At www .whitehouse.gov/news/releases/2004/03/20040319-3.html.

———. "Second Inaugural Address." January 20, 2005. At www.whitehouse .gov/news/releases/2005/01/20050120-1.html.

Canetti, Elias. *Crowds and Power.* New York: Viking, 1962.

Carter, Jimmy. *Our Endangered Values: America's Moral Crisis.* New York: Simon & Schuster, 2005.

Chidester, David. *Patterns of Power: Religion and Politics in American Culture.* Englewood Cliffs, NJ: Prentice Hall, 1988.

Clarkson, Frederick. *Eternal Hostility: The Struggle between Democracy and Theocracy.* Monroe, ME: Common Courage, 1997.

Cole, David, and James X. Dempsey, *Terrorism and the Constitution.* New York: New Press, 2002.

Cronkite, Walter. " Secrecy, Lies and Credibility." King Features Syndicate, April 1, 2004. At www.yankton.net/stories/040104/opE_20040401035.shtml.

Curry, Richard. *Freedom at Risk: Secrecy, Censorship, and Repression in the 1980s.* Philadelphia: Temple University Press, 1988.

Dean, John W. *Worse Than Watergate: The Secret Presidency of George W. Bush.* New York: Little, Brown, 2004.

———. *Conservatives without Conscience.* New York: Viking, 2006.

Debord, Guy. *The Society of the Spectacle.* New York: Zone, 1994.

Deutsch, Kenneth L., and John A. Murley, eds. *Leo Strauss, the Straussians, and the American Regime.* Lanham, MD: Rowman & Littlefield, 1999.

Domke, David. *God-Willing: Political Fundamentalism in the White House, the War on Terror, and the Echoing Press.* Ann Arbor: University of Michigan Press, 2004.

Drury, Shadia. *Leo Strauss and the American Right.* New York: Palgrave Macmillan, 1999.

Eisendrath, Craig. *National Insecurity: U.S. Intelligence after the Cold War.* Philadelphia: Temple University Press, 2000.

Ferguson, Niall. *Colossus: The Price of America's Empire.* New York: Penguin, 2004.

Formicola, Jo Renee, et al. *Faith-Based Initiatives and the Bush Administration: The Good, the Bad, and the Ugly.* Lanham, MD: Rowman & Littlefield, 2003.

Franks, Thomas. *What's the Matter with America? The Resistible Rise of the American Right.* London: Vintage, 2005.

Frykholm, Amy Johnson. *Rapture Culture: Left Behind in Evangelical America.* New York: Oxford University Press, 2004.

Fukuyama, Francis. *The End of History and the Last Man.* New York: Free Press, 1992.

———. *America at the Crossroads: Democracy, Power, and the Neoconservative Legacy.* New Haven: Yale University Press, 2006.

Goldberg, Michelle. *Kingdom Coming: The Rise of Christian Nationalism.* New York: Norton, 2006.

Hacker, Jacob S., and Paul Pierson. *Off Center: The Republican Revolution and the Erosion of American Democracy.* New Haven: Yale University Press, 2005.

Halper, Stefan, and Jonathan Clarke. *America Alone: The Neo-Conservatives and the Global Order.* New York: Cambridge University Press, 2004.

Harvey, David. *The New Imperialism.* New York: Oxford University Press, 2003.

Henrikson, Margot A. *Dr. Strangelove's America: Society and Culture in the Atomic Age.* Berkeley: University of California Press, 1997.

Hersh, Seymour. *Chain of Command: The Road from 9/11 to Abu Ghraib.* New York: HarperCollins, 2004.

———. "Selective Intelligence." *New Yorker.* March 12, 2005. At www.newyorker .com/fact/content/articles/030512fa_fact.

Johnson, Chalmers. *The Sorrows of Empire: Militarism, Secrecy, and the End of the Republic.* New York: Holt, 2004.

Johnson, Paul C. *Secrets, Gossip, and Gods: The Transformation of Brazilian Candomblé.* New York: Oxford University Press, 2005.

Kagan, Robert, and William Kristol, eds. *Present Dangers: Crisis and Opportunity in American Foreign and Defense Policy.* San Francisco: Encounter, 2000.

Kaplan, Esther. *With God on Their Side: How Christian Fundamentalists Trampled Science, Policy, and Democracy in George Bush's White House.* New York: New Press, 2004.

Kennedy, Robert F., Jr. *Crimes against Nature: How George W. Bush and His Corporate Pals are Plundering the Country and Hi-jacking our Democracy.* New York: HarperCollins, 2004.

———. "Was the 2004 Election Stolen?" *Rolling Stone,* June, 2006. At www.rolling stone.com/news/story/10432334/was_the_2004_election_stolen.

Kristol, Irving. *Neoconservatism: The Autobiography of an Idea.* New York: Free Press, 1995.

———. "The Emerging American Imperium." *Wall Street Journal.* August 18, 1997, A14.

———. "The Neoconservative Persuasion: What It Was and What It Is." *Weekly Standard,* August 25, 2003. At www.weeklystandard.com/Content/Public/Articles/ 000/000/003/000tzmlw.asp.

Kristol, William, and Robert Kagan. "Toward a Neo-Reaganite Foreign Policy." *Foreign Affairs* (July/August 1996). At www.foreignaffairs.org.

LaHaye, Tim, and Jerry Jenkins. *Left Behind: A Novel of the Earth's Last Days.* Wheaton, IL: Tyndale House, 1995.

———. *Glorious Appearing: End of Days.* Wheaton, IL: Tyndale House, 2004.

LaHaye, Tim, and David Noebel. *Mind Siege: The Battle for Truth in the New Millennium.* Nashville, TN: Word, 2000.

Laurent, Eric. *Bush's Secret World: Religion, Big Business and Hidden Networks.* Cambridge, MA: Polity, 2004.

Ledeen, Michael. *Machiavelli on Modern Leadership: Why Machiavelli's Iron Rules Are as Timely and Important Today as Five Centuries Ago.* New York: St. Martin's, 1999.

———. *D'Annunzio: The First Duce.* New Brunswick, NJ: Transaction, 2002.

———. *War against the Terror Masters.* New York: St. Martin's, 2003.

Leone, Richard C., and Greg Anrig Jr., eds. *War on Our Freedoms: Civil Liberties in an Age of Terrorism.* New York: Public Affairs, 2003.

Lerner, Michael. *The Left Hand of God: Taking Back Our Country from the Religious Right.* San Francisco: Harper, 2006.

Lienesch, Michael. *Redeeming America: Piety and Politics in the New Christian Right.* Chapel Hill: University of North Carolina Press, 1993.

Lincoln, Bruce. *Holy Terrors: Thinking about Religion after September 11.* Chicago: University of Chicago Press, 2003.

———. "The Theology of George W. Bush." *The Christian Century.* October 5, 2004.

Machiavelli, Niccolò. *The Art of War.* Translated by Ellis Farnesworth. New York: Bobbs-Merrill, 1965.

———. *The Prince.* Translated by George Bull. New York: Penguin, 2003.

Mansfield, Stephen. *The Faith of George W. Bush.* Tarcher, 2003.

McAlister, Melani. "Prophecy, Politics, and the Popular: The *Left Behind* Series and Christian Fundamentalism's New World Order." *South Atlantic Quarterly* 102, no. 4 (2003): 773–798.

McCain, John. "Torture's Terrible Toll." *Newsweek.* November 21, 2005.

Miller, Anita. *What Went Wrong in Ohio: The Conyers Report on the 2004 Presidential Election.* Chicago: Academy Chicago, 2005.

Miller, Mark Crispin. *Fooled Again: How the Right Stole the 2004 Election and Why They'll Steal the Next One Too (Unless We Stop Them).* New York: Basic, 2005.

Moore, James, and Wayne Slater. *Bush's Brain: How Karl Rove Made George W. Bush Presidential.* Hoboken, NJ: Wiley & Sons, 2003.

Moyers, Bill. "In the Kingdom of the Half-Blind." Address at the National Security Archive, Washington, DC. December 9, 2005.

Moynihan, Patrick. *Secrecy: The American Experience.* New Haven: Yale University Press, 1998.

North, Gary, and Gary DeMar. *Christian Reconstructionism: What It Is, What It Isn't.* Tyler, TX: Institute for Christian Economics, 1984.

Norton, Anne. *Leo Strauss and the Politics of Empire.* New Haven: Yale University Press, 2005.

Olasky, Marvin. *Compassionate Conservatism: What It Is, What It Does, and How It Can Transform America.* New York: Simon & Schuster, 2000.

Phillips, Kevin. *American Dynasty: Aristocracy, Fortune, and the Politics of Deceit in the House of Bush.* New York: Viking, 2004.

———. *American Theocracy: The Peril and Politics of Radical Religion, Oil, and Borrowed Money in the 21st Century.* New York: Viking, 2006.

Pinter, Harold. "Art, Truth & Politics." Nobel Lecture, December 7, 2005. At nobelprize.org/literature/laureates/2005/pinter-lecture-e.html.

The Project for the New American Century. Letter to President Clinton of January 26, 1998. At www.newamericancentury.org/iraqclintonletter.htm.

———. "Rebuilding America's Defenses: Strategy, Forces and Resources for a New Century." 2000. At www.newamericancentury.org/RebuildingAmericasDefenses .pdf.

Robertson, Pat. *The Secret Kingdom.* Nashville: Nelson, 1982.

Roy, Arundhati. *An Ordinary Person's Guide to Empire.* Cambridge, MA: South End, 1974.

Rushdoony, Rousas J. *Institutes of Biblical Law.* Vallecito, CA: Craig, 1973.

Scarry, Elaine. *The Body in Pain: The Making and Unmaking of the World.* New York: Oxford University Press, 1985.

Schmitt, Christopher H., and Edward T. Pound. "Keeping Secrets: The Bush Administration Is Doing the Public's Business out of the Public Eye." *US News and World Report,* December 22, 2003. At www.usnews.com/usnews/news/articles/031222/22secrecy.htm.

Schmitt, Gary J., and Abram N. Shulsky. "The World of Intelligence (By Which We Do Not Mean *Nous*)." In *Leo Strauss, the Straussians, and the American Regime,* ed. Kenneth L. Deutsch and John A. Murley, 407–412. Lanham, MD: Rowman & Littlefield, 1999.

Shane, Peter M., John Podesta, and Richard C. Leone, eds. *A Little Knowledge: Privacy, Security, and Public Information after September 11.* New York: Century Foundation, 2004.

Simmel, Georg. "The Secret and the Secret Society." In *The Sociology of Georg Simmel,* trans. Kurt H. Wolff, 307–378. New York: Free Press, 1950.

Strauss, Leo. *Persecution and the Art of Writing.* Glencoe, IL: Free Press, 1952.

——— . *What Is Political Philosophy?* Westport, CT: Greenwood Press, 1973.

Suskind, Ron. *The Price of Loyalty: George W. Bush, the White House, and the Education of Paul O'Neill.* New York: Simon & Schuster, 2003.

——— . "Faith, Certainty and the Presidency of George W. Bush." *New York Times Magazine,* October 17, 2004. At www.nytimes.com.

Taussig, Michael. *Defacement: Public Secrecy and the Labor of the Negative.* Stanford, CA: Stanford University Press, 1999.

Tefft, Stanton K., ed. *Secrecy: A Cross-Cultural Perspective.* New York: Human Sciences, 1980.

Unger, Craig. *House of Bush, House of Saud: The Secret Relationship between the World's Two Most Powerful Dynasties.* New York: Scribner, 2004.

Urban, Hugh B. "The Torment of Secrecy: Ethical and Epistemological Problems in the Study of Esoteric Traditions." *History of Religions* 37, no. 3 (1998): 209–248.

——— . "Religion and Secrecy in the Bush Administration: The Gentleman, the Prince, and the Simulacrum." *Esoterica* 7 (2005): 1–36.

——— . "America Left Behind: Bush, the Neoconservatives, and Evangelical Christian Fiction." *Journal of Religion and Society* 8 (2006). At moses.creighton.edu/JRS/2006/2006-2.html.

Whitfield, Stephen. *The Culture of the Cold War.* Baltimore: Johns Hopkins University Press, 1996.

Wohlstetter, Albert. "The Delicate Balance of Terror." In *The Art of War in World History,* ed. Gerard Chaliand, 1004–1012. Berkeley: University of California Press, 1994.

Woodward, Bob. *Bush at War.* New York: Simon & Schuster, 2003.

Young, Iris Marion. "Communication and the Other: Beyond Deliberative Democracy." In *Democracy and Difference: Contesting the Boundaries of the Political*, ed. Seyla Benhabib, 120–136. Princeton, NJ: Princeton University Press, 1996.

——— . "Activist Challenges to Deliberative Democracy." In *Debating Deliberative Democracy*, ed. James S. Fishkin and Peter Laslett. Oxford: Blackwell, 2003.

Zinn, Howard. Foreword to Nancy Chang, *Silencing Political Dissent: How Post–September 11 Anti-Terrorism Measures Threaten Our Civil Liberties.* New York: Seven Stories, 2002.

Index

Abu Ghraib, 22, 74–79, 87, 131
Adams, John Quincy, 134–35
Al Qaeda, 49, 71–72, 77, 149, 154–55, 176, 205
American Enterprise Institute, 96, 121, 152
Antichrist, 38, 165, 171–72, 181
apocalypse, 25, 69, 169–71, 179
Arendt, Hannah, 139, 142, 147, 195
Armageddon, 12, 17, 176, 179
Ashcroft, John, 45, 69, 80–81

Baudrillard, Jean, 140, 143, 145, 158, 160n5
Blessitt, Arthur, 42
Bush, Barbara, 43
Bush, George H.W., 2, 44, 48, 64–65, 98, 107, 197
Bush, George W., ix, 10, 22, 24, 31–55, 61–87, 89n42, 95, 97, 102, 104, 109, 123, 131–33, 139–48, 156–57, 165–69, 174–77, 185–89, 194, 202–4, 206, 209–10, 213n54; born-again experience, 42; called by God, 10, 22, 31, 40–43, 48–49, 51, 131, 176; environmental policies, 67–69, 177,
208; as floating signifier, 157, 175; and Jesus, 10, 40–42; as leader of religious right in America, 52; lies about Iraq war, 71–74, 89n42; as media creation, 140, 157, 185; messianic faith of, 147–48, 174–77; as Moses, 22, 41, 43–44, 48, 54, 131, 178, 186; as "post-truth" president, 62, 194; as prodigal son, 22, 41, 44; recommitment to Christ, 40–41; as Rorschach blot, 142, 157, 186; and September 11, 2001, 20, 48–52, 69–71; as Straussian "gentleman," 97, 102, 104, 109, 178, 196; as structural link between neoconservatives and Christian right, 3, 40, 44, 51–52, 157, 166, 169, 174–75, 178, 185; and torture, 74–79; use of religious rhetoric, 20–22, 32, 46–50, 86, 97, 131, 149
Bushist regime, 21, 25, 194–95

capitalism, 39, 53, 174, 198, 201; as a "Christian" economic system, 16, 39, 53
Carter, Jimmy, 31, 40, 54, 83, 85, 185, 197–98, 207

— 223 —

About the Author

Hugh B. Urban is professor of religious studies in the Department of Comparative Studies at the Ohio State University. He is primarily interested in the role of secrecy in religion, particularly in relation to issues of power and knowledge. He is the author of several books, including *Tantra: Sex, Secrecy, Politics and Power in the Study of Religion* (2003) and *Magia Sexualis: Sex, Magic and Liberation in Modern Western Esotericism* (2006).